CONTENTS

essential guide

to

STAGE MANAGEMENT, LIGHTING AND SOUND

Scott Palmer

Hodder & Stoughton

A MEMBER OF THE HODDER HEADLINE GROUP

Orders: please contact Bookpoint Ltd, 130 Milton Park, Abingdon,
Oxon OX14 4SB. Telephone: (44) 01235 827720, Fax: (44) 01235
400454. Lines are open from 9.00–6.00, Monday to Saturday, with a 24
hour message answering service. You can also order on our website
www.hodderheadline.co.uk

British Library Cataloguing in Publication Data
A catalogue record for this title is available from The British Library

ISBN 0 340 721138

First published 2000
Impression number   10 9 8 7 6 5 4
Year   2005 2004 2003

Copyright © 2000 Scott Palmer

Typeset by Fakenham Photosetting Ltd, Fakenham, Norfolk.
Printed in Great Britain for Hodder & Stoughton Educational, a
division of Hodder Headline Ltd, 338 Euston Road, London NW1 3BH
by J. Arrowsmith Ltd, Bristol.

INTRODUCTION

Making theatre is a difficult process – it involves dedication, enthusiasm and sophisticated teamwork across a wide range of production areas. It demands a unique range of practical, technical and conceptual skills from all those involved in supporting the work of the performers on stage.

This book concentrates on the area of technical theatre and aims to provide an introduction to the production processes involved in staging performance work. Detailed technical information and a variety of practical skills are explained in the areas of stage management, lighting and sound, and strategies are suggested which seek to maximise the individual's contribution to performance work.

Emphasis is placed on the planning and organisational skills required throughout the production period to prepare for the considerable pressures of working under performance conditions.

The purpose of this book is to support students who are training for the performing arts and entertainment industries and will be particularly suitable to those following BTEC National Diploma, GNVQ Advanced Level courses in Performing Arts and A level Theatre Studies. Much of the material will also be relevant to support study at BTEC Higher National Diploma level and degree level Theatre, Drama and Performing Arts courses which embrace professional production values and staging techniques. Because of the breadth of the subject area, this text cannot claim to provide a definitive guide to theatre production, but instead aims to highlight essential professional working practices whilst also providing detailed sources for further investigation. As such information may also prove useful to other artists, performers and directors wishing to find out more about the mechanics of theatre production and the workings 'backstage'.

The areas of lighting and sound are considered not simply from a technical stance, but also in terms of their potential artistic contribution to performance work. Too often technology is used for its own sake with little apparent awareness of its potential to contribute creatively to the events on stage. Lighting and sound design concepts are therefore introduced in the hope that students of the theatre will begin to explore the possibilities afforded by the imaginative use of these technologies.

The most exciting performance work often evolves as a result of a close artistic collaboration between the director, designers, performers and other members of the production team. This book aims to de-mystify the process of theatre production and to suggest ways of improving collaborative work so that the practical and creative contribution to performance work is maximised, thereby allowing artistic goals to be achieved in performance.

I would like to thank everyone who has given advice, support and encouragement during the preparation of this text. In particular I would like to acknowledge the support of Bretton Hall College of the University of Leeds and colleagues in the School of Dance and Theatre; Tim Banks, Joslin McKinney, Fiona Mathers, Peter Banyard; Robin Watkinson, Andrina Van Den Berg and the staff at Bolton Octagon Theatre, West Yorkshire Playhouse, Emma

Barrington-Binns, Deena Kearney, David Cusworth and Sue Davis at Strand Lighting, Louise Stickland, Harmer Public Relations, Vari*Lite Production Services, Litestructures, Zero88, Method & Madness Theatre Company and Manuel Harlan for permission to use the photograph on p26.

Finally thanks to Elisabeth Tribe, Anna Clark, Eleanor Bryson and Lisa Hyde at Hodder and Stoughton, and for the inspiration from Tanya, my family, and my students; past, present and future.

The Theatre

Who's Who in the Theatre

- **Director** – responsible for the direction of members of the cast in rehearsals to produce a polished end product. Works closely with the design team to establish a creative and coherent vision for the play. Oversees all aspects of the production. Traditionally credited with the responsibility for the overall artistic achievement of the piece.
- **Production Manager (PM)** – looks after all of the technical and production areas of the show and controls the budget. Ensures that all aspects of the production remain on schedule throughout the preparation and up to the first night. Helps to solve technical and production difficulties. Liaises with Directors and Designers. Has overall responsibility for Health and Safety backstage and on stage, including liaison with Fire Officers. In the Absence of a Technical Manager, the Production Manager will also take on the duties listed below. (See page 31 for further information on this role).
- **Technical Manager (TM)** – usually works in a venue, rather than for a theatre company. Appoints technical personnel and co-ordinates the work of all backstage staff. Draws up schedules for each week and supervises technical work. Often has responsibilities for the maintenance of the building. Liaises with visiting companies to negotiate technical details and requirements for their productions. (See page 41 for further information on this role).
- **Designer** – responsible for the overall visual aspect of the performance and traditionally the design of set and costume (see also Set and Costume Designers below). The design and final look of the stage props are also the designer's responsibility. If the designer holds a resident position at a venue, they will usually be involved in sourcing materials and assisting in the painting and texturing of the set and supervising the making of costumes. (See page 23 for further information on this role).
- **Resident Stage Manager (RSM)** – this is a position in a theatre which provides a venue for visiting companies and doesn't require an entire stage management team. Has overall control of the stage and liaises with the touring production or Company Manager to assist with moving equipment into the venue and performance work. May take on some or all of the responsibilities of the Technical Manager. (See page 41 for further information on this role).
- **Company Manager (CM)** – a senior position, usually in a touring company. Liaises with the Technical Manager and/or Resident Stage Manager of venues. Responsible for all aspects of the production during a tour, including technical issues, administration and looking after members of the cast. (See page 42 for further information on this role).
- **Stage Manager (SM)** – leads the stage management team and co-ordinates communication between all production

departments and the PM. Responsible for the stage area and the backstage environment during performance. (See page 36 for further information on this role).

- **Deputy Stage Manager (DSM)** – usually runs the show from the prompt copy, cueing all of the other departments. Sits in on rehearsals and works closely with the Director and cast. (See page 38 for further information on this role).

- **Assistant Stage Manager (ASM)** – helps in the preparation for a production by making and sourcing props. Assists with props and scene changes during rehearsal and performance. (See page 40 for further information on this role).

- **Stage Crew** – casual staff and/or resident workshop staff employed to assist with the running of a show, e.g. scene changing, spotlight operation, etc.

- **Fly Operator** – traditionally **Flyman**, whether male or female, and is responsible for operation of the flys. Flying systems enable the vertical movement of scenery, curtains, etc. during a performance. Co-ordinates the suspension of all overhead scenery and technical equipment. A Head Flyman may have one or more assistants and employ casual staff for particularly difficult shows. (See page 81 for further information on this role).

- **Lighting Designer** – usually a freelance position, or a member of the venue's permanent staff, e.g. Chief Electrician. Works closely with the Director and other Designers to create the lighting plot for the play. This involves conceiving a lighting style, drawing up the rig plan, working with the lighting team to set up and focus each light, and to agree individual lighting cues. (See page 98 for further information on this role).

- **Chief Electrician or Chief LX** – co-ordinates the work of the lighting (LX) department and is responsible for the maintenance of the lighting (and frequently sound)

systems. Supervises the setting up and focusing of lights. May also be required to design lighting and/or sound for productions. (See page 99 for further information on this role).

- **Deputy Chief LX** – assists the Chief Electrician. Usually operates the lighting or sound for productions. May be required to design lighting or sound for productions. In venues without a sound specialist may take responsibility for this area of work. (See pages 99 for further information on this role).

- **Assistant LX** – assists the Chief and Deputy LX with the rigging, focusing and operation of lights and other electrical equipment. May operate the lighting or sound for a show or assist by operating smoke machines, pyrotechnics, spotlights etc. (See pages 99–100 for further information on this role).

- **Stage Electricians** – often casual staff employed to prepare and set up on-stage electrical equipment during a performance, e.g. as part of a scene change. Typically required to operate smoke machines, dry ice machines, pyrotechnics, undertake colour filter changes on stage lights, handle microphones, etc. (See page 100 for further information on this role).

- **Follow Spot Operator (Limes)** – usually a casual employee who operates a powerful spotlight to highlight performers on top of the existing lighting. Usually (but not always) works from the rear of the auditorium. Limes is short for limelight!

- **Sound Designer** – usually freelance, but often a member of the venue's permanent staff, e.g. employed in the sound or electrics department. Works closely with the Director and other Designers to produce music and effects for productions. (See page 212 for further information on this role).

- **Composer** – usually a freelance hired to write music for a performance.

Alternatively, this work may be undertaken by the Sound Designer.

- **Head of Sound** – in many theatres this post is part of the electrics team. In larger venues the Head of Sound is not only responsible for setting up and maintaining the sound equipment, but is also involved in the designing and realising of sound for production work.
- **Sound Engineer or Operator** – technical position operating the mixing desk during the performance. In theatres without a specialist sound department this will be a member of the LX team.
- **Set Designer** – may be a freelance position or a resident post. Works closely with the Director and other Designers to establish an overall concept and visual style for the play. May also act as Costume and/or Lighting Designer. Primarily responsible for creating a scale model of the set and working drawings of individual pieces. Also responsible for designing and selecting props. May be involved in construction, painting and dressing of the set and props. (See page 23 for further information on this role).
- **Master Carpenter** – heads up the workshop team. Responsible for the construction of sets and large props, working to the Set Designer's drawings. Although a lot of theatre scenery is still made of wood, the Master Carpenter may also have to work with other materials such as steel, fibreglass, plaster and latex.
- **Assistant Carpenter** – assists the Master Carpenter in the construction of sets.
- **Head of Props** – this post does not exist in many theatres and the making of props is the responsibility of the stage management and/or workshop teams. In larger organisations there may be a team who are solely responsible for making and sourcing the props. They work closely with the Designer and members of the stage management team, who supervise the use of props in rehearsal and performance. (See page 69 for further information on finding and making props).
- **Scenic Artist** – works on the decoration of the set once it has been constructed. Paints, textures or wallpapers the set to complete the design to the Set Designer's instructions. May also be involved in the making of props.
- **Costume Designer** – may be a freelance position or a resident post. Works closely with the Director and other Designers to establish an overall concept and visual style for the play. May also act as Set Designer to provide a unified scheme. Responsible for creating costume drawings and selecting appropriate fabrics. May also be involved in the making, hiring or borrowing of individual garments. May be involved in construction, painting and dressing of the set and props. (See page 23 for further information on this role).
- **Wardrobe Supervisor or Manager** – responsible for realising all of the costumes for a production. This involves liaising with the Costume Designer and co-ordinating the making of costumes by interpreting the drawings. Costumes may be made from scratch, hired, bought or adapted from stock. The Wardrobe Supervisor is responsible for co-ordinating the work of the wardrobe staff, both in making and in maintaining costumes during the run of a show. The head of wardrobe may also be required to design costumes for some shows.
- **Deputy or Assistant Wardrobe** – assists the Wardrobe Supervisor in the realisation of costumes. Involved in the selection, cutting, dyeing and sewing of materials. Also responsible for maintenance: the preparation of costumes for each performance, washing, drying and ironing. May also be required to look after the theatre's wig collection, if there is not a specialist member of staff.

- **Dresser** – This is usually a casual post, since the role is only required from the technical or dress rehearsal onwards. Sometimes, however, the post may be filled by a junior member of the wardrobe department. A Dresser assists members of the cast with costume changes during the performance and may be involved with minor costume maintenance and running repairs.

Other traditional job descriptions are:

- **Stage Dayman** – a full-time member of the stage staff.
- **Electrics Dayman** – a full-time member of the LX staff.
- **Showman** – a part time member of the crew working for stage, props or electrics department for performances only.

Theatre Organisations

TYPES OF THEATRE ORGANISATIONS

Theatres can be divided into three categories:

1 producing theatres
2 production organisations
3 non-producing theatres.

Producing Theatres

These are large organisations with permanent buildings. The companies tend to have a large and complex staff structure. Producing theatres can also be classified into three types, according to the way in which they schedule their production work:

1 repertory theatre
2 repertoire
3 stagione.

Repertory Theatre

The company produces single shows which are staged one after the other in a season of plays. Each show has a run of a limited length, usually 3 to 4 weeks, performing every night. At the same time as this show is in performance, another production is in the final stage of rehearsals. Further productions are also in earlier stages of preparation. Some repertory theatres may also have a smaller studio venue run on the same lines and in tandem with the main space.

In the past, this was the dominant form of regional theatre, with every major town and city having its own repertory theatre and company. Financial pressures in recent years have forced many reps to scale down their own production schedules and to offer their facilities to visiting companies during part of the year, in effect becoming receiving houses for that time.

These are some well known repertory theatres:

Bristol Old Vic
Sheffield Crucible
Birmingham Rep
Belgrade Theatre, Coventry
Nottingham Playhouse
Derby Playhouse
Leicester Haymarket
Bolton Octagon
Oldham Coliseum
Royal Exchange, Manchester
West Yorkshire Playhouse, Leeds
Northcott Theatre, Exeter
Theatr Clwyd, Mold.

Repertoire

This system is used in the largest and most prestigious venues, usually where there is a large company and more than one auditorium. A longer season is planned during which

Figure 1.1 *Nottingham Playhouse is an example of a repertory theatre*

DIARY

SEPTEMBER DATE	PERFORMANCE	TIME	PAGE
Thurs 10	The Boy Friend	7.30pm Preview	3
Fri 11	The Boy Friend	7.30pm 1st Night	3
Sat 12	The Boy Friend	7.30pm	3
Sun 13			
Mon 14	The Boy Friend	7.30pm	3
Tues 15	The Boy Friend	7.30pm	3
Wed 16	The Boy Friend	7.30pm	3
Thurs 17	The Boy Friend	7.30pm	3
Fri 18	The Boy Friend	7.30pm	3
Sat 19	The Boy Friend	2.30pm & 7.30pm	3
Sun 20			
Mon 21	The Boy Friend	7.30pm	3
Tues 22	The Boy Friend	7.30pm	3
Wed 23	The Boy Friend	7.30pm	3
Thurs 24	The Boy Friend	2.30pm & 7.30pm	3
Fri 25	The Boy Friend	7.30pm	3
Sat 26	The Boy Friend	7.30pm	3
Sun 27			
Mon 28	The Boy Friend	7.30pm	3
Tues 29	The Boy Friend	7.30pm	3
Wed 30	The Boy Friend	7.30pm	3

OCTOBER DATE	PERFORMANCE	TIME	PAGE
Thurs 1	The Boy Friend	7.30pm	3
Fri 2	The Boy Friend	7.30pm	3
Sat 3	The Boy Friend	2.30pm & 7.30pm	3
Sun 4			
Mon 5	The Boy Friend	7.30pm	3
Tues 6	The Boy Friend	7.30pm	3
Wed 7	The Boy Friend	7.30pm	3
Thurs 8	The Boy Friend	2.30pm & 7.30pm	3
Fri 9	The Boy Friend	7.30pm	3
Sat 10	The Boy Friend	7.30pm	3
Sun 11			
Mon 12			
Tues 13			
Wed 14	Union Dance Co.	7.30pm	4
Thurs 15	Bhangra/Ragga	7.30pm	4
	Phil Kay	10.00pm	4
Fri 16	Gospel Extravaganza	7.30pm	4
Sat 17	Upfront Comedy	5pm & 8pm	4
Sun 18			
Mon 19			
Tues 20			
Wed 21			
Thurs 22	Who's Afraid...?	7.30pm Preview	5
Fri 23	Who's Afraid...?	7.30pm 1st Night	5
Sat 24	Who's Afraid...?	7.30pm	5
Sun 25			
Mon 26	Who's Afraid...?	7.30pm	5
Tues 27	Who's Afraid...?	7.30pm	5
Wed 28	Who's Afraid...?	7.30pm	5
Thurs 29	Who's Afraid...?	7.30pm	5
Fri 30	Who's Afraid...?	7.30pm	5
Sat 31	Who's Afraid...?	2.30pm & 7.30pm	5

NOVEMBER DATE	PERFORMANCE	TIME	PAGE
Sun 1			
Mon 2	Who's Afraid...?	7.30pm	5
Tues 3	Who's Afraid...?	7.30pm	5
Wed 4	Who's Afraid...?	7.30pm	5
Thurs 5	Who's Afraid...?	2.30pm & 7.30pm	5
Fri 6	Who's Afraid...?	7.30pm	5
Sat 7	Who's Afraid...?	7.30pm	5
Sun 8			
Mon 9			
Tues 10	V-TOL Dance Co.	7.30pm	6
Wed 11	Nottingham Ambassadors	8.00pm	6
Thurs 12	Lindisfarne	8.00pm	6
Fri 13	Steven Berkoff	7.30pm	7
Sat 14	swanflight	11.30am	7
	Ken Campbell	7.30pm	7
Sun 15			
Mon 16			
Tues 17			
Wed 18			
Thurs 19			
Fri 20			
Sat 21	swanflight	11.30am	7
Sun 22			
Mon 23			
Tues 24			
Wed 25			
Thurs 26			
Fri 27			
Sat 28	Jack/Beanstalk	2.30pm Preview	9
		7.30pm Preview	9
Sun 29			

several productions are available for performance at any particular time. Several performances of one production may be given consecutively, or may alternate with others. The continual rotation of productions within a season allows an audience to see a wide variety of shows in a short space of time. The repertoire is usually built up gradually, with one show opening whilst another is in rehearsal.

Examples of theatres operating a repertoire system:

Royal Shakespeare Company at Stratford-Upon-Avon and the Barbican Centre
Royal National Theatre
Pitlochry Festival Theatre
Chichester Festival Theatre
Peter Hall's Theatre Company.

Stagione

This system of production is rare in Britain, but common in other parts of Europe. It is a system that is particularly suited to opera production and ballet companies. In some respects there are similarities with the repertoire system, but at any given moment there is only a *small* range of productions that are available for performance. The productions are kept in the repertoire for years, but after an intensive performance run they are 'put away' in storage to be restaged at a later date. This system means that each revival usually requires major re-rehearsal and cast alterations, but it also allows major international performers to join a production for a limited number of performances.

The stagione system means that fewer produc-

Figure 1.2   *The Royal Shakespeare Company has a repertoire schedule of performances*

JANUARY 1998

		RST		Swan Theatre		The Other Place
Thu	15 Jan	7.30	Twelfth	7.30	Romeo	7.30	Zucco
Fri	16 Jan	7.30	Merchant	7.30	Fair	7.30	Goodnight
Sat	17 Jan	1.30m	Merchant	1.30m	Fair	1.30m	Goodnight
Sat	17 Jan	7.30	Merchant	7.30	Fair	7.30	Goodnight
Mon	19 Jan	7.30	Twelfth	7.30	Romeo	7.30	Zucco
Tue	20 Jan		No mat	1.30m	Romeo		No mat
Tue	20 Jan	7.30	Twelfth	7.30	Romeo	7.30	Zucco
Wed	21 Jan	7.30	Twelfth	7.30	Romeo	7.30	Zucco
Thu	22 Jan	1.30m	Twelfth	1.30m	Romeo		No mat
Thu	22 Jan	7.30	Merchant	7.30 ▼	Romeo	7.30	Goodnight
Fri	23 Jan	7.30	Merchant	7.30	Fair	7.30	Goodnight
Sat	24 Jan	1.30m	Merchant	1.30m	Fair	1.30m	Goodnight
Sat	24 Jan	7.30	Merchant	7.30	Fair	7.30	Goodnight
Mon	26 Jan	7.30	Twelfth	7.30	Romeo	7.30	Zucco
Tue	27 Jan		No mat	1.30m	Romeo		No mat
Tue	27 Jan	7.30	Twelfth	7.30	Romeo	7.30	Zucco
Wed	28 Jan	7.30	Merchant	7.30	Fair	7.30	Goodnight
Thu	29 Jan	1.30m	Merchant	1.30m	Fair	1.30m	Goodnight
Thu	29 Jan	7.30	Merchant	7.30	Fair	7.30	Goodnight
Fri	30 Jan	7.30	Twelfth	7.30	Romeo	7.30	Zucco
Sat	31 Jan	1.30m	Twelfth	1.30m	Romeo	1.30m	Zucco
Sat	31 Jan	7.30	Merchant	7.30	Romeo		No eve

FEBRUARY 1998

Mon	2 Feb	7.30	Merchant	7.30	Romeo	7.30	Goodnight
Tue	3 Feb		No mat	1.30m	Romeo		No mat
Tue	3 Feb	7.30	Twelfth	7.30	Romeo	7.30	Zucco
Wed	4 Feb	7.30	Twelfth	7.30	Romeo	7.30	Zucco
Thu	5 Feb	1.30m	Merchant	1.30m	Fair		No mat
Thu	5 Feb	7.30	Merchant	7.30	Fair	7.30	Goodnight
Fri	6 Feb	7.30	Merchant	7.30	Fair	7.30	Goodnight
Sat	7 Feb	1.30m	Twelfth	1.30m	Romeo		No mat
Sat	7 Feb	7.30	Twelfth	7.30	Romeo	7.30	Zucco
Mon	9 Feb	7.30	Twelfth	7.30	Romeo	7.30	Zucco
Tue	10 Feb	7.30	Twelfth	7.30	Romeo	7.30	Zucco
Wed	11 Feb	7.30	Twelfth	7.30 p	Romeo	7.30	Zucco
Thu	12 Feb	1.30m	Merchant	1.30m	Fair		No mat
Thu	12 Feb	7.30	Merchant	7.30	Fair	7.30	Goodnight
Fri	13 Feb	7.30	Merchant	7.30	Fair	7.30	Goodnight
Sat	14 Feb	1.30m	Merchant	1.30m	Fair	1.30m	Goodnight
Sat	14 Feb	7.30	Merchant	7.30	Fair	7.30	Goodnight

tions are in rehearsal and performance at any one time, and so organisation is easier. Savings can be made by restaging existing popular productions again and again over a period of years. It is also argued that a higher standard of production results from the intensive periods of rehearsal and performance that this production system requires.

Production Organisations

These are companies which produce theatre shows but which do not own their own theatre venues. There are basically two types of these companies:

1 commercial production companies
2 non-commercial touring theatre companies.

The Commercial Production Company

These are often quite small organisations based in an office with only a few permanent staff. Because they need to keep overheads to a minimum, they operate without the permanent backstage and front-of-house staff found in theatre venues. A typical company may only include the Producer, Production Manager, Business Manager and a few secretarial staff as permanent employees. They work to bring together a team of theatre professionals to realise a particular project. This involves appointing a director, designers, actors, and freelance production personnel. Each show is put together from scratch and is independent of the last. The duration of the production is often not known. At any moment the producer may decide to cut the losses and close the show. Successful productions, in contrast, can run for years and are often reproduced internationally.

Initially, to keep overall running costs down to a minimum, the production manager will negotiate with external suppliers to provide the scenery, and if the production is to be staged at a London theatre, to hire the lighting and sound equipment. If the production is to tour the country, a series of venues are arranged. If the show is targeted at the London West End, the location, size and type of theatre is vital.

Because the aim of the production company is to make money, every show is a package that is put together to provide an attractive investment opportunity. This often means casting 'star' actors and, if the production is destined for London's West End, securing a suitable venue. The project is then sold to potential investors. (The largest London productions may need to run for over a year, playing to full houses, before they begin to show a profit!)

Examples of commercial production organisations:

Really Useful Theatre Company
Bill Kenwright Productions.

Non-Commercial Touring Theatre Companies

There are a large number of theatre companies which rehearse and tour performances throughout the country because they do not have their own venue. The most prestigious of these companies receive grants from Regional Arts Associations and are registered with **Equity**. Smaller companies may also receive grants and often belong to the **Independent Theatre Council** (ITC). Typical companies will have a core of permanent staff and hire additional freelance staff for each project.

Below is a rough guide to a classification of performance companies. Remember that large-scale companies can produce small-scale work from time to time and that the boundaries between these categories are fluid. For example, Hull Truck Theatre Company tour small-scale, medium-scale and large-scale productions.

Large-scale touring companies:

English Touring Theatre
Rambert Dance Company
The Royal Ballet
Opera North
Northern Ballet.

Medium-scale touring companies:

Theatre de Complicite
Shared Experience
Out of Joint
Oxford Stage Company
Northern Stage
Compass Theatre
Siobhan Davies Dance Company
Hull Truck.

Small-scale touring companies:

Paines Plough
IOU
Frantic Assembly
Forced Entertainment
Trestle
Red Shift
Most Theatre-in-education (T.I.E.) companies.

Non-Producing Theatres

These are also known as **receiving houses** since they only *receive* visiting companies. They provide venues for the variety of production organisations already described. Non-producing theatres tend to require only a small permanent staff who look after the building and liaise with visiting companies. Most receiving houses rely on a regular crew of casual staff who are hired to augment the existing theatre staff.

There are two types of non-producing theatres:

1 West End theatres
2 Regional receiving houses.

The West End Theatre

These are owned by large organisations with an interest in the arts or leisure industries and are hired for open-ended runs. The building is usually hired with a minimal staff and little equipment. Everything else that is required is brought in by the production company. Productions may close after a few weeks or like the musical *Cats*, may stay in the same venue for years.

Regional Receiving Houses

There is a network of non-producing theatres that spans the length and breadth of the UK. From Aberdeen to Plymouth and from Aberystwyth to Norwich, a variety of venues provide fully equipped facilities for touring companies to hire usually for a week at a time.

Examples of large-scale receiving houses (over 800 seats):

Manchester Palace
Manchester Opera House
Theatre Royal, Plymouth
Nottingham Theatre Royal
Bradford Alhambra
Leeds Grand

Derngate, Northampton
Sheffield Lyceum
Grand Opera House, Belfast
Edinburgh Festival Theatre
New Theatre, Cardiff.

Medium-scale receiving houses (350–800 seats):

Wakefield Theatre Royal and Opera House
Theatr yr Werin, Aberystwyth
Eden Court Theatre, Inverness
Lawrence Batley Theatre, Huddersfield.

Small-scale receiving houses (under 350 seats):

Most studio theatres and Fringe venues
The Green Room, Manchester
Georgian Theatre, Richmond
Battersea Arts Centre, London
Chapter Arts Centre, Cardiff.

A number of venues are designated as **Arts Centres**. These have a variety of different sized venues available for touring productions. For example, the Warwick Arts Centre, in addition to a gallery and a film theatre, has:

Concert Hall – 1471 seats
Theatres – 573 seats
Studio Theatre – 150 seats.

SUMMARY

Companies With Theatres

- *Repertory theatre* – at any one time has one production in performance, one in rehearsal and several in planning.
- *Repertoire* – several productions are available at any one time. A rotation system can offer the audience a different play each night during a week. Has several productions in performance and several in planning or at rehearsal stage.
- *Stagione* – a small number of productions are available at any one time. Intensive rehearsal followed by lots of performances close together. Productions are rotated over several years and re-rehearsed with new casts as required.

Companies Without Theatres

- *Commercial* – these aim to make profits by putting together a business package to realise particular scripts. Each production is separate and rents space in a West End theatre or tours to regions. Some productions may run for many years and return high profits for their investors.
- *Non-commercial* – these are grant funded and stage regional and national tours to re-

ceiving houses. Usually a single production is toured at a time.

Theatres Without Companies

These are known as receiving houses. West End theatres are hired on open-ended runs. Other theatres are part of the national touring circuit and are hired by the week.

The Stage

WHAT IS A THEATRE?

What do we think of if we are asked to imagine a theatre? Many of us would think of an ornate, late Victorian building with plush seats arranged in stalls, a dress circle and side boxes. And, of course, a stage. But a theatre can be any place in which a performance occurs. It doesn't need to have a defined stage area, curtain, raised seating or the ability to black out daylight. Indeed, it has been argued that all that is required for theatre to take place is an empty space and an actor to walk across it.

TYPES OF STAGE

Performances take place in a wide range of venues both indoors and in the open air. There is a variety of options for arranging the performance area in relation to the audience. The decision about where the audience are to be positioned to view the performance will have a fundamental impact on the nature of the performance and wide ranging implications for the design, the direction and the atmosphere of the performance event itself.

Figure 1.3   *A plan showing the typical layout of a theatre*

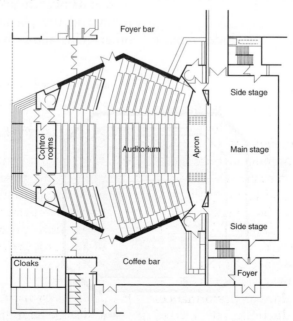

Essentially there are four main types of stage arrangement:

1 the thrust stage
2 the end stage
3 the traverse stage
4 the arena stage.

Many venues are adaptable and are able to offer more than one staging format. Some theatres, particularly those built in the second half of the twentieth century, are able to offer totally **flexible staging**. Often, however, compromises have to be made to accommodate some or all of the formats, so even a flexible venue is unlikely to suit each staging form equally.

The Thrust Stage

The first large performance venues were Greek **amphitheatres** in which the steeply raked auditorium was arranged around a semi-circular playing area, backed by a walled *skene*. This is a typical thrust stage arrangement. The semi-circular stage protrudes into the auditorium and is surrounded on three sides by seating. At one extremity of such a stage, the actor has a significant portion of the audience to the sides and behind him. The sweep of these auditoria is typically an arc of around 220°.

Variations of thrust stages include typical Elizabethan playhouses, such as The Globe and The Swan. These have a rectangular stage and end stages with a large apron. This variation of stage also places a significant proportion of the audience to the sides. The sweep of the auditorium is over 180°. Action on a thrust stage is, therefore, often viewed against a background of other members of the audience.

Examples include:

- Greek amphitheatre at Epidaurus, circa 4 BC
- Olivier Theatre, Royal National Theatre
- Quarry Theatre, West Yorkshire Playhouse
- The Globe, Southwark, London
- The Swan, Stratford upon Avon
- Crucible, Sheffield
- Chichester Festival Theatre
- The Young Vic, London
- Salisbury Playhouse
- Almeida Theatre, Islington, London.

The End Stage

This form of staging became common in theatre once performances moved indoors. Actors played at court, in halls or in converted tennis courts.

The audience are arranged at one end of the room and the playing area is situated at the other. This allows most of the action to take

Figure 1.4   *A thrust stage*

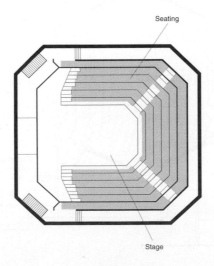

Seating

Stage

Figure 1.5   *An end stage*

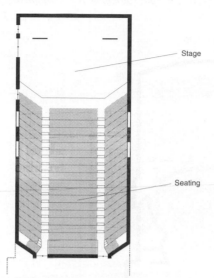

place against the stage wall or a scenic backdrop. Typically, the sweep of the auditorium seating is below 135° and, since the audience are situated in a single block it is usually necessary to improve their sightlines by raising the stage platform. In larger venues also the auditorium is raked and there are often balconies.

Examples include:

Mermaid Theatre, London
The Green Room, Manchester
Hampstead Theatre, London
Courtyard Theatre, West Yorkshire Playhouse, Leeds
Norwich Playhouse.

The Proscenium Stage

A type of end stage is found in the **proscenium arch theatre**. This format developed mainly due to scenic requirements in the seventeenth and eighteenth centuries. It became the dominant staging form of the nineteenth and much of the twentieth centuries.

The end stage arrangement is enclosed with the playing area separated from the audience by a wall – the proscenium. This has an opening. In older theatres the proscenium is decorated in an elaborate manner and appears as a picture frame through which all the action is viewed. Scenery

can be changed easily behind the proscenium. A front curtain is often used during such changes, as well as to indicate Act divisions.

To improve visibility, older proscenium stages were often raked (sloping from back to front), although more modern theatres with a proscenium tend to have flat stages with a steeply raked auditorium instead. Due to the nature of the picture frame stage, where all of the action must be viewed through the narrow opening in the proscenium, it is difficult to arrange large numbers of spectators close to the stage. The geometry of such spaces is dictated by the sightlines and narrow auditoriums are common due to the restriction of the width of the proscenium arch.

Examples of proscenium arch theatres include:

Bristol Old Vic
Bath Theatre Royal
Palace Theatre, Manchester
Lyceum, Sheffield
Theatre Royal, Northampton
Cambridge Arts Theatre
Royal Shakespeare Theatre, Stratford-Upon-Avon
● and the vast majority of theatres in London's West End including the Royal Opera House, Covent Garden.

Figure 1.6   a *A proscenium stage is a type of end stage format* b *A proscenium with cut cloths*

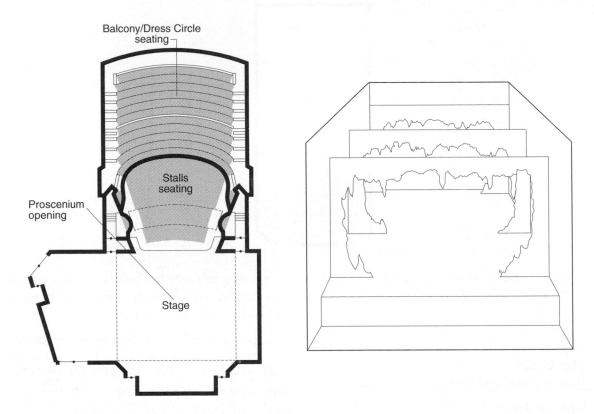

Some more modern proscenium theatres are:

Belgrade Theatre, Coventry
Lyttleton Theatre, Royal National Theatre, London
Birmingham Repertory Theatre
Chester Gateway
Glyndebourne Opera House
Plymouth Theatre Royal.

The Traverse Stage

This is a fairly unusual arrangement of stage space, with the audience situated on either side of the playing area. The action is always seen against the other bank of audience members. There are very few performance venues that are set up permanently in this format. Many smaller, flexible studio theatres are able to offer the traverse stage as one in a range of possible formats.

Examples of theatres which can offer a traverse stage:

The Traverse, Edinburgh
Old Fire Station, Oxford.

Advantages of the Traverse Format

Relatively large numbers of audience members can be seated close to the action. It can be appropriate artistically: a restoration comedy might invite the audience to reflect on its own society by placing the audience in traverse. *The Seagull* at the West Yorkshire Playhouse in 1998 was staged in traverse at the Courtyard Theatre and worked particularly well to heighten the discussion about the nature of theatre which occurs within the play.

Figure 1.7 *A traverse stage*

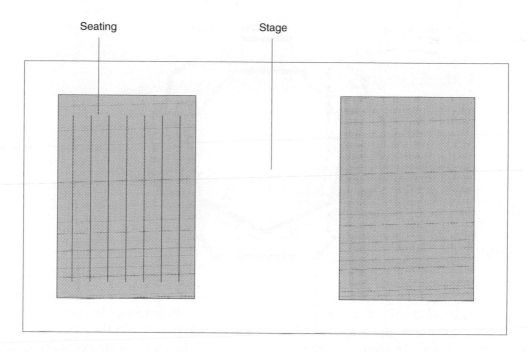

Disadvantages

Scenery must be minimal, except at the sides of the acting area and actors always have audience behind them. The stage area is limited to a relatively narrow strip.

The Arena Stage

This format is also known as an **island stage**, **theatre-in-the-round** or **centre stage**. The auditorium encircles the stage entirely. The circular stage is a performance space which has ancient origins and it has had many advocates in modern theatre, notably **Stephen Joseph**.

Out of necessity, all of the actors' entrances are made through the audience or from under the stage and during the performance their backs are towards one section of the audience at all times. This fact restricts the distance from which the performance can be fully appreciated and may be one reason why venues that are designed for permanent in-the-round staging are relatively small in size. The other difficulty is in getting large numbers of audience members close to the acting area, so auditoriums are usually steeply raked, or tiered. Although arena stages can be very exciting performance spaces, there are significant difficulties for actors and the whole production team.

Examples of arena stages are:

Royal Exchange Theatre, Manchester
New Victoria Theatre, Stoke-on-Trent
Stephen Joseph Theatre, Scarborough
The Orange Tree Theatre, Richmond, Surrey.

OPEN STAGE OR CLOSED STAGE?

Whilst the proscenium stage provides many advantages in terms of the mechanics of staging, there is always a very definite division between actor and audience, which can be problematic. The proscenium is, therefore, an end stage format which creates a **closed stage**.

Figure 1.8   *An arena stage*

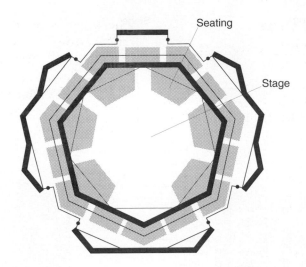

Although the barrier of the proscenium can be alleviated by the addition of an apron or forestage, the auditorium and stage areas remain distinctly separate. In contrast, the **open stage** (open end stage, arena, thrust and traverse formats) is often regarded as a more dynamic performance venue, since there is a sense of unity between actors and audience.

Since the Second World War, a number of theatre buildings have been designed or adapted to remove the artificial barrier of the proscenium arch, but to retain the flexibility of a closed end stage. In these the proscenium opening was not gilded as an elaborate picture frame, but rather became a natural (and wider) termination of the auditorium walls and ceiling. A false proscenium can always be added when required to reduce the size of the stage opening.

Site specific staging

Promenade Productions

This is the oldest format of actor–audience relationship. The spectators are mobile and can follow the action wherever it occurs. This can even take the opposite form to an arena stage, with the audience in the middle and the action around the edges of a space (as in the Mediaeval tradition of loci or houses). It is also the form that street performers use.

There are a number of performance groups who specialise in exterior, site specific promenade performances. Some events can even involve a few miles of walking! Another variation is the **installation**: the audience moves (sometimes as individuals) through an environment which has been designed to contain many small acting areas.

Promenade performances can take place in 'found spaces' or in existing theatre buildings, usually in flexible studio theatres where the seating can be removed or retracted. There may be little permanent scenery or definition of stage area. Throughout the performance the action shifts continually around the space and the audience mingle with members of the cast in what can be a dynamic experience.

DESCRIBING THE STAGE AREA

Describing an End Stage

An end stage is traditionally divided into segments, so that precise areas of the stage can be identified when necessary. The area nearest the audience is referred to as **downstage** and the part furthest away is **upstage**. Think of the physical attributes of the raked stage which goes up at the back to help the sightlines from the auditorium.

The other edges of the stage are always described from the actor's perspective, so, **stage left** is the right area of the stage as the audience views it. **Stage right** is the left area of the stage as viewed from the auditorium. The stage is bisected by a **centreline** which is usually marked on the stage for setting purposes.

Figure 1.9   *Remember that the stage is described from the actors' perspective*

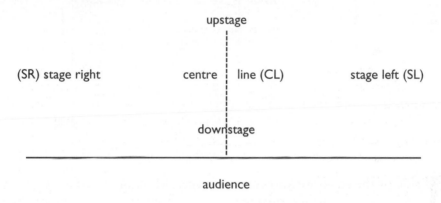

We can identify nine basic areas of the stage (Figure 1.10).

Figure 1.10   *Nine areas of the stage*

Upstage Right (USR)	Upstage Centre (USC)	Upstage Left (USL)
Centre Stage Right (CSR)	Centre Stage (CS)	Centre Stage Left (CSL)
Downstage Right (DSR)	Downstage Centre (DSC)	Downstage Left (DSL)

audience

For more detailed descriptions we may wish to subdivide the stage further.

It may be necessary to indicate locations of ac-tors and props with greater precision (Figure 1.11).

Figure 1.11   *A more detailed stage plan may be used to locate actors and props*

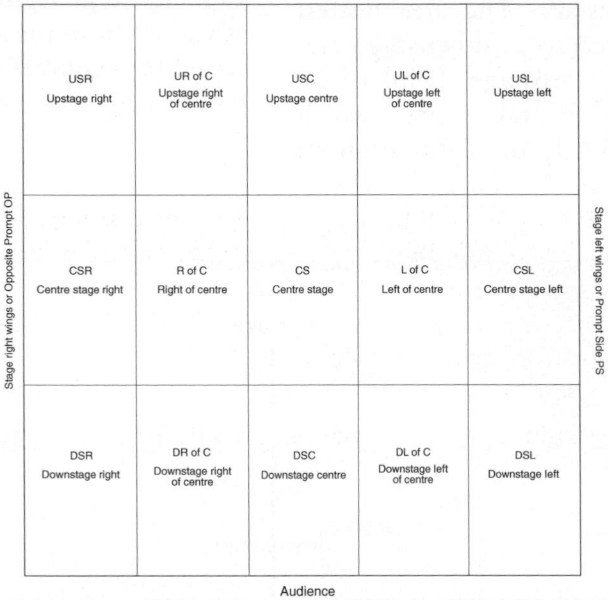

USR Upstage right	UR of C Upstage right of centre	USC Upstage centre	UL of C Upstage left of centre	USL Upstage left
CSR Centre stage right	R of C Right of centre	CS Centre stage	L of C Left of centre	CSL Centre stage left
DSR Downstage right	DR of C Downstage right of centre	DSC Downstage centre	DL of C Downstage left of centre	DSL Downstage left

Stage right wings or Opposite Prompt OP (left side)

Stage left wings or Prompt Side PS (right side)

Audience

The areas at the side of the stage are known as the **wings**. Moving a chair further **onstage** means moving it towards the centreline of the stage. Moving it **offstage** means moving it away from the centreline of the stage and to-wards the wings.

Figure 1.12   *This diagram shows one method for describing areas of an arena stage*

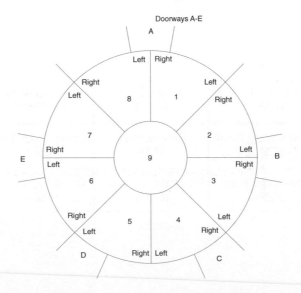

In proscenium theatres, stage left is also known as **prompt side** (PS), traditionally the side of the stage for the Deputy Stage Manager's prompt desk. Stage right is known as **opposite prompt** (OP). The prompt desk is actually situated stage right in some venues and this is known as a '**bastard prompt**'!)

TECHNICAL DRAWINGS

All those involved in staging theatre need to be able to understand technical drawings.

Plans are technical drawings of the building and stage area from above. They are always drawn to scale – usually 1:25 or 1:50 (imperial scales of 1:24 and 1:48 can still be found). Plans are used for different purposes: a lighting plan will show the hanging positions and the lights being used; a ground plan will show the stage area with masking and scenic items.

A **section** is a view from the side of the stage. Sections may be required for organisation of the setting or for calculating lighting beam angles.

An **elevation** is a front view of the stage or scenic piece for example.

Figure 1.13   *This example of a plan view shows the sightlines from the edges of the auditorium and how the wings are hidden from view*

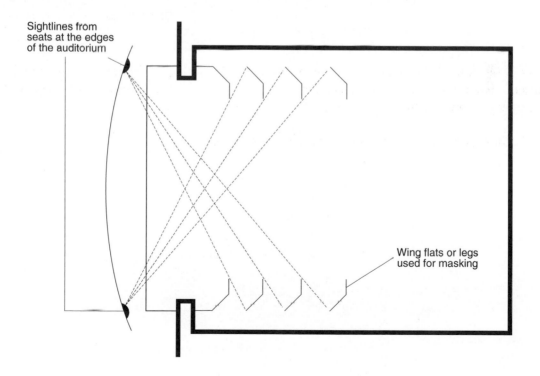

Sightlines from seats at the edges of the auditorium

Wing flats or legs used for masking

Figure 1.14   *This example of a section view shows the borders which are used to mask the equipment hanging above the stage*

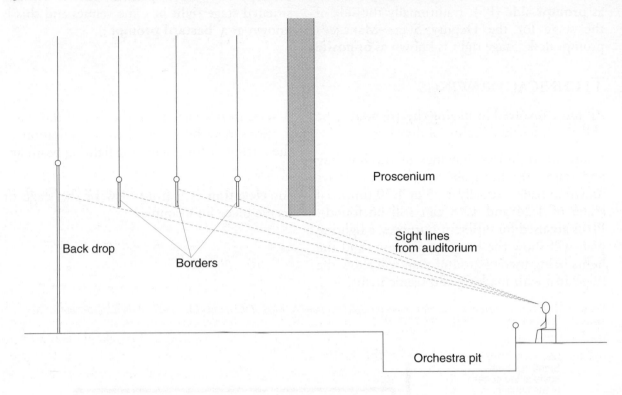

PRODUCTION PLANNING

The Process of Production

Producing theatre is a collaborative act. To be able to mount a performance successfully, the co-operation of a large number of people, all working towards a common goal, is required. The process of production can be exhausting, as well as exhilarating, since staging a live performance is a complex task, fraught with potential pitfalls.

Extensive planning and preparation will be undertaken in the weeks or even months before the opening night. Despite this effort, there is no guarantee that all will go perfectly.

The pressure of producing a performance event for a live audience concentrates the mind! On the day of the performance, the production team rely on all of the planning, rehearsal and preparatory work that has been put in previously. This effort helps to mitigate the sudden rush of adrenaline which accompanies the anticipation immediately before the start of a performance. Just as performers hope that the rehearsal period has equipped them to work in front of an audience, members of the production team also rely on their careful preparation, so that any apprehensiveness does not affect the performance.

The best performances are those where the actors and technical staff work together to 'get it right'. It is difficult for either to work in isolation. The mechanics of production should be so practised as to seem invisible to the spectator, whilst setting off the show to best advantage.

The process of production is not separate from the final event. The planning involves a combination of conceptual, artistic processes and practical, technical activities. A great variety of skills and a large number of people are required to achieve the effect that is desired in performance.

THE PRODUCTION TEAM

Because of the diverse range of activities required to stage an event, there are a wide range of job titles. These may differ slightly between organisations and performance type. However, each role will have distinct areas of responsibility, which are agreed in advance.

The production process for staging theatre is perhaps the most complex and has the most roles. Some organisations may not have the resources or need to employ a full range of staff.

Smaller companies may combine roles: a stage manager may have to handle the setting, lighting and sound. Larger theatre organisations may have whole departments and even additional specialists, such as head of props and wig makers. Live music events require a small core of staff to plan and co-ordinate the production, but they rely upon a large number of crew or 'roadies' to realise the performance at each venue.

THE STARTING POINT FOR A PRODUCTION

Most productions begin with a **script** which will be interpreted by the Director and Designers. However, some productions may start from an idea or a general theme and may not have a written text until fairly late in the rehearsal process. Devised performances like this will, therefore, evolve in a slightly different manner.

A traditional theatre production tends to begin with a written text which has been selected by the artistic board, production company or by an individual director for a particular reason. The play may have a particular relevance to the place and time; a particular treatment or production concept may communicate specific ideas to an audience. Alternatively, the play may have been chosen on the grounds that it will be popular and, therefore, a commercial success. Whatever the reason for choosing to stage a particular script, permission must be obtained before the production process can begin.

Securing the Rights

It is usually the task of a senior member of the theatre staff to establish whether rights are payable on a script. This may be the duty of the Production Manager, Director or Administrator. If rights are payable, it is essential that **permission** is sought and approval given before rehearsals begin. Rights may still be payable, even if the audience are not being charged for their tickets.

Agent or Publisher?

Establish who holds the rights. Copyright details and contact addresses are published in the front of playscripts. For unpublished work, it is necessary to deal with the playwright or their agent directly. Original play scripts can be performed without a fee if they are out of copyright. Works are protected by copyright during the lifetime of the author and for 70 years after their death. However, translations, adaptations and modern works do attract fees.

Request Permission

A phone call will usually be sufficient to establish if the play is currently available for performance. There are often restrictions on both amateur and professional productions of plays and musicals. Some may be withdrawn temporarily. Many contemporary plays and musicals are not available for amateur productions, since the copyright owner may consider that a non-professional production will prejudice future professional presentations of the same script.

A **Free Licence** may be granted to schools and colleges if the play is being staged purely for educational purposes and where the audience is entirely 'in house'. This arrangement precludes any audience members travelling to the venue 'from their ordinary place of overnight residence', and should be applied for *in advance* of rehearsals.

Following an initial enquiry, you will need to write with full details of the production:

venue(s)
amateur, student or professional cast
number and dates of performances
seating capacity of each venue
ticket prices.

If permission is granted, you will be notified of the fee for each performance:

- For plays there will be a straight fee per performance. The fee will vary according to the published charging bands and the scale of your production. Amateur and student productions usually pay considerably less than professional companies.

- For musicals, permission is usually granted on the basis of a percentage of box office takings, in addition to an advance fee for the hire of librettos and orchestra scores. [The usual rates are between 7½% and 15%]. It is common for a musical to incur a royalty payment of 12% of gross or total box office takings.

Conditions of Permission

The granting of a licence to perform a piece of work is usually given on the understanding that the published work will not be altered in any way. This means that lines cannot be cut, choreography amended or music rearranged. Specific written permission must be sought in advance if you wish to do any of these things.

Licenses for performance are usually given to amateur and educational groups on the understanding that it is made clear on all promotional material that the audience will witness an amateur performance. Also, that the name of the author is included in all announcements and on all programmes.

THE PRODUCTION CONCEPT

Before rehearsals begin, the play is discussed in detail by the Director and members of the production team. There are discussions with the design team to formulate a coherent artistic concept for the play. A series of pre-production or design meetings will be held to discuss these creative ideas. Practical, technical and financial considerations can impact on the design ideas, forcing modification of the original scheme.

In a devised performance, the creative process usually evolves as an integral part of rehearsals and involves substantial input from members of the cast and other members of the production team. Whilst this is an exciting way of working, it usually results in the details of the production becoming fixed at a much later stage of the production process.

Collaborative work in the early stages of a production is vital if there is to be a coherent response to the text which has been chosen. Decisions may be taken at a relatively early stage in the production process, which have far-reaching consequences for the final production.

Initial designs and directorial requirements will be drawn up and presented to a larger meeting where they will be scrutinised by the Production Manager and Heads of Departments. Any potential difficulties and problem areas should be highlighted at this stage. The proposed designs will be costed and a production budget will be agreed with a breakdown of costs for each area of the production.

KEY STAGES IN THE PRODUCTION PROCESS

Pre-Production

This is the period when the play is planned, the concept established, designs submitted and preliminary work undertaken to make sure that everything is ready for the move into the venue. Rehearsals will take place, the set will be built and painted, costumes and props found, made, or hired, lighting plans drawn and sound recorded. Specialist equipment may be borrowed or hired.

The Fit-Up or Get-In

This is the moment when the company moves into the performance space. Usually, they will inherit a 'black box', literally an empty stage without scenery, masking (bits of set which block the audience's view of the wings, etc) or lanterns on the rig. The fit-up involves assembling the set, the lighting rig and the sound equipment.

The Production Week

During the production week final touches are made to the set and masking is put in place. The lighting is focused and plotted cue by cue. Sound effects are plotted. The cast rehearse on stage. A technical rehearsal is held in which each scene change and technical effect is practised until it is correct. The technical rehearsal is followed by one or more dress rehearsals, each of which is a complete and continuous run of the play in full costume. These take place under performance conditions.

The Run

This is the period of performances from the opening show to the last night. Apart from crewing the shows, there may be additional work for technical and stage management personnel, and actors, during the daytime. They may be involved in re-rehearsing or perfecting parts of the show currently in performance, or could even be preparing for the next show to be staged.

The Get-Out or Strike

This is the several hours of technical work involved in returning the venue back to the 'black box' state. The set and masking are taken down, props and costumes packed away, lighting and sound equipment de-rigged. For weekly shows the get-out will usually occur on the Saturday night and will continue into the early hours of Sunday morning.

Post-Production

This is the period immediately following the last performance. Costumes may need to be cleaned and stored back in the wardrobe. Props, lighting and sound equipment are stored. The set is usually broken up unless it is likely to be used again in the future. Some wood may be reclaimed for future use. All hired equipment is returned to the suppliers. The prompt copy, plans and all other documentation are gathered up by the stage management team and filed in the Production Manager's office. A post-production meeting is often held to discuss any difficulties that arose during the production period, in the hope that any similar problems can be avoided in future.

A PRODUCTION CHRONOLOGY

This is a timescale for a typical show in a regional repertory theatre. The times given are the months, weeks and days before the opening night, on the run up to the performance.

Pre-production Planning	
6 months	Season of plays are planned by Artistic Director and approved by Administrative or Financial Director, Production Manager, Head of Marketing and Board of Directors. Preliminary budgets are fixed.
5 months	Marketing begins. Designers are contracted. Information, such as technical drawings and specifications are sent to the design team.
3–4 months	A design meeting is held. Initial design ideas are submitted. Auditions are held. Casting is carried out.
2 months	Final designs are approved. The production is costed.
6 weeks	The set model and technical (working) drawings are produced. Costume drawings are produced. There is a design production meeting: technical and design staff meet to discuss all technical and design aspects of the production. Potential problem areas are identified and discussed and a budget breakdown is established. The model and drawings are used by workshop carpenters to build the set.

5 weeks	Set building continues. Wardrobe staff source fabrics and begin costume-making.
4 weeks	The Stage Manager begins to source props. The prompt copy is prepared. Sound experimentation and recording is undertaken.
3 weeks	The first read through happens and designs are presented to the cast. Rehearsals begin.
2 weeks	Programme details are finalised and sent to the printers. All props should be present in rehearsal. Costume fittings are done. Sounds are presented to the Director and used in rehearsal.
1 week	The last performances of the current show in repertory are going on. The first run through in rehearsal is carried out. Most of the marketing and publicity activity happens at this stage; media interviews take place. The printed programme is delivered. The final preparations for the fit-up are made. The lighting plan is finalised. Sound recordings are completed. Costumes are completed. Collections of props are finalised and hire equipment is collected.
4 days (Sun)	Get-in and fit-up of new production. Set installed on stage. Light and sound equipment rigged.
3 days (Mon)	Lighting focus and plotting are completed and the sound plot is finalised. Set work continues.
2 days (Tue)	The technical rehearsal happens today. Final painting and dressing of the set is done.
1 day (Wed)	Dress rehearsals and preview performance
Opening night (Thurs)	Final dress rehearsal and the opening (press) night.

On the Monday following the opening night rehearsals for the next play in repertory begin.

The Role of the Designer

The Designer contributes to the production by interpreting the play, text or music to produce a visual (or in the case of the Sound Designer, an **aural**) response. The Designer needs to be able to communicate clearly to a wide variety of people, if the design is to be realised effectively. The Designer needs to work with directors, other designers, actors, the stage management team, technicians and other members of the production team.

THEATRE DESIGN

There are four main areas of theatre design:

1 set
2 costume
3 lighting
4 sound.

Designers try to combine all four aspects to create an imaginative environment for the world of the play. As well as contributing to the atmosphere, setting and lighting also define the limits of the acting area. Design involves more than creative ideas, it also involves putting ideas into practice. Design goes beyond the communication of the realistic environment (the historical period, location, season and wealth of the characters), it also expresses the style and mood of the play. The design elements are often important in communicating elements of the sub-text and underlying themes.

Set Design and Props

Settings provide a visual reflection of the world of the play and will express the mood, spirit and style in which the production is presented to the audience. Props (short for properties) complement the set design and contribute to the overall effect.

Costume Design

At its simplest, costume provides clothes for the performer. Costume can also communicate historical period, season, age of the wearer, their social status, occupation, personality, emotional state and individualism, for example. Costume design includes the design of shoes, hats, and accessories such as jewellery, purses, wallets, handbags and parasols, if appropriate.

Lighting Design

The illumination of the performers can also create mood, atmosphere, sense of place and time. In addition, lighting can communicate more complex themes, emotions and abstract ideas. Colour, direction and level of light are particularly important in creating the environment on stage.

Sound Design

Sound design involves the use of sound effects and music either as spot effects or used to underscore specific sequences. Sound can be live or recorded. The expressive quality of the sound will have a direct psychological effect on the audience. Sound influences emotions and mood. The level and direction of the sound can also be important signals to the audience.

TASK

Arrange to see a play (or think of one that you have seen recently). Pay special attention to all the design features: set design, costume design, lighting design and sound design. What do you think the design team were trying to convey by the way that they used different design features? Was the set design used to give a sense of realism or fantasy to the play? Were the costumes appropriate to the historical period, or had the Designer used modern costumes for a historical drama? If so, why do you think they did this? Were there any aspects which seemed to conflict, perhaps bright sunny lighting but sinister sound? Could you detect any underlying messages through the use of design? Analyse in as much detail as you can.

Design Skills

Once the overall artistic concept has been established, the Designer will decide which elements to accentuate and which to use subtly. Composition of the stage area is a key consideration and this involves an understanding of elements such as:

- space
- time
- volume
- perspective
- line
- form
- colour
- tone.

Designing requires creative, artistic thinking and practical, problem-solving skills. When designing, there are many different aspects of the production to take into account:

how, where and when the action happens
the performers' requirements

the Director's vision
the style of the piece
the artistic interpretation of the text
the communication of meaning
how to create the world of the play
the limits of the particular stage environment.

THE CONTRIBUTION OF DESIGN

The Designer's contribution to a production may be immense. The Designer may be responsible for the characteristic look of a show but may not receive the appropriate acknowledgement. For example, Sally Jacobs, who created a striking stage and costume design for Peter Brook's famous production of *A Midsummer Night's Dream*, is rarely mentioned.

In Europe during the late twentieth century, a trend for '**conceptual design**' has emerged. This is where a director works closely with one designer, who is responsible for all aspects of the design for a production. This implies an overall, unified design which can be very striking. A designer with such an important role is sometimes called a **scenographer** and the term for their work is **scenography**.

TASK

Investigate the contribution of directors, designers and scenographers (see below) to modern theatre. You may like to consider the work of some of the following practitioners:

Adolphe Appia
Edward Gordon Craig
Robert Edmond Jones
Vsevolod Meyerhold
Erwin Piscator
Bertolt Brecht and Casper Neher
and the contemporary work of Josef Svoboda, Ralph Koltai, John Bury, John Napier.

Directors whose productions tend to have a strong scenographic influence include Peter Brook, Peter Stein, Robert Wilson and Robert Lepage.

ANALYSING DESIGN

To learn more about stage design, you may find it helpful to analyse the work of others. Here is a brief checklist to help you think about design:

Does the design express the mood and style of the play?
Do different aspects of the design complement or clash to good effect?
Does the design work for the actors on stage, or hinder their performance?

Does it communicate time and place?
How does the design comment on the world in general and the specific themes of the play?
Does the design engage you and make you think?
Is the design one unified theme or does it set up layers of possible meanings that communicate in performance?
Does the design stimulate and excite you?
Can you suggest *practical* ways to improve the design?

TASK

This is a design case study of Chekhov's *The Cherry Orchard*. Study the picture of the setting for the 1998 Method and Madness touring production of the play.

Figure 2.1   *Stage set from* The Cherry Orchard, *1998 Method and Madness tour*

The play was written in 1904, is set in Russia and is about the rise of industrialisation, the coming of the train, and the decline of the land-owning classes. The passing of time and the setting of the orchard dominate the drama. Most of the characters in the play are self-obsessed and incapable of action. The loss of the trees at the end of the play symbolises the passing of a social order and provides an astonishing prediction of the coming Revolution.

The opening Act is set in a room, known as the nursery, in a large house. These are the stage directions:

Dawn is breaking and the sun will soon be up. It is May. The cherry trees are in bloom, but it is cold and frosty in the orchard. The windows of the room are shut.

Consider the dramatic elements in the photograph. Knowing something about the play you should be able to respond to the above image.

What does the design scheme for this production convey to you?
What is the most dominant feature?
What does the choice of furniture communicate to you?
What do you think is the significance of the toy train?
What do the ladders at the back of the set represent? (Do they suggest anything else other than the trees of the orchard?) How do the ladders relate to other aspects of the setting?
Can you comment on the floor and the lighting?

THE PROCESS OF DESIGN

A close, collaborative relationship between the Director, design team and performers is vital, if the design is to respond to changing needs and to match the overall artistic intentions of the production. However, methods of working often prevent such a close collaboration between members of the company. Often key design decisions are taken well in advance of the rehearsal period. The budget and production schedule are usually drawn up months in advance, which may create restrictions. The Director may already have a definite and distinct way in which they wish to work. Indeed, the Director may already have worked on key elements of the design before the Designer has even become involved.

The traditional theatre approach is for the Set Designer and Director to work together to establish a conceptual approach to the piece before other members of the design and production team are involved. This is not ideal since early decisions may restrict the contribution of others in the design and production team.

The ideal collaboration allows all members of the design team to contribute ideas at an early stage and to influence the development of *all* the design areas, and even directorial decisions. Performers can also contribute if decisions have not been finalised before rehearsals begin.

Preparation Before Meeting the Director

Designers usually go through a number of preparatory stages. These are outlined below.

Consider the Initial Stimulus Material

Designers need to read the text and attempt to imagine the play on stage. For musicals, opera and other music-based performances, the score, libretto and/or recordings provide the starting point.

It is best to read through the material in a single session, preferably without interruptions. At this point, it would be usual to note down any initial responses to the stimulus material. It is important to understand the narrative, key moments, main themes and to get a feel for the style of the play.

TASK

Imagine you are a designer preparing a new show. Select a script to think about, read through and then answer the following questions:

What do you think the play is about?
Why did you choose this play?
What relevance does it have?
Do you think a contemporary audience would come and see a production of this play?
When is it set? Where?
What does the first reading of the play suggest to you? Any particular atmosphere? Mood? Theme or motifs? Colours? Shapes? Tones? Textures? Patterns of light and shade? Directions of light? Sounds? Music? Volume direction of sound?

Research and Early Design Ideas

The next stage would be to re-read the text. This time the Designer would note down any specific references to the world of the play in the text and any stage directions which would influence the design approach. References to any of these things would be important:

particular events in the play
historical period
locale
season
time of day
weather conditions
temperature
costume
any changes in emphasis or mood
lighting effects such as lightning, a light being switched on, a candle being lit, a power cut or the sun setting
sounds such as a baby crying, a car arriving, or a radio being switched on
specific music titles, composers or general indicators. Such as 'magical music', 'frenetic music'.

Designers have to investigate the world of the play in detail. They have to understand the ideas expressed in the text and alluded to in the sub-text. Further research into specialist areas may be required:

historical period or specific events
political or philosophical concerns
key themes and motifs
individual locations and environments
implied style of the play.

Where Do Ideas Come From?

In addition to the text, the Designer should be alert to a range of other stimuli. These will include visual materials from books, magazines, photographs, paintings and sculpture for example. These can be very helpful for developing original design ideas and for use as examples to assist in the communication of those ideas to others.

A good tip is to build up a scrapbook of interesting visual material over a period of time. This will often spark creative thought and stimulate new design ideas. Examples of architecture, furniture, and costume may be particularly useful.

Lighting Design Ideas

Photographs of observed light effects in the world around us are a valuable reference for any designer, who may need to achieve a naturalistic summer sky, for example. Photographic examples of flat light, harsh shadows, directional light, winter sunshine, moonlight and so on can be extremely useful as future reference material for a lighting designer. Likewise, a multitude of images selected from printed material, newspapers, magazines, fine art, advertisements, picture libraries, CD-Roms, the Internet and other performances will provide stimulus material from which to develop ideas.

Sound Design Ideas

The Sound Designer will build up a collection of sound references which are used to generate original effects. Recordings may also provide a creative spark and stimulate new design ideas.

Music from the period of the play being designed may be helpful. Other pieces of music may help to create particular atmospheric or emotional moments in the performance.

As far as possible, the Sound Designer should gather original recordings of sound for performance work. Although sometimes this is impractical – a recording of the Space Shuttle taking off for example – many sounds can be recorded in the 'wild' or created in the studio.

Synthesisers, computers and effects units are able to create an infinite variety of sounds. Experiment with a variety of objects, textures and sound equipment to create all sorts of effects. A comb, recorded as it is run along a desktop, processed and slowed down can give an ominous rumble, for example.

TASK

Listen to a range of music recordings and keep a portfolio with notes on specific composers and pieces of music. What do individual pieces of music communicate to you? Concentrate on feelings, mood, and atmosphere.

Research some of the following composers and their styles of music. Identify when individual composers were working. This will help you in the future to match music or composers to a particular time in history and to select appropriate styles of music for a scene.

Composers:

Monteverdi	Liszt
J.S. Bach	Schubert
Vivaldi	Strauss
Purcell	Wagner
Handel	Tchaikovsky
Beethoven	Mussorsky
Mozart	Sibelius
Haydn	Vaughan-Williams
Brahms	Elgar
Chopin	Grieg
Schumann	Debussy
Berlioz	Ravel.

You may also like to research the music and theories of some of the following twentieth century composers: Schoenberg, Stockhausen, Stravinsky, Britten, Boulez, Tippett, Satie, Kurt Weill, John Cage, Phillip Glass, Arvo Part and Brian Eno.

Sound can also be sourced and downloaded from the Internet. However effects from library recordings should be used carefully and sparingly. Copyright may be an issue when using pre-existing recordings. Many theatres have a licence that allows copyright material to be replayed in performance. You need to check this and may need to complete a PRS return.

Do not worry about borrowing ideas from others – observing what other people do is an essential part of the creative process! The Designer must select what is appropriate for their project and develop those ideas in the new context. If original material is used in an unchanged form, it should be credited and permission should be sought if copyright is an issue.

The Designer uses the results of all their research to draw up an **Initial Scene Synopsis** (see pages 44 and 219). This is useful preparation for the first meeting with the Director.

Working with the Director

The Design Meeting

A design or pre-production meeting will be convened and is attended by the Production Manager, Director and other members of the design team. It is important to establish some of the practicalities and parameters for the production, which may prove to be limiting factors on the design plans. Certainly, it is essential to establish:

- the venue(s) in which the production will be staged
- the staging format, e.g. end stage, in-the-round, thrust or traverse (see pages 9–14) – this will have a major impact on the lighting design, the sound installation and where the speakers are placed
- the technical facilities available to you (types of equipment, system limitations, control facilities, potential rigging positions, etc).
- the time scale and schedules involved
- the overall budget and the budget allocated to each specific design area.

At the design meeting, the Director will discuss the main ideas and concept for the play. At this point, it is important to agree on the overall style of the production. The Director's vision may challenge the early design ideas, so it is important for the Designer to use this opportunity to understand the way in which the Director intends to approach the piece and the reason why.

Questions to ask the Director

It is important that the Designer questions the Director closely to gain an insight into what they hope to achieve. These are the sorts of questions that might need answers:

- How does the Director think the lighting or sound will contribute to the overall piece?
- Are there any additions to the script? Any cuts?
- What are the minimum requirements for the lighting or sound?
- Does the design need to represent location, mood, period, help to define style and/or acting areas?
- What is the style of the production?
- Are any pieces of music that the Director considers significant to the piece and, if so, why?

TASK

If you are working on the initial stages of a production, draw up a list of specific questions to ask the Director. Use your list as a guide during a production or design meeting to consolidate your own design ideas.

Practical and Technical Considerations

The Production Meeting will help you to establish the practical limits which must be applied to your design ideas.

Practical restrictions may include:

Time – the largest amount of time will be spent on research, field recordings and preparing the design. The greatest pressure of time is during the production week when the design needs to be realised in the space, plotted and rehearsed. This part of the process often takes longer than anticipated!

Personnel – an appropriate number of skilled technicians will be required to assist in realising the design. They will be needed to rig and operate equipment in the venue.

Equipment – a **Technical Specification Sheet** should be available from each venue with the relevant information on it. It is important to note that difficult rigging positions, inadequate or poorly maintained equipment, and insufficient cabling will limit the design. It is likely that the design will have to be modified for each theatre on a tour.

Budget – the Designer may need to hire equipment such as projectors, effects, intelligent lights and radio microphones. This will have a major impact on the whole production budget. The Designer may also need to buy colour filters, lighting accessories, music or effects CDs, tape and digital storage media such as MiniDiscs. The Designer can justify this expenditure on both artistic and practical grounds but will need to make a special case for extra funds.

The Designer and Rehearsals

The Designer's role does not stop once the practicalities have been established. The Designer attends rehearsals as often as time allows and maintains a close contact with the Director and co-designers throughout. Working alongside actors in rehearsal can be very rewarding. It provides the Designer with new ideas as the performance develops.

The design can evolve with the rest of the production and also respond quickly and imaginatively to changing ideas and new requirements.

Further chapters on lighting and sound can be found later in this book.

The Role of the Production Manager

The Production Manager oversees the work of all of the technical and backstage areas of the production. They are responsible for budgeting, scheduling work and co-ordinating the various production departments. The Production Manager is ultimately responsible for ensuring that all aspects of the production are completed within budget, according to the Designer's and Director's wishes and in time for the first public performance. For these reasons the Production Manager has to be conversant with *all* aspects of production.

So, the Production Manager oversees the cost-effectiveness and technical planning of the entire production process. They provide the link between the artistic, technical, administrative, and financial departments of the company or theatre and seek to resolve conflicts between these areas.

The Production Manager's key areas of responsibility:

- To advise on technical and production issues.
- To ensure performance rights are secured for each production.
- To establish a budget for each production.
- To cost design proposals.
- To allocate the budget breakdown.
- To monitor production costs in the context of the overall production budget.
- To undertake risk assessment of all production work.
- To be responsible for Health and Safety on stage and backstage.
- To ensure building regulations and other legislation are adhered to.
- To liaise with local Fire Officers and other licensing authorities.
- To draw up the production and technical schedules.
- To monitor and maintain the schedule and reschedule if necessary.
- To chair production meetings.
- To hire technical and production staff, including casual staff.
- To ensure staff and performers fulfil their contractual obligations.
- To supervise get-in and fit-up of production.
- To run the technical rehearsal and troubleshoot as necessary.
- To watch the dress rehearsal and give

technical and production advice as necessary.

- To monitor performances via the **Stage Management Show Report** and troubleshoot as necessary.

BUDGETING

The overall budget divides into two parts:

1 **Production costs** (those incurred in preparing the show for performance)
2 **Running costs** (expenses incurred during the run of the show).

The budget for a production should be realistic and agreed by all departments at an early stage. Each area of production or department will be allocated a figure according to the requirements of the production. Some shows may need to hire a lot of lighting equipment and effects, whilst others may be designed to use existing equipment. The budgets should reflect the likely demands. The Production Manager should always have a contingency fund to pay for unforseen expenses.

The Production budget should be reviewed regularly as work progresses. Funds may need to be reallocated as the production requirements alter.

SCHEDULING

The Production Manager creates a schedule that makes the most of the existing resources. The most important resources are *time* and *staff*. Wasteful use of either will impact on the budget.

The Production Manager must establish a **critical path**, which shows what needs to be done by when. The ultimate deadline is the first night of a show. In reality, the Production Manager treats the last dress rehearsal as the final deadline.

Time in a theatre building is very precious. It is expensive to maintain the building and its staff without the income generated by an audience. Consequently, the number of days left 'dark' is kept to a minimum. This means that pressure is exerted on all members of the production team to work quickly. Thorough planning and preparation, together with intelligent scheduling, are the keys to a successful production week.

See pages 22–23 for a typical production schedule.

The Production Manager holds regular production meetings to monitor the progress of each show. The Director and members of all of the production departments attend and this provides an opportunity to check that all is going smoothly, and to raise any problems. The Production Manager needs to set the agenda for this meeting and to chair it effectively.

The production week exerts the maximum pressure on all who are involved in the production process. It requires the careful co-ordination of all departments, who each require access to the stage at the same time! Although, with sensible scheduling, many different activities can take place in the same space simultaneously, one department's work often precludes the work of another, e.g. lights over the stage can't be focused whilst set construction is taking place, sound plotting needs silence.

Like budgets, schedules should not be imposed, but agreed by all departments in advance. It is important to establish precise deadlines and to acknowledge any expectations which are unrealistic.

The Production Manager's experience of theatrical production techniques is used to draw up a realistic schedule that incorporates a logical sequence of events and maximises the time available.

OTHER ROLES

Arbitrating

The Production Manager is often called upon to arbitrate between individuals with differing priorities and concerns. Good interpersonal skills are vital to be able to handle potentially explosive situations in a tactful way. Having an overview is important. Extensive experience and knowledge of theatre practice should allow the Production Manager an air of objective calmness whilst under considerable pressure.

Invisibility!

A good Production Manager will work unseen, constantly monitoring the production process and tackling issues that arise before they have had time to develop into problems.

chapter three
STAGE MANAGEMENT

The Stage Management Team

The stage management team are an essential element of any theatrical production. They co-ordinate the work of all of the other production departments and enable information to flow continuously between them. A regular flow of information from the rehearsal room to other members of the company is vital during any pre-production period. It is essential that this flow is a two-way process and that communication of information also occurs from the production departments back to the Director.

The stage management team must work together as a unit. In some venues and in small companies there may only be one team member, the Stage Manager, but in other organis-ations, the stage management structure may be more elaborate (see Figure 3.2). Historically, Assistant Stage Managers were known as Acting Stage Managers and, in addition to their stage management roles, they were required to appear in front of the audience, acting minor parts in the play!

Although different organisations use markedly differing staffing structures, a typical stage management team for a theatre performance would contain:

- **Stage Manager** (SM) (see page 36).
- **Deputy Stage Manager** (DSM) (see page 38).
- **Assistant Stage Manager** (ASM) (see page 40).

Figure 3.1 *A two-way flow of information is vital*

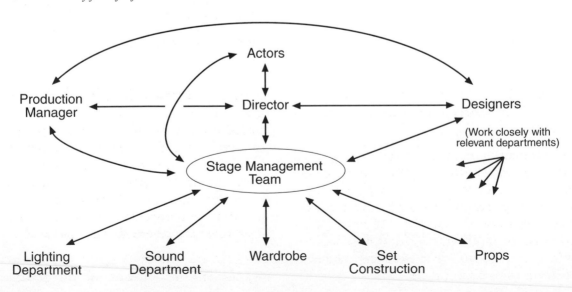

Figure 3.2   *Typical structures for stage management teams in different companies*

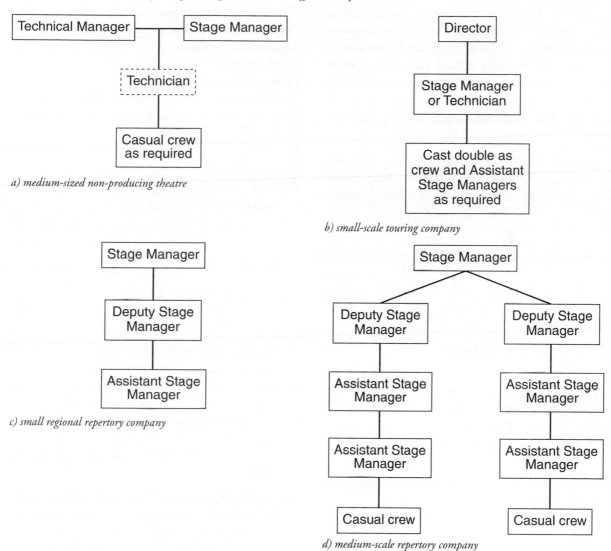

a) medium-sized non-producing theatre

b) small-scale touring company

c) small regional repertory company

d) medium-scale repertory company

- **Stage Crew** (as casual staff, these are not strictly members of the stage management team).

The ultimate aim of the stage management team is to achieve the smooth running of the show onstage in the most efficient way possible. In organisations working under Equity rules, the Stage or Company Manager is responsible for ensuring that working conditions are not violated and that overtime payments are made when appropriate.

There is no definitive list of the duties expected of a member of the stage management team. Indeed, members of the stage management team staff should be prepared for almost any eventuality. Stage management personnel are often put under enormous pressure, are expected to respond to changes and to take on additional responsibilities, more often than not when there is a severe shortage of time!

Precise duties will depend upon the size of the organisation, the nature of the production and the working methods of the performance company. There are minimum guidelines for the number of members of the stage management team in Equity registered companies (see below), but the actual number of stage management personnel will vary between organisations and from show to show, depending on the individual production requirements.

Whatever the duties expected of a member of the stage management team, they should be able to demonstrate the following qualities:

Meticulous organisation
Efficient time management
Excellent inter-personal skills
Appear unobtrusive
Be observant
Have a sense of humour
Have the ability to keep cool under pressure
Have the ability to think and respond quickly
Be friendly and considerable
Be flexible
Be firm yet fair
Be able to stand up for themselves when necessary.

MINIMUM STAGE MANAGEMENT STAFFING

These are the required minimum staffing requirements for Equity registered companies.

For repertory no less than:

1 SM
1 DSM
1 ASM.

(No member of the team should act or understudy.)

For repertoire not less than two teams, each consisting of:

1 SM
1 DSM
1 ASM.

(No member of this team should act or understudy.)

For companies registered with the Independent Theatre Council the minimum requirements are:

2 Team members for productions involving nine or more performers.
1 Dedicated Stage Manager for productions involving less than nine performers.
On minimal tours of less than four performers, a minimal set and short get-in time, it may be possible to operate without a dedicated SM.

The following section is offered as a guide to individual stage management roles in a traditional theatrical context. These roles are also discussed in more detail as this chapter develops.

The Role of the Stage Manager

The Stage Manager's job will vary considerably depending on the nature of the venue as well as the type of organisation and the complexity of the show.

Working directly to the Production Manager

(see page 31 for this job description), the SM is the senior member of the stage management team and, as such, is responsible for overseeing the work of all stage management personnel and for co-ordinating everything that happens backstage. During the rehearsal and production period the SM ensures that all of the production elements are correct and in the right place at the right time. Ensuring that there is a regular and efficient communication between production departments and the rehearsal room is the key to achieving this goal.

The SM controls the props budget and co-ordinates all of the scene changes and the running of properties during the performance. During the run of the show, in the absence of the Director, the SM has the overall responsibility for maintaining the quality of each performance and for ensuring that it is exactly as the Director intended.

In some theatres, especially when the production is not technically complex, the SM may not be involved during the performances. In fact, it is a distinct advantage for the SM to be free from specific performance duties, to watch the performance from 'out front'.

In repertory theatre, the SM may be released from specific tasks during performances. This allows the SM to concentrate on the pre-show planning and the production process of the next show in rehearsal. However, the SM still keeps an overview of the play in performance, so that they are able to troubleshoot any stage management problems.

In venues where the Deputy Stage Manager cues the performance from a control room and is not available on stage, the SM may be involved in the organisation of the stage and backstage areas during the performance. Although, if the show was a relatively straightforward one the Assistant Stage Manager could fulfil this role.

As the senior member of the stage management team, the SM directs the tasks of individual members of the team and can also stand in or 'double' for other members at any time during the production process.

When members of the company are engaged on Equity contracts, it is usually the responsibility of the SM to monitor the actual hours worked by actors and stage management personnel. The SM may also have to calculate overtime payments and act as the Union representative on behalf of the company.

1 The pre-production and rehearsal period

- To attend all Production Meetings and ensure that all decisions taken are minuted.
- To ensure all members of production staff have access to the script.
- To co-ordinate the stage management team.
- To delegate workload fairly and hold regular stage management meetings to check on progress.
- To establish and maintain an effective communication system with all other production departments, designers and the Production Manager.
- To assist the Director in drawing up a rehearsal schedule.
- To distribute copies of all rehearsal notes and minutes of production meetings.
- To attend the first rehearsal or read through.
- To organise the setting up of rehearsal spaces.
- To supervise the marking out of the set.
- To respond to rehearsal notes and production developments.
- To hold the petty cash budget for props.
- To compile the props list.
- To supervise the hire, buying, making and insurance of props.

- To maintain the property log or record book (see page 77).
- To devise the props setting list (see page 89)
- To establish show personnel requirements.
- To devise scene change plot.
- To ensure credits appear in the program and publicity material as appropriate.
- To deputise for the DSM and ASMs when necessary.
- To monitor rehearsal calls to ensure that Equity contracts are adhered to.

2 The production week and fit-up
- To supervise the stage management team and assist in the fit-up.
- To allocate tasks to members of the stage management team.
- To organise transport of items to the venue.
- To organise the backstage area, including props tables.
- To ensure Health and Safety, fire regulations etc. are adhered to.
- To attend lighting and sound plotting sessions, supervising scene changes.
- To maintain the company notice board and the Cast/Crew register.
- To organise the allocation of dressing rooms.
- To ensure cue lights and communication sets are available and working.
- To supervise distribution of props, taking particular care with valuable or potentially dangerous items and instructing cast members as necessary.

- To maintain and replace props as necessary.

3 During the performance
- To prepare the performance area, set and stage prior to the half hour call.
- To undertake pre-performance checks, paying attention to potential fire and health and safety risks.
- To run scene changes according to scene change plot.
- To cue ASMs, crew and cast as appropriate.
- To assist actors, resolve problems arising during performance and maintain discipline backstage during show.
- To attend and contribute to the Director's post-performance notes session.
- To undertake post-performance routines.
- To ensure that copies of the Show Report are given to the Director and Production Manager.

4 During the strike and post-production period
- To supervise onstage management team during strike and get-out.
- To ensure that the theatre and dressing rooms are clean and tidy.
- To organise transport and ensure the speedy return of all props and furniture.
- To finalise financial records and complete petty cash returns.
- To collect together all production documentation and file for future reference.

The Role of the Deputy Stage Manager

The Deputy Stage Manager is in many ways the most important member of the production team since they are the only person who is in permanent contact with the Director, actors and all technical departments on a day-to-day basis. The DSM will be present at every rehearsal and so will probably understand the elements of a production better than any other member of the production team.

The DSM cues and acts as the prompter in rehearsal and performance, keeping the prompt copy accurate and up to date. This aspect of the DSM's work is discussed in more detail on page 55. Working 'on the book' entails close work with actors and the Director, so interpersonal skills are of paramount importance. In rehearsal, a good DSM is a priceless asset to the Director and cast. In performance, the ability to cue a show correctly from the prompt copy has a major impact on the technical and artistic success of the production.

The role of DSM is a highly privileged and responsible one that requires dedication, concentration and excellent organisational skills. The working relationship with the SM is crucial to the success of the production and it should ensure that rehearsal information is efficiently communicated to all relevant production departments and that appropriate information is also conveyed back to the Director.

In proscenium theatres the DSM cues the performance from the prompt desk. In many venues, however, the DSM may have to cue the show from a control room at the rear of the auditorium. In both cases, the DSM will be able to communicate to technical staff through communications headsets ('cans') and often by a cue light system as well.

In musical theatre, opera and ballet, it is essential for the DSM to be able to read a musical score, since cues will often need to be given on a particular note. For dance, it is vital that the DSM develops a technique to record movements so that cues can be given precisely.

1 The pre-production and rehearsal period
- To assist the SM.
- To attend and keep records of all production meetings.
- To prepare a prompt copy.
- To compile a character plot.
- To compile cast and crew lists.
- To assist the Director and SM in drawing up the rehearsal schedule.
- To attend all rehearsals.

- To work closely with the Director, recording blocking (see page 60) in the prompt copy.
- To ensure the prompt copy is accurate, clear, legible and up to date at all times.
- To note cue points and other information in the prompt copy.
- To complete rehearsal notes for every rehearsal.
- To copy rehearsal notes to the SM and assist in distributing them.
- To prompt the cast (as required by the Director).
- To provide substitute props and collect them back at the end of every rehearsal.
- To keep a record of the running times of scenes and acts.
- To run the rehearsal in the Director's absence.
- To ensure the actors are given appropriate breaks in rehearsal.
- To assist with the organisation of rehearsal and wardrobe calls.
- To liaise with the rest of the SM team.
- To provide support to the Director and cast.

2 The production week and fit-up
- To assist the SM with the fit-up.
- To attend lighting and sound plotting sessions.
- To indicate cues and standby cues in the prompt copy.
- To ensure all calls and cues are neat and can be clearly understood.
- To assist with scene change rehearsals.

3 During the performance
- To give front of house (FOH) calls if required.
- To give cast and crew pre-show calls.
- To give backstage calls and cues as appropriate.
- To control the running of the performance according to the prompt copy.
- To maintain discipline in the control room and on 'cans'.
- To time each performance.

- To complete the show report and copy to the SM, Director and Production Manager.

4 During the strike and post-production
- To assist the SM with the strike and get-out.

- To ensure returns of all props and furniture are made.
- To give the prompt copy to the SM for filing.

The Role of the Assistant Stage Manager

Assistant Stage Managers hold junior positions in the stage management team and are responsible for supporting the SM and DSM to ensure that everything runs smoothly in both rehearsal and performance.

Specific duties will be assigned by the SM and are likely to be concerned with the finding, servicing and setting of props. ASMs will therefore find themselves assisting in the rehearsal room, as well as shopping for props and running errands. The ASM should be present in the rehearsal room as much as possible to support the DSM and may well have to deputise for the DSM on occasions by working 'on the book'. Duties may also extend to operating sound and other technical equipment in rehearsal and performance. Occasionally ASMs may be required to appear on stage as part of the performance in a minor 'walk-on' role. This opportunity is very useful to gain an insight into the role and craft of the actor.

1 The pre-production and rehearsal period
- To assist in the setting up of the rehearsal space as required, (marking out for example).

- To attend rehearsals and assist with props and furniture.
- To locate substitute props and supervise their use in rehearsal.
- To assist the SM and DSM as required, e.g. collecting, buying and making props.
- To compile props setting lists for stage left and stage right, and to create a provisional scene change plan.

2 Production week, fit-up, performance and strike
- To assist the SM during the fit-up.
- To undertake allocated duties, such as supervision of transportation and storage of props, organisation of props tables and compilation of final props setting lists.
- To assist with the dressing of the set.
- To assist with scene change rehearsals.
- To undertake duties during the performance according to the cue sheet.
- To appear on stage in costume and act a walk-on part as required, e.g. a servant.
- To assist with strike and get-out.
- To assist with the return of all props and furniture.

Stage Management in Different Organisations

Different organisations work in different ways and have varying ways of approaching stage management. These are discussed below.

REPERTORY THEATRE

A typical stage management team in a regional repertory theatre would contain:

- A Stage Manager (SM) to lead the stage management team and co-ordinate communication between production departments. In some theatres the SM would be responsible for everything that happens backstage, co-ordinating scene changes and running the properties. Often however, the SM is free from specific tasks during a performance and, instead, concentrates on the pre-show planning for the next production in the repertoire. They would maintain a supervisory role during the rehearsal and production process of the new production as well.
- Two Deputy stage Managers (DSM), one working on the book in production and one assigned to the next production in rehearsal.
- A team of Assistant Stage Managers (ASM), usually two for each production.
- Stage crew.

A RECEIVING HOUSE

The Resident Stage Manager or Technical Stage Manager

Non-producing theatres and other entertainment venues do not require a full stage management team, but will have one or more stage technicians headed by a Resident Stage Manager. This team is concerned with assisting the members of each visiting company to get their production ready for performance. The team's knowledge of the building is often invaluable: they can advise on the idiosyncrasies of the venue and help to troubleshoot any problems that arise.

The main role of the Resident Stage Manager is to liaise between the visiting company and the venue staff, but they also have responsibility for:

- coordinating the venue staff during the fit-up.

- monitoring time and ensuring appropriate rest breaks are taken
- assisting with the running of the show in performance as required.

In addition, the Resident Stage Manager may also be responsible for:

- technical liaison with the company before they arrive at the venue
- agreeing show staffing requirements

- scheduling venue staff hours for the week
- recruiting casual staff to assist with get-in, crewing the show and working the get-out
- negotiating the 'get-out' fees for resident staff.

In larger venues, however, many of these tasks may become the responsibility of the more senior Technical Manager.

LARGE-SCALE PRODUCING COMPANIES

The Company Manager or Company Stage Manager

This is a role found in large scale producing companies, commercial and West End theatre. The Company Manager holds a senior position, similar to that of a Production Manager (who acts on behalf of the producers in a financial and administrative capacity, see page 31). Where these duties are combined with a direct involvement in the running of the show in performance, the post-holder is referred to as a Company Stage Manager. Therefore, in addition to the usual stage management responsibilities, the CSM maintains a financial overview of box office receipts and organises the weekly payment of company members and venue staff.

When accompanying a production on tour, the Company Stage Manager is in effect a touring Production Manager and Stage Manager combined. They are responsible for liaising with each of the venues in advance (and therefore they work closely with the host venue's Resident Stage Manager). The Company Stage Manager on tour is responsible for the fitting-up of the show in each venue and the overall running of a production in performance. They

are also concerned with ensuring contractual arrangements are maintained by the cast, production and venue staff, collating box office receipts and organising weekly pay to staff.

Pre-Production Responsibilities

- employing production staff
- establishing contractual arrangements
- monitoring contractual arrangements
- co-ordination of production departments
- liaison with venue(s).

In Performance Responsibilities

- sole responsibility for running the show
- may cue the show from the prompt copy
- payment of staff, both in the company and in the touring venue
- documentation and monitoring of box office takings
- monitoring contractual arrangements of performers
- monitoring contractual arrangements of SM and technical staff
- monitoring contractual arrangements associated with the venue
- may run understudy rehearsals directing actors from the prompt copy.

SUMMARY

The stage management team is an essential department in theatre production. They are able to take on a large amount of the organisation

and planning required in staging a production. A calm, efficient approach should reassure colleagues and, when this is combined with a thorough knowledge of all production aspects, it will promote additional confidence amongst the company and make the task of directing and performing an easier one. As Sir Peter Hall states, 'It is impossible to make good theatre without good stage management.'

Planning for Rehearsals

A large part of the stage management role is concerned with anticipation – planning for the possible as well as the probable. Before the rehearsal process begins, the stage management team have a considerable amount of preparation work to undertake.

The overall aim of the stage management team should be to create the optimum conditions for rehearsals to take place. It has been said that each minute's delay in rehearsal or production could be regarded as the fault of the stage management team since they should have foreseen the problem and developed a strategy to prevent it from impacting on the production! Although this may seem an extreme viewpoint, it is useful to consider that, as a member of the stage management team, every second that you can 'save' by being efficient will help to deliver additional rehearsal time. Therefore, if you are able personally to deliver more productive rehearsal time for the Director and actors, your individual contribution will lead directly to an improvement of the overall quality of the production.

WORKING FROM THE SCRIPT

Initial Scene Synopsis

The Stage Manager usually reads the script through once without taking any notes. This allows them to get a feel for the entire play, its plot, characters, style and tone, before making any detailed notes. After reading the text through, it is useful to draw up an **Initial Scene Synopsis**, which lists each individual scene, its location and additional information such as the time of year, time of day and any indication of weather conditions.

Production Analysis Chart

Having read the script the Stage Manager will re-read it, making detailed notes of all technical requirements, as well as any acting or stage directions that could cause problems. This detailed knowledge of the script is invaluable during the pre-production and planning process.

The Stage Manager creates a **Production Analysis Chart** (see Figure 3.3), which provides an overview of possible cues and identifies issues to be solved during the planning process. The Production Analysis Chart raises a series of questions such as:

How can we make it look as if a character is jumping out of a window on stage?
How can we move items of scenery quickly?
How do we create the explosion?
How can we make it look as if an actor is flying?
How can an actor exit stage right and appear quickly stage left?

The Production Analysis Chart can be used to document a large amount of information such as:

* the page in the script where a specific requirement arises
* character entrances and exits
* particular costume or make-up requirements
* scenic setting requirements, such as the number and location of doors

Figure 3.3   *An example of a production analysis chart*

ACT/Sc. page no.	Character Info. include costume + make up	Stage (scenic + locations)	Props	LX Q	Sound Q	Special FX	Other Notes
ACT 1 THE VISIT by Friedrich Dürren-matt		"Guellen" a run down Swiss town. name means "liquid manure"	Benches Other station paraphernalia?	"Hot autumn sun" Time of day?	Background atmos? Thunderous train		Possible complex series of sound (+ lighting?) cues at the opening of the play.
p11	MAN 1, 2, 3, + 4 similarly dressed. Shabby "Everyman figures"	Station platform	Benches. Bunting Flags + signs.		Express trains pass through but do not stop.		
p11	MAN 5 = Painter. very shabby.		Banner			Does painter require real paint?	
p12	Stationmaster		Green Flag. Whistle		Bell rings. Train clatter. Right to left.		
p12					Bell rings. Train clatter.		
p13	Mayor + entourage shabbily dressed.		Chain?				
p14			Notebook		Bell rings. Train passes right to left		

- scene change information
- props – many will be obvious, others may be implied – a scene set in a kitchen may require a whole set of props
- lighting cues such as the time of day, year, weather references, interior or exterior location, reference to a fireplace or lamp and other specific effects
- sound cues, such as voices or a telephone ringing
- titles of music referred to in the script
- whether microphones or hidden speakers are likely to be required
- special effects which could include trick props, pyrotechnics, flying, UV sequences, gauze effects, projection, water, fire, rain, snow and bubbles, for example
- other notes: this column should be used for anything that hasn't been recorded elsewhere! Make a note of factors that need to be taken into consideration as a result of details noted in a previous column e.g. a blackout in the lights column will require adequate working lights backstage. Some special effects will require further consideration on safety grounds: a candle flame or an explosive effect may both need special permission from the licensing authority.

The information from the Production Analysis Chart is used to provide additional lists as a basis for further work. It may be appropriate to enter the details onto a computer spreadsheet, making it easy to manipulate the data to produce the additional lists without having to write out the information again.

These provisional lists may be prepared:

- probable lighting cues
- probable sound cues
- an initial property requirements list (see page 71)
- initial scene change plot
- initial costume plot (what each character is wearing at each point in play)
- special effects list
- a character plot (see below)
- provisional rehearsal and production schedules.

The Character Plot

The Stage Manager creates a character plot that shows in detail which characters appear in which scenes of the play. This information is required to draw up the rehearsal schedule and future rehearsal calls. Many classic plays are divided into Acts and separate scenes, so compiling a character plot is a relatively simple matter. However some texts are not so straightforward and it is necessary to subdivide the play into manageable chunks using page references. One way is to divide the play into '**French Scenes**'. The term originates from the strict structure of seventeenth century French neoclassical plays. The divisions between each French Scene mark the occasions when a character enters or leaves the stage. These divisions are very useful to identify smaller segments for rehearsal calls.

The Character Plot may include brief notes on each individual character describing their age, character type, social standing, attitude, and any reference to their physical features.

TASK

Choose a play and draw up a character plot. Examine the script and subdivide it into appropriate segments for rehearsal purposes. Where Act and scene divisions are minimal or non-existent, sub-divide these into smaller French Scenes. Ensure that the appropriate page and line numbers are referenced clearly.

The stage management budget

The Stage Manager confirms the stage management budget with the Production Manager and establishes precisely what the amount allocated to stage management is supposed to cover. The Stage Manager may be expected to provide refreshments during auditions and rehearsals. A petty cash float may be required.

Remember that receipts are needed for every item that is bought.

Meeting the director

The Stage Manager and the Director need to establish a rapport and the beginning of a working relationship. The initial meeting is used to discuss the production and to establish a method of working. Different Directors work in different ways, so the Stage Manager might ask:

- How does the Director see the process of rehearsals? Will there be a period of improvisation before blocking begins?
- How should the rehearsal schedule be broken down?
- Is the Director happy for you to devise a provisional rehearsal schedule?
- How rigidly does the Director want you to adhere to the schedule for each day? Is it flexible?
- When will rehearsal props and furniture be required?
- Does the Director want a reminder before breaks are called? How much warning do they require?
- What policy would the Director like to establish regarding visitors at rehearsals?
- When will the actors be 'off-book' (i.e. not prompted)?
- What are the guidelines for prompting?
- Is there a convenient time to discuss matters arising each day?
- Are there any other expectations of the SM or DSM?

Auditions

Stage management team members are sometimes involved with auditions. It is usual for one member of the team to look after the actors in the waiting area, and one to introduce individuals to the director and to read in if necessary. The process is very nerve racking for the actors and it can be a demanding task to ensure that the process runs smoothly.

Stage Managers may be required to:

- meet the artists on arrival, check names, telephone numbers and the contact details of their agents
- supply additional copies of the script
- arrange a comfortable waiting area, access to toilets and a telephone
- arrange changing facilities, particularly for any dancers
- provide tea, coffee and ashtrays
- prepare the audition space with furniture, sympathetic lighting or a piano that has been tuned, as required.

Following the audition the Stage Manager may be asked to:

- prepare a list of addresses and telephone numbers of actors who are selected complete with contact details for their agents
- draw up a schedule charting the dates when actors are not available for rehearsal due to prior commitments (if important costume or wig fittings have been agreed in

advance then these should also be added to the chart)

- prepare a list of addresses and telephone numbers of all other important contacts including members of the stage management team, the Director, designers, wardrobe staff, external suppliers and hire companies

- organise the distribution of scripts and contact lists (scripts should be numbered and checked out so that there is a record of who each copy has been issued to).

PRODUCTION AND DESIGN MEETINGS

These meetings can take place before the auditions, so the production may have progressed conceptually and technically before the actors are cast.

Production meetings enable the team to study the set model, ground plans and other technical drawings and give an opportunity to question the Director and designers about their intentions. The Production Analysis Chart can be used in this context to raise possible problem areas.

The stage management team should emerge from the production meeting with a clear idea of the aims of the production, the extent of their responsibilities, and the range of problems to be solved. Decisions agreed and taken at production and design meetings should be minuted by a member of the stage management team and circulated to relevant production departments and individuals.

THE REHEARSAL SCHEDULE

The Stage Manager and the Director meet to establish the role of the stage management team in rehearsals and how the rehearsal room should be organised for the first rehearsal or read through. They may well collaborate to draw up the rehearsal schedule for the production. The character plot and the information about cast availability are invaluable when assisting the Director to finalise the rehearsal schedule.

Booking Rehearsal Space

The Stage management team may be responsible for finding appropriate rehearsal rooms. If this is the case, the search for a space should begin as early as possible. Certainly, a member of the team is expected to check the facilities prior to the start of rehearsals. Here are some points that the Stage Manager takes into account when deciding upon an appropriate space:

- How large is it? What is the size of set, stage and acting area? Is there room to spare?

- How many people can it accommodate?
- How many rooms are there?
- Would additional spaces be useful for musical or dance rehearsals, or small group work with an assistant director?
- How long is the space available
- Is time needed after the opening night or is stage space available then
- When is it first available?
- Are alternatives needed for some dates?
- How much does it cost? Is it within the available budget?
- How accessible is it? Is it near the theatre or venue? Is there public transport? Parking?
- What about access? Is a key available? Is there a caretaker? What times will the building open and close?
- If not on the ground floor, are there access problems? Are there any members of the company with special needs?
- Does the size of the staircase or lift prevent

elements of set or furniture reaching the space? Are the doors large enough to get items of set into the room? Is the ceiling high enough?
- Would the Company have sole use of the space?
- Can props be left out, or does everything need to be cleared away at the end of each rehearsal?
- Is there a safe storage area? Is it lockable?
- What about acoustics? Are they suitable or acceptable?
- Is this a musical production? Is a piano available? Is it tuned?
- Is the room reasonably soundproof? Will external noise interfere?
- Does anyone mind how much noise the company makes?
- Are there are rules associated with the building that might cause problems? Is smoking allowed?
- Are the lighting, heating and ventilation adequate? Are they included in the charge for use of the space?

- What about the number and location of electric sockets?
- Is the floor suitable? Is it smooth? Is it sprung (essential for dance)? Can PVC tape be used for marking out? Are there any other limitations?
- Are there toilets? Changing facilities? Showers?
- Are there mirrors? Is there somewhere to hang costumes? Are additional rooms available for fittings?
- What about refreshments? Is there a room or kitchen to make coffee and tea?
- What facilities are nearby? Shops? Cafes? Restaurants? Pubs?
- Is there a blackout? Is it important?
- Is there a telephone? Does it accept both incoming and outgoing calls? What is the number?
- Is furniture available or would this have to be organised?
- Is there a cleaner? If not is cleaning equipment available?

PREPARING THE REHEARSAL ROOM

Marking Out the Stage

The stage management team is responsible for marking out the stage area. It is necessary to assess the size of the rehearsal room to decide where the stage should be marked out. For an end stage, there will have to be sufficient room down stage for the Director, cast and Deputy Stage Manager to sit and work. There should also be space for the wings each side of the stage if possible.

If the performance is to be staged in-the-round, traverse, or as a promenade, it is important to indicate, through the mark out exactly how the playing area relates to the auditorium. Page 15, and Figures 1.10 and 11.1 show how to describe a stage. Some modification to these systems may be required to describe positions on a marked out rehearsal stage area.

If there are not too many lines and marks indicated on the rehearsal room floor following the marking out of the set (see below), it may be helpful to mark out the separate acting areas on the floor with tape. If this would be confusing to the cast, the different segments could be indicated by faint chalk lines instead. Whatever the solution, the different areas should be clearly understood by all of the stage management team.

Marking Out Methods

There are two ways of marking out the set or stage plan on the rehearsal room floor:

1 using two fixed points
2 using setting and centre lines.

Figure 3.4   *The two fixed points method is one of two ways to mark out a stage set*

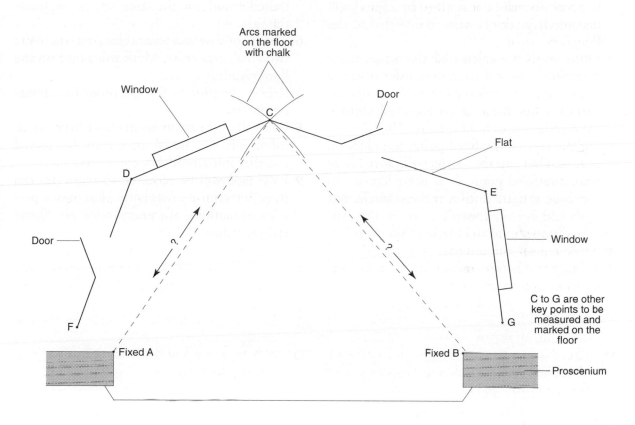

Equipment needed:

two or three people
scale plan of the stage setting
a 1:25 scale rule (and/or a ruler and calculator)
a set square (for the setting and centre line
    method)
at least two long tape measures
sticks of chalk
a snapline and reservoir filled with chalk dust
    (available from a builder's merchants)
coloured PVC tape.

Using Two Fixed Points

1 Once you have decided roughly where the
stage will be in the rehearsal room, mark the
two fixed points on the floor. The two fixed
points may already be indicated on the plan
down stage of the acting area. If the production is to be staged on a proscenium stage,
the two onstage, upstage corners of the
proscenium arch walls become the two fixed
points. On open stages, the two down stage
corners of the stage area can be used as
alternatives. All measurements are taken
from these points, which are now fixed in
space.

2 On the scale drawing, measure from one of
the fixed points to the first mark that you
wish to establish on the floor. If you have a
scale rule, you will be able to convert the
measurement on the plan to the actual measurement on the floor with ease. If you do
not have access to a scale rule, then you have
to measure the distance on the plan and then
calculate the floor measurement by multi-
plying by 25 (for a 1:25 plan). Take care

when measuring distances on the plan. Any small errors will be magnified by 25 and will become large errors when transferred to the floor!

3 Once you have calculated the actual measurement, you will have to transfer it to the floor. This is achieved by positioning the end of a tape measure on the fixed point – get a colleague to hold it there. Then, pivoting the tape at the fixed point, use chalk to draw an arc at the correct distance away from the fixed point. It is not necessary to continue this arc until it makes a circle, but it should be big enough to cover the estimated position of the mark on the stage.

4 Now repeat the exercise for the desired point, but this time measuring from the second fixed point on the plan.

5 Scribe a second arc on the floor at the required distance in the same way as you made the first.

6 The point that you want is located where the two chalk arcs cross. Mark this point on the floor clearly.

7 Repeat the process for the other key points on the set.

8 Once all of the main points have been established on the floor, they can be joined together initially with a chalk snapline.

9 PVC tape will be required to mark out the stage set semi-permanently. For more permanent marking of scenery, windows, doors etc. see below.

TASK

Mark out part of a stage set using the plan shown in Figure 3.5 and the method outlined above. You will need an area of 3m².

Figure 3.5   *Use this plan to mark out a stage set*

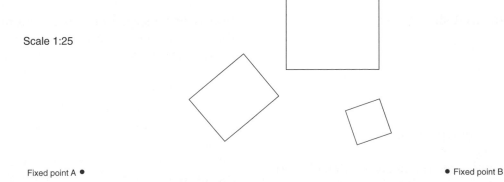

Using Setting and Centre Lines

The **Setting Line** (S/L) is a specified line drawn on the stage plan from which all positions for the scenery are measured. The setting line runs across the stage. It may be the front edge of the stage, the down stage limit of the acting area or the line to which the house tabs fall in a proscenium theatre.

The **Centre Line** (C/L) is the line that divides the stage in two, running parallel to the wings. It therefore, bisects the setting line at right angles. Many centre lines are marked on the stage itself by a slight groove. However, many are not! Do not assume that the centre line corresponds exactly with the centre of an auditorium or that it is mirrored by the position of an overhead grid or lighting bar!

The Method:

1 Assess the size of the rehearsal room to decide where the stage should be positioned.
2 Measure the lengths of the S/L and C/L on the plan and transfer them to the floor by marking them with a chalk snapline or PVC tape. Use one of the long tape measures and lay it down on the marked C/L. This will make transferring measurements to the stage floor much quicker!
3 On the plan, use a set square to draw lines out from the C/L to intersect with the corners of the set.
4 On the plan, where each line crosses the

Figure 3.6 *Alternative method for marking out the stage*

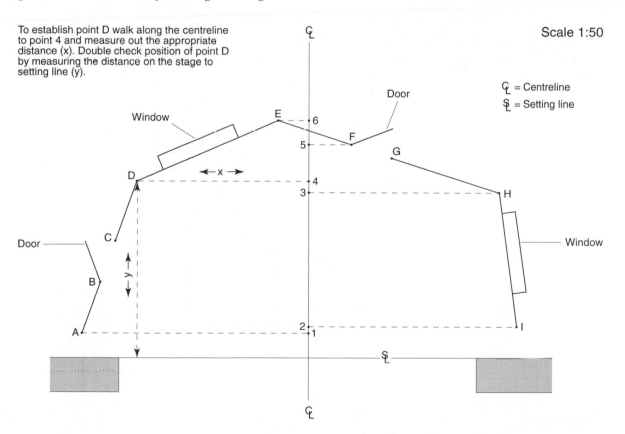

To establish point D walk along the centreline to point 4 and measure out the appropriate distance (x). Double check position of point D by measuring the distance on the stage to setting line (y).

Scale 1:50

℄ = Centreline
℄ = Setting line

C/L, mark its position with a number on the plan and a short chalk line on the floor.

5 On the plan, measure a line from the C/L outwards to the point of the set that you wish to locate on the stage (e.g. point D below)

6 Convert the plan measurement to an actual distance on the floor.

7 On the floor, walk along the C/L until you locate the correct mark e.g. mark 4 for point D.

8 Transfer the measurement to the floor by using the second tape measure. Mark this point clearly on the floor with chalk.

9 Repeat the exercise for the other corners of the set.

10 Double check floor measurements by using the S/L instead of the C/L.

11 Finally join up the chalk marks using the chalk snapline to create an outline of the set.

12 PVC tape will be required to mark the stage set clearly on the floor. (see below)

TASK

Mark out part of a stage set using the plan shown in Figure 3.7 and the method outlined above. You will need an area measuring 2.5m².

Figure 3.7   *Use this plan to mark out a stage set*

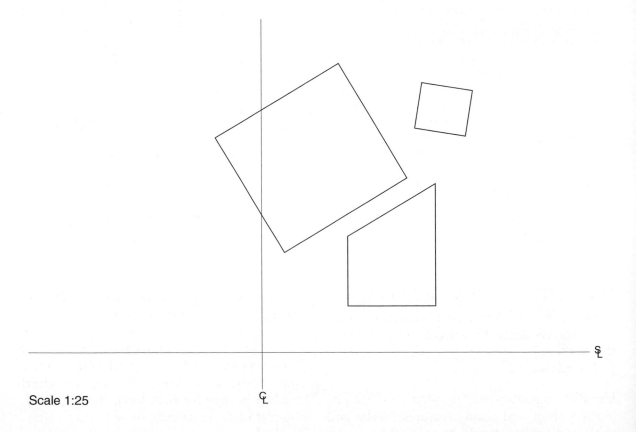

Scale 1:25

Figure 3.8 *Note how windows, doors and other features are shown when marking out on a rehearsal room floor*

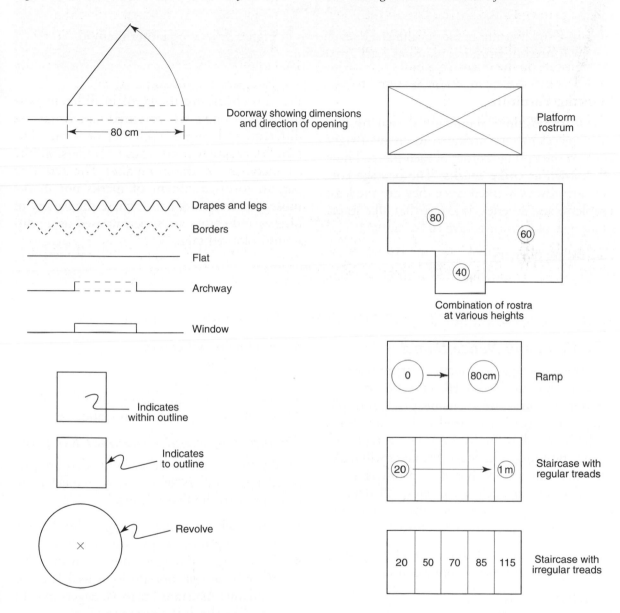

Marking Windows, Doors and Rostra

Once the walls of the set have been established, it is relatively straightforward to measure along the chalk line to locate the positions of doors and windows.

Use PVC tape to mark the position of all important stage and scenic features. Walls and solid scenic items should be marked by a con-tinuous line of tape. Gaps should be left where there are arches and doorways for example. Practical doors should be shown opening on or off stage with an appropriate arc of tape. Windows should be indicated with a dotted line. Heights of rostra should be clearly marked in tape for each level. Ramps, revolving platforms and treads should also be clearly marked.

TASK

In a small group mark out the stage set shown in Figure 3.6, using either method. You will need to work in an area at least 7m × 5m.

Marking Furniture

Furniture positions should be shown by two short pieces of tape arranged to create a right angle at the upstage corner of each piece. These are known as **spike marks**. The upstage corners are always marked since they are the least visible to an audience. It is rare that all corners of a piece of furniture have to be marked.

Indicating Scenery

Where there is more than one setting, or where the same furniture is placed in different positions on a single set, coloured tape is used to differentiate between each Act or scene. The series of complex marks can be understood by all members of the company. The resulting pattern forms a system of marks not unlike those seen in sports halls, where the variety of pitches and courts are superimposed using differing coloured tape.

OTHER RESPONSIBILITIES OF THE STAGE MANAGEMENT TEAM

The Company Notice Board

The stage management team is responsible for the **company notice board**. This should be located in a central and accessible place. A duplicate notice board may need to be maintained in the rehearsal room, if this is not close to the theatre building. The Stage Manager will make sure that the notice board location is mentioned in the first rehearsal notes. All relevant information pertaining to the production should then be posted on this board.

These are examples of things which should be posted on the company notice board.

- rehearsal calls
- contact numbers
- accommodation details
- production schedules
- rehearsal notes
- maps of the area
- details of touring dates, theatres, phone numbers, maps, accommodation, etc.

Prompt Copy and Rehearsal Kit Box

Finally there are two other items that are prepared by members of the stage management team prior to the first rehearsal:

- The Deputy Stage Manager should prepare the prompt copy (see page 55).
- The Stage Manager should ensure that there is an appropriate Rehearsal Kit Box available; Assistant Stage Managers may be asked to check the contents.

TASK

Consider what items will be required in rehearsal. What might members of the stage management team be expected to provide? Remember that the team is expected to be able to deal with all eventualities! Draw up a list of contents for a new SM Kit box. How does your list compare to the one printed below? What items are missing? Do you think any are unimportant? If so, why?

Contents of the Rehearsal Kit Box

- The prompt copy and associated documents
  - rehearsal schedule
  - contact list
  - rehearsal calls
  - character plot
  - provisional cue lists
  - groundplan of set or theatre stage
  - maps of local area
  - bus or train information, car parking information
  - cast list and emergency contact numbers
- spare scripts
- ring binder
- plain A4 paper
- 2B pencils
- pens
- notebook
- pencil sharpener
- erasers
- scissors
- snapline and chalk
- scale ruler
- set square
- long tape measures
- PVC tape in assorted colours and widths
- stopwatch
- watch
- sewing repair kit
- small first aid kit (tweezers, nail file, paracetamol, throat lozenges, plasters, dressings, bandages, antiseptic)
- tissues
- safety pins
- matches
- sellotape
- hole reinforcers
- stapler and staples, staple remover
- paper clips
- drawing pins
- blutak
- bulldog clips
- calculator
- glue
- gaffa tape
- dictionary
- diary
- lockable box for valuables and petty cash
- screwdrivers
- pliers
- torch
- dressmaking pins
- hair pins
- mirror(s)
- extension lead
- corkscrew, bottle opener or penknife.

The Prompt Copy

The **Prompt Copy** or 'the book' is the most important document in the process of play production. It is created by the Deputy Stage Manager and maintained by them throughout the rehearsal and production process.

It comprises the full copy of the script, with any cuts or additions marked on, notes regarding actors' movements, delivery and pauses, details of all technical cues, such as lighting, sound and fly cues, scene changes, property requirements and backstage calls to cast and crew. The prompt copy becomes a complete and definitive record of everything that should happen as part of the performance and, once the technical cues have been added, it is used by the Deputy Stage Manager to run the show. After the dress rehearsal, the prompt copy becomes the official record of the production as it was performed, and should be filed away safely for future reference.

During the production process, the prompt copy should be stored in a *safe place*, known to

TO42543

all of the stage management team. It should **never**, in any circumstances, be allowed to leave the theatre building and should not be considered to be the property of any one individual, even though the Deputy Stage Manager will have worked hard to record information on its pages. Having a *duplicate* prompt copy is a good idea and it should be maintained by an Assistant Stage Manager. If a duplicate prompt book is to be made up, it must be identical to the original in every respect.

Although there are no strict rules or international standards associated with the marking and layout of a prompt copy, it needs to be *clear, legible* and *logical*! Any experienced stage manager should be able to pick up the prompt book and cue a show from it without difficulty.

MAKING A PROMPT COPY

Before rehearsals begin, the prompt copy is created by placing pages of the script opposite blank pages. The cues are written on to these.

There are two main ways of making up a prompt book:

1 the window method
2 the two copy method.

The Window Method

It may not be possible to photocopy the script for copyright reasons. If so, this method is the cheapest, since it only requires the break up of a single copy of the text. Each page of the script is then mounted within a plain sheet of A4 paper, which can be very time consuming. Mounting can be done by cutting an appropriately sized window out of the sheet of plain paper and securing the script page behind the window using sellotape. The script can be inserted into the window in a number of different ways according to personal preference. The centre window is the most difficult and time consuming to achieve, so with a lengthy script, an alternative variation, requiring less cutting and taping, may be preferred. Each A4 window page is inserted into an appropriate ring binder and interleaved with plain A4 paper, divided into cue columns (see below). The aim is to achieve alternate pages of script and cues.

Figure 3.9   *The window method is one of two ways to make a prompt copy*

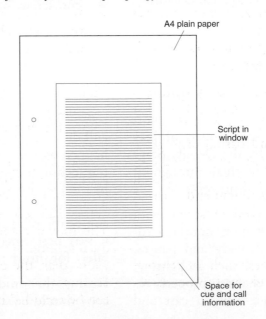

A4 plain paper

Script in window

Space for cue and call information

Figure 3.10   *The two copy method*

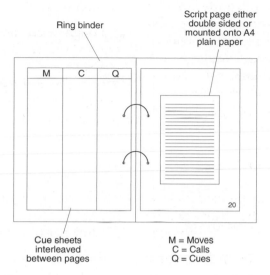

Ring binder

Script page either
double sided or
mounted onto A4
plain paper

M	C	Q

20

Cue sheets
interleaved
between pages

M = Moves
C = Calls
Q = Cues

The Two Copy Method

This technique is quicker since windows are not required. Instead, two copies of the text are 'broken up' and the pages separated. Each page is secured by glue or tape to a plain A4 sheet of paper. Since play texts are printed on both sides, it is necessary to use the second copy of the script to show the reverse of each page that is glued down. The reverse side of each printed page is attached to the same prompt copy page, in effect sandwiching an A4 page between two pages of the script. These pages are inserted into a ring binder and interleaved with plain A4 paper, divided into cue columns. Again, the aim is to achieve alternate double sided pages of script and cues.

If the text is not protected by copyright, it is possible to photocopy each page, enlarging it for clarity. The A4 photocopies can then be glued together, or cut and pasted onto plain A4 paper (as in the two copy method). Alternatively, they could be photocopied as an enlarged, double-sided document and inserted into a ring binder, as described above.

Cue Pages

Cue pages contain information about progress in rehearsal and are used to cue the play accurately in performance.

Cue pages include columns for documenting:

Moves – a record of each important move or action that cast members make during the piece.

Cues – a sequential list of technical cues, identified precisely and numbered appropriately.

Calls – courtesy calls for cast and backstage staff, to alert them to key moments when they are required on stage. If front of house calls need to be given, they also appear in this column.

Props – details of property movements during the show. There is not usually a separate column for this information, which is incorporated in the moves or calls column.

There is no single recommended method of organising all of the information outlined above, but it may be helpful to note the following pieces of advice. The cue column should always be adjacent to the text page. The calls column usually contains the least amount of information and can be narrower. Property details can also be recorded in this column. The moves column is usually located at the outside edge of the page. This needs to be wider than the calls column, as it contains a larger amount of information. Property details can be recorded in this column if preferred.

Figure 3.11 *Cue pages have various columns for noting aspects of the performance – this sheet is from a dance performance*

Music and action notes	Time	Q
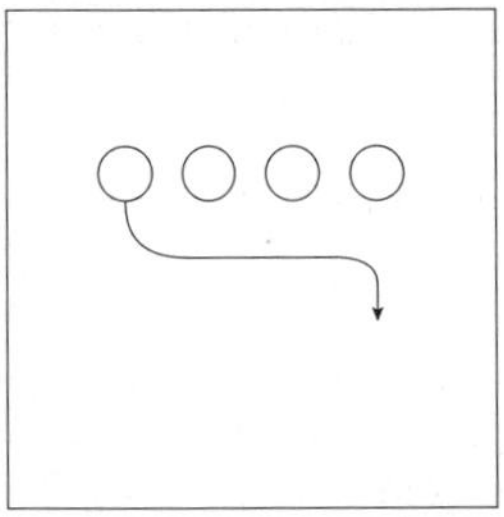 1'52" Tempo changes	1'52"	LxQ6 GO
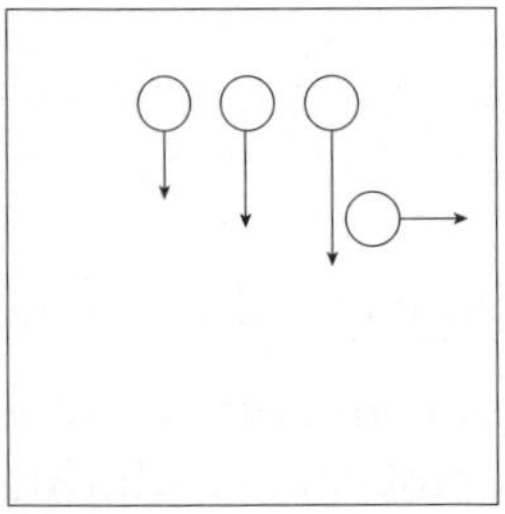 Louise splits off	2'20"	standby LxQs 7-10
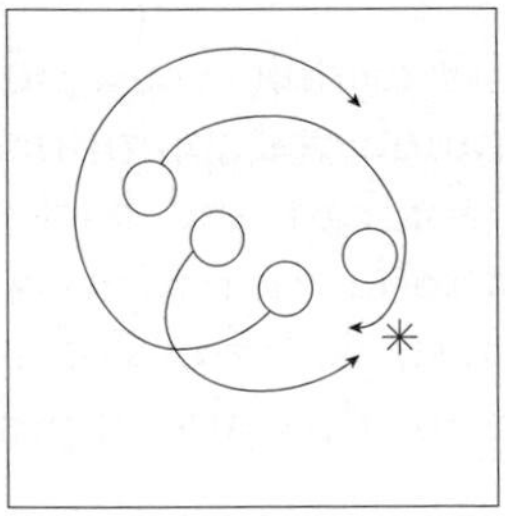 *Give Q when Tanya is in position	3'04"	*Visual LxQ7 Go
Music fades out	4'33"	LxQ8 Go
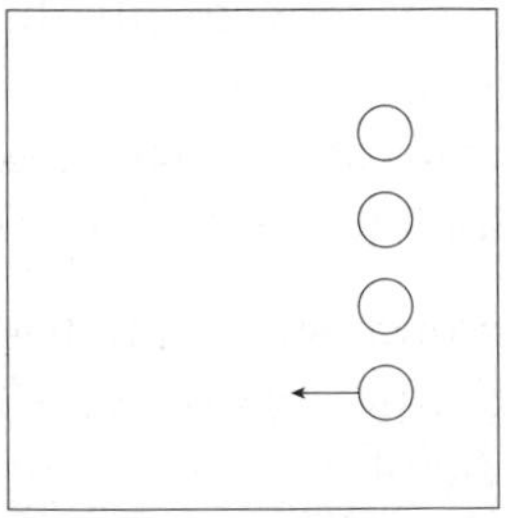 Hands up section in space		
Claire splits	5'22"	*Visual LxQ9 Go
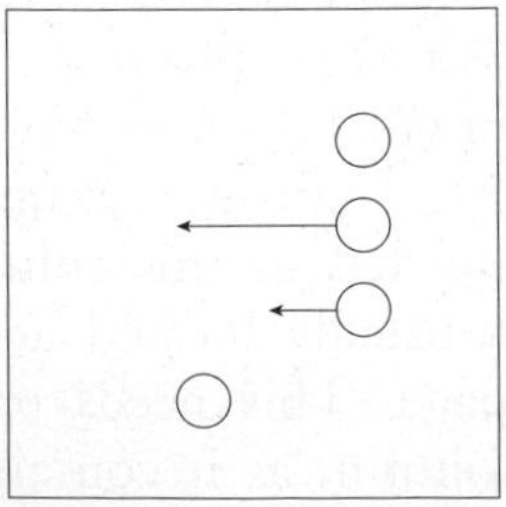 Marilyn Monroe bit All fall to floor as tempo changes	5'40"	LxQ10 Go
		F.O. Standby LxQs 11-18 sound Qs 4 and 5 Fly Qs 2 and 3

Figure 3.12   *These are two facing pages from a prompt copy showing all the markings that the Deputy Stage Manager has made*

Maudie No way. Buzz off Moth.[1]		[1] Stands up in kind of protesting way.
Moth Come on love, get them in. Let's have a few and forget all this. You pay, I'll order.		
Maudie No.		
Moth But Maudie, my Maudie.		
Maudie No, I'm stopping the tap. I shall not be used.		
Moth Used. Used. Well if that's[2] how you feel I can always go you know.		[2] C X towards the bar trips over the S.R bar stool.
He walks down the bar a bit, stops, looks back, walks down the bar a bit, stops, looks back. Falls over a stool, Picks it up, laughs to cover embarrassment, limps back to her.		
Maudie, I've been thinking,[3] all what you're saying's so true and right as always. I'm losing everything, my flair, my waistline, what's next to go – you? Will it be you next?		[3] Walk around the bar
Maudie (unmoved)[4] You'll try anything won't you, just to get into my handbag. The romantic approach, the comic approach, the concern for me approach, the sympathy approach. Does it never end?		[4] C X back to the table around the back of the bar
Moth You forgot ⬚sexy⬚ in there.	STANDBY LXQ 9	
She swings for him, he ducks.		
No Maudie. You're right again. What does a princess like you see in a loser like me?		
Maudie I don't know. Well I do. You're romantic, like something on the fade. I love that.[5]		[5] C when gets to table stands in front of B + chair
Moth (moving in) Oh Maudie, my Maudie.		
As he does, she starts to melt again, he starts to reach into her handbag, she suddenly sees this and slams it shut on his hand.[6]		[6] after B swings for C he steps out of the way off the raised platform.
Maudie Stop!	SQ 7 SQ 8	
Moth Aw Maud. How can I prove I'm ⬚genuine⬚ to you? Here take everything on me, everything, ⬚everything⬚. (Starts [7]	LXQ 9 GO STANDBY LXQ 10	

(page one – script)   (page two – cues and moves indicated opposite the text)

Task

Using photocopied extracts from a play text, make up three or four pages of a prompt copy using the window method. Repeat the exercise using the two copy method explained above. What are the advantages or difficulties of each method? Which do you prefer and why?

Early work in the prompt copy

The Deputy Stage Manager works from the prompt copy throughout the entire production process from the first read through. They ensure that all rehearsal decisions are recorded on the appropriate pages. As well as pens, pencils, a sharpener, eraser and a ruler, the Deputy Stage Manager may find that a dictionary and stopwatch are useful.

Marking the prompt copy

Figure 3.13 *Cuts from the script must be shown clearly*

of her purse, and extends it to her.] Where's your book full of little theatre notices and stills that show you in the back-ground of . . .

CHANCE: Here! Here! Start signing . . . or . . .

PRINCESS [pointing to the bathroom]: Or WHAT? Go take a shower under cold water. I don't like hot sweaty bodies in a tropical climate. ~~Oh, you, I do want and will accept, still . . . under certain conditions which I will make very clear to you.~~

CHANCE: Here. [Throws the chequebook towards the bed.]

PRINCESS: Put this away. And your leaky fountain pen. . . . When monster meets monster, one monster has to give way, AND IT WILL NEVER BE ME. I'm an older hand at it . . . with much more natural aptitude at it than you have. . . . Now then, you put the cart a little in front of the horse. Signed cheques are payment, delivery comes first. Now, Chance, ~~please~~ pay close attention while I tell you the very special conditions under which I will keep you in my employment . . . after this miscalculation. . . .

Forget the legend that I was and the ruin of that legend. Whether or not I do have a disease of the heart that places an early terminal date on my life, no mention of that, no reference to it ever. I've been accused of having a death wish but I think it's life that I wish for, terribly, shamelessly, on any terms whatsoever.

When I say now, the answer must not be later. I have only one way to forget these things, I don't want to remember and that's through the act of love-making. That's the only dependable distraction so when I say now, because I need that distraction, it has to be now, not later.

All early work in the prompt copy should be in pencil, as there are likely to be many alterations as the rehearsals progress. Although there are many variations of annotating the prompt copy, there is a system of notation and cueing that is widely used and understood.

Identifying Cuts

The prompt copy is adjusted whenever any cuts to the text are made. Alterations may be identified by the Director prior to rehearsals or indicated during the first read through of the text. Cuts can be individual lines, parts of a speech, or whole pages of text. This should be shown clearly by ruling through individual lines in pencil, or by drawing a diagonal line through large areas of text, taking care to identify where the cut begins and ends (see Figure 3.13).

Recording Moves or Blocking

Each actor's moves during the play (the **blocking**) are recorded clearly and accurately, either in writing or in diagrammatic form. These two methods are discussed in more detail below. This information is recorded in pencil, as the blocking often has to be rubbed out and rewritten as rehearsals progress and the scene develops. It is quite tricky keeping up with changes in blocking during rehearsal, particularly when the cast and the Directors are experimenting and trying out different moves. So, each significant movement by a member of the cast on stage is noted in detail in the moves column of the prompt copy and referenced to an appropriate point in the script on the facing page. If the blocking is particularly complex and the action is proceeding quickly, the Deputy Stage Manager may experience difficulty getting it all down. In this case, the Assistant Stage Manager may be asked to prompt while the Deputy Stage Manager concentrates on making notes.

To indicate the blocking for a scene involving crowds or a large number of principal actors, it is sensible to use a series of annotated diagrams rather than a written method.

Written Shorthand Notation Techniques

Moves can be recorded in a written shorthand. They should be identified by the character's name and not the name of the individual actor. Using abbreviations will save time and make the written information clearer. Look at the following example of blocking taken from Macbeth:

1 M	→	DSC (Macbeth moves Down Stage Centre)
2 LM	X	DSR (Lady Macbeth crosses to Down Stage Right)

Abbreviations for position follow conventional descriptions of the stage area (see page 15). The numbers refer to the first and second moves on this particular page of script. Here are some more abbreviations which are often used:

→	moves to
X	crosses to (a diagonal movement across the stage)
⌒	circles or arcs around something or someone
sits	sits on chair or sofa – it may be necessary to describe which chair the actor is to sit on or the actor's position on a sofa
rises	stands up from chair or sofa
enters	moves from off-stage to on-stage
exits	leaves the stage
→ A	moves towards character A

Diagrammatic Notation

This involves drawing plan diagrams of the stage showing key elements of the set. Characters are identified by their abbreviations and the moves are shown as numbered arrows. The numbers of the arrows correspond to the sequence of individual moves which are noted on the script. Several moves from one actor or the moves of more than one person can, therefore, be shown on a single plan drawing.

Figure 3.14   *Symbols like this are used as a shorthand to record blocking*

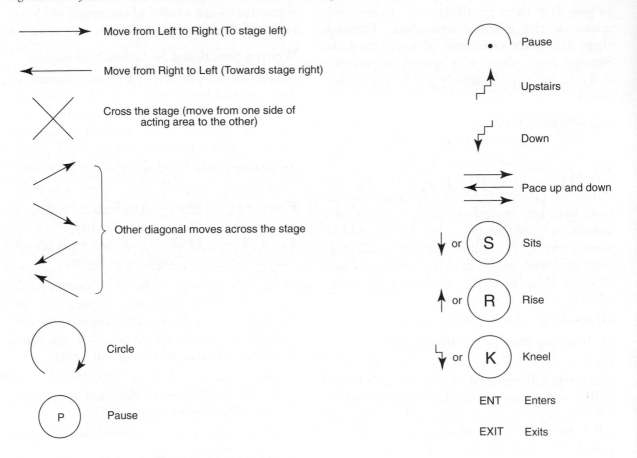

Move from Left to Right (To stage left)

Move from Right to Left (Towards stage right)

Cross the stage (move from one side of acting area to the other)

Other diagonal moves across the stage

Circle

P   Pause

Pause

Upstairs

Down

Pace up and down

↓ or S   Sits

↑ or R   Rise

↓ or K   Kneel

ENT   Enters

EXIT   Exits

Marking Moves on to the Script

Whether blocking details are represented in shorthand or diagrammatic form, they are written in the moves column opposite the relevant line in the script. Each move is identified numerically from the top of each new page and the corresponding number is added to the line in the script where the move commences. It is important to locate this number at the precise point of the line when the actor starts to move.

Here are some variations showing how moves are cross-referenced on the script:

[1] *Example of move 1 commencing before a line.*
Example of [2] *move 2 occurring on the line.*
Example of move 3 beginning on the [3] *line, but a little later.*
Example of move 4 commencing after a line has been delivered. [4]

Pauses should also be marked on the text, where they have been directed or where actors have decided to punctuate their delivery for dramatic effect. A pause can be identified using the musical symbol above the appropriate part of the script. For example:

Hamlet: To be ⌢ or not to be, ⌢ that is the
*   question.*

Musical notation can be adapted to indicate additional elements such as rhythm or tempo.

Not everyone is familiar with these symbols so it is important to include a key at the beginning of the prompt copy. Stressed words may be indicated by underlining, staccato delivery by dots above the appropriate words and tempo changes by crescendo and diminuendo symbols.

TASK

In a group, rehearse an extract from a script. Using a copy of the script pages and some blank cue pages, take turns to practice recording the blocking. You may need to stop the rehearsal from time to time and ask the actors to repeat the blocking that has been decided.

Which moves and actions were difficult to describe and why? As a group discuss how you could indicate moves in shorthand or with a diagram? Are some movements only possible to describe in longhand?

Recording Additional Information

It is not always possible to record all the information that is required in abbreviated shorthand or in diagram form. Complicated moves and additional actions may have to be described in full in the moves column. Symbols may be used to locate these moves in the text. Remember to show the symbol in the moves column, next to the description, and in the script. For example:

i   carefully stubs out cigarette in ashtray
√   shakes umbrella three times
∞   pours milk into two cups from jug. Pours tea from teapot, carelessly spilling it into the down stage saucer.
Δ   kicks black chair stage right

Adjectives may be required to describe the movement precisely or to record an actor's motivation, for example "saunters slowly", "rises energetically", "strides angrily", "flops onto bed with an air of resignation" etc.

In rehearsal, it is helpful to note occasions when actors have needed prompting. A system using abbreviations can be employed:

C   an actor called for (forgot) a line
P   the text has been paraphrased

L   the actor was late with a line or a cue
Pr pronunciation was incorrect
J   a passage or a speech was missed out
H   additional words have been added to the script, known as 'a handle'
S   Text was spoken out of sequence

Recording Calls

As mentioned previously, calls are recorded in the cues sheet calls column or cue column. Front of house and backstage calls may be recorded. Backstage calls are for performers and/or technicians and crew. They warn performers that they will be required on stage and they alert stage crew and technical staff of imminent scene changes, for example.

Five minutes before the beginning of the play the actors receive a beginner's call from the Deputy Stage Manager. Before every entrance thereafter, the relevant actors receive a warning call informing them that they will be required on stage in approximately five minutes. The calls are made alphabetically and use the actor's surnames rather than the character names. Traditionally, calls were organised with the male actors first, females next and children last:

'Act 2 Beginners Please.
Mr Banks
Mr Smith
Mr Williams
Miss Andrews
Miss Peto-Cook
Miss Terry
Master Collins
This is your Act 2 Beginners' Call. Act 2
Beginners please.
Thank you.'

Other rehearsal documentation

Rehearsal Notes

One of the most important duties of the
Deputy Stage Manager is to ensure that any rehearsal developments are communicated to
production team members outside of the rehearsal room. There may be production
queries or directorial decisions to be recorded
in the form of **Rehearsal Notes**.

Each day's rehearsal notes are given to the
Stage Manager for photocopying and distribution. The Deputy Stage Manager should file
one copy of the notes in the prompt copy.
Each rehearsal notes sheet should be numbered
consecutively and should include details of:

the production title
the date of the rehearsal
the distribution list
the name of the originator of the notes
each item requested or queried.

The rehearsal notes should be as precise as
possible so that instructions will not be misunderstood. A mirror is needed, but what type of
mirror? Hand mirror? Wall mirror? Full
length? What size or shape is required? What
style or colour?

Both the Stage Manager and the Deputy Stage
Manager are responsible for communicating
production information and developments
back to the Director. If there are difficulties as-

Backstage staff may also be called for scene
changes:

'Members of the crew this is your call for
Act 3 Scene change. Act 3 scene change.
Thank you.'

Recording Cues

As mentioned before, the column nearest the
text in the prompt copy is reserved for technical cues. This is discussed in much more detail
later in the book (see pages 79–83).

sociated with directorial requests made at production meetings or in rehearsal notes, these
should be clearly communicated to the
Director.

The Call Sheet

The **Call Sheet** will be drawn up and posted
by the Stage Manager following the day's rehearsal. It should indicate:

the date of the next rehearsal
the place
the times
the individual actors' names
the scenes to be rehearsed
breaks in the rehearsals
the time at which the call ends
the name or signature of the Stage Manager
where the call sheet will be distributed

Copies of the Call Sheet are displayed
prominently and distributed to all staff who
are requested to be present. The stage management team should keep at least one copy
for reference and file one in the prompt
copy.

When compiling the calls list the Deputy Stage
Manager must remember to refer to the details
of actors' contracts to ensure that they are allocated appropriate breaks and that the total
hours of rehearsing does not exceed the daily
or weekly maximum.

Figure 3.15   *An example of rehearsal notes*

THE WRITING GAME

REHEARSAL NOTES

NO.7

WEDNESDAY 4/3/92

STAGE MANAGEMENT/PROPS

1. The front of Mrs Baxter's script should read "Those Golden Days" by Valerie Baxter.
2. Could the lights and shadows script contain Leo's dialogue on p32.
3. There will be a props progress meeting with stage management on Thursday 27/2/92 in the rehearsal room.

LX

1. Could the socket for the kettle S.R have a manual switch which can be either operated from prompt corner or the LX box, as the kettle needs to boil at a specific time.
2. Cue light positions are: 1 Up-stairs bedroom
                                1 Bathroom
                                1 D.S.L Wing
                                1 D.S.R. Wing

SOUND

1. Could I have a copy of the answerphone dialogue when it is recorded for rehearsals please.
2. Can you possibly find the following:
     Miles Davis – "A Kind of Blue"
     John Coltrane – "Ballades" (this may not be the right title)

WORKSHOP

1. Just a note to confirm that the sides of the bedrooms and bathroom (S.L+S.R) are open i.e not boxed in.

GENERAL

There will be a run of the play at 2.00pm tomorrow Thursday 5/3/92 in the rehearsal room. The bust of "Aubrey" has been moved to underneath the stairs but will still be seen.

SARAH
D.S.M

Working in Rehearsals

There should be at least two members of the stage management team in the rehearsal room at all times. The Deputy Stage Manager is usually the most senior member of the present team and will be on the book. The other, usually an Assistant Stage Manager, will deal with props and be able to run errands. The Stage Manager should be aware of daily developments in the rehearsal room and will visit rehearsals on a regular basis. However, for most of the time, they will be involved in co-ordinating work elsewhere.

It is vital that all members of the stage management team are aware of how to work in the rehearsal room and appreciate the degree of sensitivity that is required when working with directors and actors.

The Deputy Stage Manager sits facing the acting area and in reasonably close proximity to, if not alongside, the Director. It makes recording in the prompt book easier if the Deputy Stage Manager sits in the same place in relation to the stage at every rehearsal. However, later in rehearsals, once blocking has been set, it may be appropriate to shift places so that the stage can be observed from a variety of viewpoints.

PREPARING FOR REHEARSALS

The stage management team are responsible for making ready the rehearsal room and should:

- arrive at the rehearsal room in good time
- set out the stage for the first scene to be rehearsed
- lay out props on the props table
- prepare refreshment facilities, if appropriate
- as actors arrive, check them against the rehearsal call list
- attempt to trace anyone who has not arrived
- make introductions
- ensure that the actors understand the stage markings on the rehearsal room floor
- advise actors about substitute props
- point out props which are delicate, particularly valuable or in any way hazardous or awkward to use.

During rehearsals the Deputy Stage Manager will:

- mark all moves in the prompt copy
- time whole scenes as they are run
- ensure that the rehearsal room stays absolutely quiet once rehearsals are in progress

- keep an up to date props list
- monitor the rehearsal times
- liaise with the Stage Manager to ensure that actors and stage management on Equity contracts do not exceed the maximum permissible working hours
- keep rehearsal notes (see previous page)
- ensure that appropriate breaks are taken
- inform the cast of calls for the next day.

The Assistant Stage Managers will:

- assist the Deputy Stage Manager as requested
- maintain a duplicate prompt copy if required
- keep a note of amendments to lines
- organise the props, substitute props and the layout of the stage area
- supervise the use of props during the rehearsal
- undertake all scene changes as required
- prepare props and keep the props lists
- check that props are retrieved at the end of each session.

THE DEPUTY STAGE MANAGER – DIRECTOR RELATIONSHIP

Working closely with a director is a great privilege and is an opportunity to learn about the process of play production. Undoubtedly, working with some directors can be difficult at times. However, other directors make the experience in the rehearsal room a pleasurable one and are able to create a great atmosphere of team spirit.

The Deputy Stage Manager needs to ascertain at an early stage how the Director would like them to work. The Deputy Stage Manager is the primary source of help, support and encouragement for both the Director and the actors during the rehearsal process. They will need to establish a rapport with the Director, as they will be spending considerable periods of time together. Some directors may invite or insist that all relevant members of the stage management team join in with the actors' warm up. This can help to generate a great company spirit. However, the Director's main focus is the actors and they may be so involved with coaxing a performance that they do not pay much attention to the stage management team.

The Deputy Stage Manager is often called upon to be the Director's second pair of eyes and may be asked to give an opinion on a scene or on an individual actor's movement or speech. Members of the stage management team should not offer an opinion unless asked to do so!

It is the Deputy Stage Manager's duty to warn the Director when the actors are due for a break. These are stipulated in Equity contracts.

Running Rehearsals in the Director's Absence

The Stage Manager or Deputy Stage Manager will sometimes be called upon to run a rehearsal in the Director's absence. These rehearsals will often give the actors the opportunity to reacquaint themselves with the blocking that has already been set, or to run through their lines. The Deputy Stage Manager may well be asked to preside over a speed run of the play, where actors go through their moves and deliver their lines as quickly as possible without worrying about what sense this conveys to an audience! This is a useful test of memory.

On the occasions when the Deputy Stage Manager is left in charge, they should not be tempted to make any changes.

PROMPTING

In the rehearsal room, the Deputy Stage Manager is expected to prompt actors when required. This is a key duty, especially once the Director has stipulated that actors must work without scripts. It is important to learn how to prompt sensitively, to be able to judge how long to leave an actor to try and remember the words before offering the correct lines. An early prompt may be unhelpful, if the actor is attempting to recall lines at a relatively early stage in the rehearsals. A more definite prompt will be required later in the production process, when actors are more confident and most lines have been learnt.

The Deputy Stage Manager should check with the Director before rehearsals begin, to establish how prompting should take place. Each director will have a preferred method for giving prompts. Some directors may insist that

the cast get themselves out of trouble, whilst others may request that the line is given immediately it appears that an actor is struggling. This is one reason why it is essential to mark pauses on the script where they are directed (see page 63). Giving a prompt during an actor's dramatic pause can be very embarrassing and can destroy the creative atmosphere of a rehearsal environment. Some individual performers or directors may prefer to agree a system for prompting. An actor may indicate the need for a prompt by calling 'line', 'prompt' or by using an agreed signal, such as a click of the fingers.

Whether the Deputy Stage Manager is required to prompt in performance or just during rehearsals, it is important that the prompt should be confident and done with deliberation. Occasionally a key word may be all that is required for an actor to regain concentration. When an actor drys completely, it is essential that a complete phrase or line is offered.

WORKING WITH ACTORS

It has been said that stage management personnel need to get used to working with excitable, conceited, self-centred, temperamental, volatile, sensitive, nervous and explosive people! Tact and patience may be required. Stage management staff should never lose their temper or raise their voice to a member of the cast. Even though it may be difficult on occasions, keep calm and steady at all times.

Members of the stage management team should not align themselves with particular actors. It is far better to take a professional approach and to appear kind, friendly and supportive to the whole cast, rather than to selected individuals. A professional approach to the rehearsal situation is vital if the stage management contribution to the production process is to be maximised.

REHEARSING MUSICALS AND DANCE SHOWS

Rehearsals for musicals often take place in a number of rooms at the same time. Therefore, a large stage management team may be required. A typical arrangement may be:

Room 1   Blocking of scene with the Director
Room 2   Scene run through with the Assistant Director

Room 3   Dance rehearsal with the Choreographer
Room 4   Singing rehearsal.

Duplicate prompt copies may be required for some of the rooms.

THE END OF THE REHEARSAL

The stage management team are responsible for leaving the rehearsal room tidy at the end of the working day, so that it is ready for the next rehearsal. They are also responsible for clearing the room on the last day of rehearsals.

End of Rehearsal Checklist

- Check that the cast are aware of the next rehearsal call.
- Tidy the space.
- Retrieve personal props.
- Pack all props away carefully.
- Attend to the refreshment area (if applicable).
- Write up the rehearsal notes and convey them to the SM for distribution.

- Ensure that the prompt copy is safely stored.

Last Rehearsal Checklist

Before leaving the rehearsal room for the last time stage management should:

- pack all props away carefully for transit (include an inventory to show what has been packed where!)
- check that the room is as clear and tidy as possible
- remove all items and paperwork associated with the production
- remove taped marks from the floor.

Props

Stage Properties or 'props' are an essential element in most dramatic presentations and their importance to the world of the play cannot be underestimated. Props can signify specific periods in time, locations, styles, and also convey information about the characters who own and use them on stage. A well-chosen prop will complement and enhance the impression communicated by the setting, costumes and action. An ill-considered item will not just look out of place, but may serve to destroy the audience's belief in the world portrayed onstage.

Props can be classified as one of three types:

1 furnishings
2 dressings
3 hand props.

FURNISHINGS

These are used by actors as an integral part of the stage environment. For example:

tables
chairs
beds

– thrones
– altars
– chaise longues
– telephones.

DRESSINGS

These are decorative items. They may be referred to in the stage directions or in dialogue between characters, but are not actually handled by actors during the performance. For example:

– pictures
– photographs
– books
– plants
– clocks
– ornaments.

HAND PROPS

These can be divided into either personal props or costume props. For example:

- personal props
  – letters
  – newspapers
  – glasses of wine
  – snuff boxes
  – pens
- costume props
  – swords
  – umbrellas and walking sticks
  – spectacles

The responsibility for furnishings and dressings is usually agreed between the Stage Manager and the Designer at an early stage of the production process. The suitability of all props is the responsibility of the Designer, but the whereabouts of each individual prop is ultimately the responsibility of the Stage Manager.

The Designer may be very definite about the look of a particular property. There are often very important artistic reasons why a designer or director may require a specific prop.

CHOOSING PROPS

Unless props are chosen to contrast or to be deliberately out of place, they should reflect the period and location of the rest of the setting. Properties will also signify the styles, taste, class, wealth and social standing of the characters who use them. Some props may need to look unrealistic or to be used non-naturalistically. Others may work primarily on a symbolic or metaphorical level.

TASK

Build up a personal props journal using drawings, photographs and pictures from magazines and reference books. Supplement these images with pictures or descriptions of detail taken from items from particular periods in history.

Divide your journal into the three props areas and collect information on each type. Your collection will be very useful when it comes to researching future productions.

TASK

Try and find pictures of chairs from the following periods and styles:

Mediaeval
Tudor
Jacobean
Georgian
Rococo
Victorian
1920s Art Deco
1960s.

THE PROPS LIST

Once it has been decided which props will be sourced by the stage management team and which will be the responsibility of the Designer, a detailed props list will be drawn up. As much information as possible should be obtained so that the precise object that is required can be found. Any uncertainties should be resolved with reference to the Designer and the Director. Early production meetings are also useful to establish precisely how a prop is to be used in the production. These questions may be asked:

- Why is it needed
- Who uses it and when?
- How is it to be used? Is it likely to break (spares may be required)?
- Does it need to work? Is it practical? (i.e. Does the gun need to fire? Should the cuckoo clock strike? Will the jam tarts be eaten?)
- What size does it need to be?
- Is colour, texture, shape or size important?
- What style or period?
- Does it need to appear new or old? Should it communicate opulence, social standing or poverty, for example?

Figure 3.16   *An example of a props list*

Column ITEM	DESCRIPTION	BUY	HIRE	Borrow	MAKE	STOCK	Donated	NAME, ADDRESS + CONTACT No.	Collection Date	Return Day	Returned ?	Page Scene
Plastic Flowers						✓						1 p8
2 × SINGLE BEDS	Interesting Bed heads. Need sheets, quilts etc.			✓				Mr. Miller at Walnut Antiques	20/3			1 p8
Briefcase	old, battered					✓						1 p9
Spade						✓						1 p9
Shopping Bag	details?	✓		?		?						2 p10
Sealed Envelope	with letter inside				✓							2 p11
Sink Unit	with practical taps				✓							2 p11
Kettle	electric					✓						2 p12
Coffee, Tea Bags	spoons + milk	✓ £10										2 p12
Car keys						✓						2 p12
Pot Plants	Yucca, ferns etc.						✓	Hazel at Clough Garden Centre. *Credit in Programme needed	21/3			3 p14
Astroturf	About 2m² cost?	✓										3 p14
Portable radio				✓		✓						3 p15
Garden gnome	stereotypical – red hat fishing line?			✓								3 p15
Standard lamp	Practical					✓						4 p18
Red Telephone	1960's style with dial			✓				speak to B.T.				4 p19
Birdcage	ornamental – large enough for a parrot		✓					Howarth Wrightson Cost £15 a week.				4 p20

The props list may alter as rehearsals progress. Some props may be cut and other, new props may be required. It is essential, therefore, that the stage management team keeps in close contact with the Designer throughout the rehearsal period.

FINDING PROPS

The Props Stock

Most theatre companies have a stock of basic props. Some props, therefore, can be sourced from this collection. It may also be possible to adapt props to suit. Even if an item is not entirely suitable for use in a particular production, it can often be modified. Some props may not need to look realistic in close-up, but will work from a distance. Wooden automatic machine guns can look just as menacing as the real article, when seen on stage in a proscenium setting. However, the same prop would not work well where the audience are positioned close to the acting area. Similarly, green pieces of paper with rough markings might make adequate prop banknotes in some situations, but would not work well for a production staged in-the-round. Props sourcing is, therefore, more difficult in certain staging conditions, since attention to detail can be important.

If a prop cannot be found or adapted from one in stock, then it will need to be bought, hired, borrowed or made.

Researching Suppliers

Access to a telephone, a copy of the local phone book, the Yellow pages and a Thompson Local Directory are essential to assist in the sourcing of props. Each show will probably have at least one item that proves a challenge to find:

Yorrick's skull in *Hamlet*
An period dentist's chair for *The Little Shop of Horrors*
A gattling gun for *Sergeant Musgrave's Dance*
A turn of the century telephone for *Wait Until Dark*
A tiger skin rug for *Me and My Girl*.

Any production that is set in a foreign location or in a specific historical period may cause headaches in the sourcing of props. A large amount of research may be required to locate a particular item. Sometimes, lateral thinking is necessary: even when a telephone enquiry produces a negative response, always ask for any ideas or contacts that might help.

Consider issuing a press release to the local papers explaining how difficult it is to find an old washboard, a Victorian school desk, a large, pink, stuffed elephant, for example. The more bizarre the prop, the more likely this will generate interest! However, do not rely upon members of the public to solve all props sourcing difficulties.

Using the Telephone

It is important to approach potential lenders of props in the right way. A polite, confident telephone manner is essential. It helps to know which individual or department to speak to; most organisations have a telephone switchboard operator who will answer first. Remember that everyone these days is extremely busy and they may not understand the world of the performing arts. Be prepared to explain.

Borrowing Props

Extensive borrowing of properties may be necessary if production budgets are limited, or if the props budget has already been exhausted! Borrowing of props is only possible for short performance runs. Tact is extremely important when attempting to source these items. Use of the telephone is often essential to source items in the first instance, but often a call in person can be more rewarding.

Often a local amateur or repertory theatre may

be willing to lend props from their own stock. Some of the professional companies now provide a commercial service and make a small charge for hiring. Use tact when contacting the props department or stage management team of a theatre. Find out first when is a good time to make the initial approach. Study the production schedule. Don't even bother attempting to make an enquiry during a production week or near to the first night of a new show! Be punctual for any appointments. Remember they are doing you a favour! Think about transportation of any items in advance and, if necessary, book an appropriate vehicle to collect the props at a pre-arranged time.

Retailers may be willing to lend items on a sale-or-return basis. Obviously, if the material is damaged and can't be resold, the company will have to pay up. Some non-profit organisations, such as charity shops, might also be willing to lend articles.

When borrowing a property bear these points in mind:

- When is it convenient to view or to collect the item?
- Transport? What size? Car? Van?
- Is insurance required?
- Credits should be printed in the programme: the wording and spelling should be correct. It is a good idea to send a copy of the programme to the company or individual concerned.
- If an individual object has been particularly difficult to locate or is particularly

valuable, it may be appropriate to offer the owner complimentary tickets to the show. However, this should be an occasional occurrence rather than a rule of thumb!

- When collecting the prop, establish a date and a time when it is convenient to return the item. Note this information.

Buying Props

Unless it is to be borrowed, acquiring a prop will have an impact on the budget. Many props can be bought at shops, market stalls or specialist retail outlets. Flea markets, car boot sales, second-hand and charity shops can all be useful, especially for cheap domestic items for stage dressing (e.g. crockery, glasses, clocks, ornaments) and, costume and hand props (e.g. watches, spectacles, walking sticks).

Furniture can often be found in second-hand stores, markets and local auctions. Antique furniture is probably beyond the budget, but it might be worth asking if the retailer would be willing to lend or hire an item for a small fee or in exchange for a free advertisement in the programme!

Keep all receipts and make sure the retailer will refund the item if it is not suitable.

Hiring Props

There are a large number of companies that specialise in hiring props for the stage, film and television. Whilst hiring can be rather expensive, it may be worthwhile for those props that are considered essential to a production. Although it is possible to reserve a particular prop over the telephone, always go and look at the item to check that it is suitable.

If hire charges are expensive, it may not be possible to acquire particular props for the entire length of the rehearsal period. If the budget will allow, the prop should be available for the last week of rehearsals. If not, it will have to be obtained in time for the technical rehearsal.

It is always worth negotiating on price. If a production and performance lasts for 10 days, it is worth trying to secure the property for a single week's hire charge. Personal charm and a polite approach can do wonders!

Choosing Between Possibilities

You may well be able to locate a number of choices for a prop. If you are asked to find a King's throne, it is likely that you will be able to find several examples. It is a good idea to record the details of each choice on paper. Note details such as the size, shape, colour, style and decoration, as well as the hire cost and whether there are any other implications, e.g. arranging insurance or transportation difficulties. The weight of any prop that needs to be moved in full view of the audience should also be taken into account.

Possible thrones for production of *Henry V*:

Description	Size/weight	Price
Gold Rococo chair with arms, red velvet seat and back	Large	£35/week
Ornate carved wooden throne, high back, wooden seat, lions carved on arm rests	Large	£50/week
Silver/metallic chair with arms, plain and futuristic, very shiny, reflective finish	Light weight	£30 for production week and the run!
Plain wooden arm chair with solid high back, chunky plain legs	Heavy	Free from local theatre

A quick sketch or a photograph may help when sharing this information later with the Designer or Director. Keep any photographs for future reference, irrespective of whether you actually then hire the article!

To Hire or to Buy?

When hiring, multiply the weekly hire charge by the length of the run in weeks. Compare this with the likely purchase price, less a pessimistic resale value for the item. If the buying cost less the resale value is significantly greater than the cumulative hire charge, then it is probably sensible to hire. If the property is likely to be used again in a future production, it is worth investing in the item and putting it into stock.

Making Props

Props can be constructed from scratch or adapted from existing items. The Designer may provide sketches or technical drawings. The precise detail is often important (size, shape, colour, texture, should it appear to be new, or old and battered?). Discuss each prop that is to be made with the Director, Designer, and other members of the stage management team to find out how the prop is to be used. Consider what materials are appropriate to make the item and research a range of construction methods. Bear in mind that there may be several modifications to a prop during the rehearsal process as it gets used by the cast, and several versions may be required!

Practical Props

These behave like the real article even if they are not necessarily real:

- a stove which glows red when the door is opened (cheated with a red electric light positioned inside)
- a telephone which rings until the receiver is picked up (operated by the Deputy Stage Manager by a ringing device on the prompt desk)

- an oil lamp which glows when turned on (battery powered effect with electronic flickering flame).

Food

Acting is difficult. Acting and eating is doubly difficult! It is important to ensure that the process is as easy as possible for the actors. Tables should be set identically each time with cutlery and crockery and with the food placed in the same position, so as not to confuse. Actors need to work with the actual props and correct sized table as early as possible in the rehearsal process.

An actor will not consume the same amount of food as they would at a meal in reality. Make sure that portions are small, especially if the actor has to clean the plate by the end of the scene.

Food that doesn't have to be consumed on stage can be made from materials such as plastic, plaster, papier mache and wax.

Alternatives are often used for practical food, but it must appear real and be palatable! You may need to find alternatives for difficult foods. Ingenuity is often required to find edible substances that imitate the real food. Oysters, for example, can be cheated by using a teaspoonful of pale jelly in a shell. Actors who are vegetarians appreciate substitutes for meat.

- A fried egg can be created by using blancmange with half an apricot or cut white bread with half a peach on top.
- Bacon can be cheated by using a slice of banana coloured with food dye.
- Cooked meat can be substituted by a slice of ham or represented by bread soaked in gravy.

Health and Safety

For health reasons stage food should be covered until it is required on stage and it should be prepared in hygienic surroundings. Store surplus food in air tight containers and/or refrigerators as appropriate.

Drinks

Alcohol should be not consumed in large quantities on stage. Here are some examples that can be used as substitutes. Experiment to achieve the precise colouring.

- Cold tea can be diluted to represent whisky, sherry or rum.
- Diluted cola also works well and is more palatable.
- Water or lemonade can be used for gin or vodka.
- Weak lime cordial looks like white wine.
- Blackcurrant juice or a diluted concentrate can be used for red wine. Experiment with different dilutions for a Beaujolais, a Rosé or a Claret.
- Some wine merchants are able to supply ginger ale in sealed champagne bottles which will pop just like the real thing. Professional props companies also supply such items.
- For beer (and some wines) non-alcoholic versions are available.

Other Practical Props

- **China** – don't use valuable china! Antique china can be represented by cheap white crockery decorated to suit the required period.
- **Ash trays** – use wet sand in the bottom of the ash tray to help extinguish cigarettes.
- **Cigarettes** – no real alternative except menthol varieties. If using matches, leave a couple sticking out of the box so that the actor doesn't need to struggle to extricate one.
- **Bottles** – use real ones if only a few are needed. Sugar glass vessels can be made if bottles need to smash on stage, but this is a time consuming and fairly messy process. Breakaway bottles can be bought but are relatively expensive.
- **Telephones** – modern telephones can be bought or borrowed and can be made to

ring with an appropriate transformer and ringing device. Many prompt desks incorporate these. Older telephones can be slightly more difficult to source. British Telecom depots have provided old dial telephone units in the past. Other telephone manufacturers may be willing to loan or supply replica models of older telephones, such as the candlestick variety.

- **Flowers** – silk or plastic flowers will often suffice and need little care! Real plants need to be looked after carefully throughout the run.
- **Money** – money can be problematic if it is to be used in close proximity to an audience. Bank notes of appropriate denominations can be created fairly easily using computers, scanners or photocopiers. They can be colour printed or photocopied in black and white and hand coloured with pencils or crayon. Make sure that they cannot be mistaken for the real thing when seen close up, or you could be charged with forgery! Consider asking around for unwanted banknotes from foreign countries. These work well as substitute currency.
- **Stationery** – letters should be as authentic as possible, and should contain the exact wording if read out on stage. Use appropriate paper and ink (not biro) if the play is a period drama. Envelopes can be sealed with a wax stamp for authenticity.
- **Books** – these can be covered, distressed or broken down as necessary. Existing titles may need to be hidden or removed.
- **Weapons** – there are strict rules governing the use of dangerous knives, offensive weapons and handguns. All should be strictly controlled within the theatre. The care and use of a weapon should be carefully demonstrated to an actor and practised at the technical rehearsal. Weapons should be issued to individual cast members immediately before they go on stage and taken back from them as soon as they leave the stage. When not on stage, such

props should be locked away for security reasons. It is a legal requirement that guns and ammunition are locked away when not in use; ammunition should be stored in a fireproof metal box.

More About Guns

Firearms which have been de-activated to Home Office standards and verified professionally are not considered to be firearms for legal purposes. Correspondingly, there are no controls on their possession or use in the theatre. However, they should still be kept securely within the building at all times. Replica guns that fire blanks can be used on stage and can be hired from specialist companies. However, the performance venue will need to hold a special firearms licence. In addition, there are strict limitations on the type of weapon that can be used and the amount of ammunition that can be stored in the building. Firearms have to be registered with the local police station in advance – even if the gun is a replica that cannot fire.

As an alternative, some toy revolvers that use caps produce a loud bang and are not subject to restrictions. Sports starting pistols can also be used without restrictions, but most are designed to be used in the air at arms length and the blast is often emitted at the top of the pistol. Actors should be instructed carefully so that the gun is kept well away from the face when operated.

The ABTT publish a comprehensive guide on firearms and ammunition as part of their *Code of Practice for the Theatre Industry* series of publications.

Firearms Procedure

1 All gun effects should be tested at the technical rehearsal, which should be stopped for the effect to be demonstrated so that everyone knows what to expect.
2 Guns should never be left unattended, even on the props table, whether loaded or unloaded.

3 Blanks should be counted out into a cartridge box, which should be secured safely.

4 Guns and ammunition should be locked away when not in use.

5 Guns should never be pointed at people, even in fun. The Director should take expert advice from a firearms specialist if in doubt about the safety of a move.

6 Guns should never be fired in close proximity to other people, either on stage or off stage. *Blanks can kill.* A gun fired close to a person's head can cause severe damage to hearing.

7 If a performance requires a gun to be fired at an actor at close range, it is safer to use a gunshot effect off stage.

8 Always have a spare gun ready to fire off stage in case the one onstage fails to go off.

THE PROPERTY LOG BOOK

It is essential that an accurate props log book is kept recording all the hired and borrowed items for a production. This information used to be kept on a chart kept in a file, but today it is becoming increasingly common to find this information stored on a computer database in the stage management office. The recorded information, whether on paper or in database form is the same. The props log book:

- chronicles all props ever used in the theatre
- can provide a record of who owns borrowed props, past and present, and shows where they are stored at the theatre
- enables the stage management team to locate props quickly for future shows

- is vital for the co-ordination of returns after the production has finished.

The information required for each article should include:

- a detailed description (if photographs can be included this is particularly useful
- a note of the production
- the delivery note if appropriate
- name, address and telephone number of owner
- whether borrowed or hired, and the hire rate if appropriate
- value
- insurance details.

THE PROPS STORE

The stage management team often use a small room or a number of large cupboards to store props. Many repertory theatres rent cheap additional storage space for larger items, often a considerable distance away from the theatre itself. The props store should be organised in a logical way and should be cross referenced with the property log book. It should be easy to locate a particular item when it is required!

REHEARSAL PROPS

Props or substitute props are required early on in the rehearsal process. Substitute props are used when the final version has yet to be bought, borrowed or made.

Substitute props can be useful as a way of experimenting during rehearsal. The precise size and shape required of an object may only become clear through use.

A substitute prop should be replaced as soon as the real prop is available. This gives the actors the maximum amount of time to become acquainted with using it. However, because some props might be damaged or broken in rehearsal, it may be decided to withhold delicate or precious items until the production week.

ORGANISING PROPS TABLES

Props tables are usually located off stage and provide a way to organise the props during the performance. Usually, there will be one props table on either side of the stage. Sometimes more are required and tables may be located at every entrance and exit.

Each props table should have a list detailing the props that are held there. Tables may be labelled in sections, so that it is easy to see at a glance which props are in use and if any are missing. If there is room, there may be a key line drawn around each prop to show where it belongs. It may be appropriate to divide the tables into sections according to each Act or scene of the show.

PERSONAL PROPS

Particular care is required when monitoring personal props. These props are used exclusively by a particular actor and are carried by them onto the stage. Often the prop may need to be kept about their person, e.g. in their pocket. Such items may include money, keys, spectacles or a snuff box, but can also include larger items such as a notebook, newspaper or walking stick. The Stage Manager should decide whether the actor is to be responsible for the prop during the performance or whether the stage management team should look after it. It is essential to establish where the personal prop will be left, once it is finished with on stage. If this location is the actor's dressing room, the prop should be retrieved as soon as it is practicable to do so. At the very least, a sweep of relevant dressing rooms should be included on the pre-show checklist. Many Stage Managers prefer to relocate the item immediately after the show, rather than wait to attempt to find it as part of the pre-show check.

PROPS MAINTENANCE AND REPLACEMENT

The stage management team should constantly monitor the state of props both in rehearsal and performance. Running repairs are often required and food must be kept fresh.

When breakages occur, replacements must be found. (Hopefully, the stage management team will have foreseen the possibility of a breakage and will have spares at the ready!)

If the replacement for a prop is not identical to the original, it is important and courteous to tell the actors. There is a well known story of the actors in a long run of a play 'drying' on seeing a different carpet on the stage!

Be Prepared

Props that are essential to the performance should have a substitute, in case there is a problem. Gun shots, door bells and telephones ring out at crucial moments and need to be heard! Other mechanical props can also let actors down, e.g. cigarette lighters. Have a substitute ready. Make sure that other props are as easy to pick up and use as possible.

Using the Prompt Copy in Production Week and Performance

We have already seen how the prompt copy is used as an integral part of the rehearsal process. The 'book' is also important during the production week and in performance, since it contains all of the essential production information.

GIVING TECHNICAL CUES

We have covered notation for recording actors' moves (pages 60–63). The Deputy Stage Manager also needs to understand cue notation and conventions for giving instructions and guidance to other members of the production staff in the final preparatory stages of a show. Whilst the majority of scene change cues are pencilled in during the later stages of rehearsals, the precise positioning of lighting and sound cues is not determined until the plotting sessions in the production week. The Deputy Stage Manager writes each individual cue in the cues column (see Figures 3.11 and 3.12) opposite the line in the text where the cue is given.

Word Cues

Each cue is identified specifically and numbered sequentially. The precise location for the cue to start is indicated by drawing a box around the appropriate word in the script. A line is also drawn across the page to link the word to the cue column.

In the following example, lighting cue 28 begins on Marcello's last word. It would appear like this in the prompt book:

```
                    HOR:  Heaven will direct it.
LX Q28 GO   MAR:  Nay, let's follow him.
                          (Exit)
```

The word 'Go' should always be spoken last, as it determines precisely the instant that a cue is realised. So, the above example would be given as: 'Elecs cue twenty-eight ... Go' and not, 'Go elecs cue twenty-eight'

Similar conventions to those on page 62 are followed depending on whether the cue needs to be given on a line, after the line, or before a line. The cue word is boxed, rather than numbered. Cues should be marked in pencil only, since they may change during or after the technical rehearsal.

Often more than one technical department will need to be given a cue at the same time:

```
                ROM:  But he that hath
                      the steerage of
                      my course
                      Direct my sail!
                      On lusty gentle-
                      men.
LX Q22, SOUND
Q12, and FLY Q3
GO              BEN:  Strike, drum
                              (Exit)
```

Where there are lots of cues to be given at the same time, they may be grouped together for clarity:

```
LX Q22
FOLLOWSPOT Q9
SOUND Q12
FLY Q3
TRUCK Q2
REVOLVE Q3 GO        and so Goodbye!
```

Where the 'Go' is to be given simultaneously to a group of operators, as in the above example, it is practice to place the lighting cue first in the string, sound follows and then other technical department's cues are listed. Keeping to this system avoids possible confusion and operators will be used to hearing their cue in a familiar order.

However, when cues are not given together, they must follow the order in which they are required on stage.

A close sequence of cues near the beginning of a show might look like this:

SOUND Q1 GO   LIONS: | Roar! |

when drums heard on sound track
FLY Q2 GO
as music ends
LX Q2 GO
Visual as monkeys enter USR
LX Q3 GO

MONKEYS: You can't
catch us!

Visual cues

In the above example the cues need to be given at a time when no words are being spoken on-stage. This happens frequently in theatre productions and is very common when cueing dance productions. In this case, the musical score and/or dance notation, together with a stopwatch, can be used to identify cues precisely. In the above example, the fly cue is given by the Deputy Stage Manager once there is an audible change in the music.

A cue which is given on a particular movement or character entrance it is known as a 'visual' and the Deputy Stage Manager will give the 'Go' as soon as the visual cue is seen on stage. The prompt copy is marked appropriatly:

LX Q53 GO   *VISUAL when A enters USR

Some cues can be difficult to cue accurately. This may be due to visibility problems or timing. A good example might be an actor entering a dark stage and switching on a lamp.

Timing the lighting cue to match the actor's actions can be difficult. On such an occasion, the operator may respond to the visual cue without waiting for a 'Go' instruction. Instead, the operator will be given a **standby cue** with a reminder that it is a visual. The notation is:

Standby LX Q4 (Visual)

The Deputy Stage Manager will say 'Standby Elecs cue four, this is a visual.'

Similar situations may arise for some sound cues, e.g. an actor switching on a radio or turning off a television set.

Follow On Cues

There will be moments on stage with no action and no speech, but still require cues. In this case, the next cueing instruction is given after a specified time has elapsed. This is called a **follow on cue**. This sequence gives a series of follow on cues for a blackout situation:

LX Q17 GO   Ghost exits

(B/O)
F.O. after 5 secs
SOUND Q6 GO
F.O. after 3 secs
LX Q18 GO
F.O. (when scene change is complete)
LX Q19 & SOUND Q6A GO

In this series of cues only LX Q17 (the ghost's exit) is rooted to a specific aspect of the text. The lighting cue (blackout) is given when the ghost leaves the stage. The following cue, Sound Q6 will be given 5 seconds after the previous 'Go'. The next lighting cue, LX Q18 is given 3 seconds after the sound cue. Finally, the next two cues are given, but only once the stage is ready.

Some follow on cues should happen straight after another cue has been given. These are identified as immediate follow on cues:

LX Q8 GO	As music ends

Immediate Follow On
Fly Q4 GO

The fly cue should be given as soon as the lighting change has begun. This sequence would be given as:

'Elecs cue eight Go ... Fly cue four Go.'

TASK

Practise getting the timing right when cueing such sequences. Make sure that you are clear that the 5 second follow on refers to the time duration between each of the 'Gos'. Being a second out can make the difference between a cue that looks or sounds perfect and one that jars.

PLOTTING SESSIONS TO DECIDE CUES

As we have discussed, it is important that cues are added to the prompt copy in a logical and ordered manner.

Usually scene changes (including fly cues) will be decided or plotted at a **scene change rehearsal**. In complex shows, this rehearsal may be scheduled prior to the technical rehearsal. For many shows, however, the scene changes will be set informally between the Stage Manager, Fly operators and the stage management team at a convenient point in the fit-up schedule. Precise timing and positioning of cues can be amended at the technical rehearsal, but the majority of the cueing points will have been identified at the rehearsal stage, since it is obvious where most changes are required.

Cues for each technical area should be plotted in the correct order from the beginning of the show, to avoid possible confusion. If cues are added at a later stage the original cues are never renumbered.

Whatever the process of plotting, it is essential that the Deputy Stage Manager is absolutely sure where each cue should be given, and must not let the Director or Designer press on before the location for each cue has been indicated precisely in the prompt copy.

Adding Lighting and Sound Cues

Once the scenic changes have been set, the Lighting Designer can work with the Director to establish individual lighting states. During the **lighting plotting session**, the Deputy Stage Manager assists by noting each cue in order in the prompt copy. Sometimes, if the lighting board is computer controlled, the cues may need to be identified in a slightly different manner to match the way that the computer memories are identified: LX Q1.1, LX Q1.5, LX Q2.1, etc.

The process of plotting each cue usually takes several minutes, possibly longer for complex sequences.

Sound cues are added during a separate **sound plotting session**, where each cue is replayed and appropriate volume levels are set. Again, cues are identified numerically, e.g. Sound Q1, Sound Q2, etc.

Often cues are needed to modify an existing sound. These cues are identified by a letter. For example, a storm on stage may require a rain and thunder effect. The sound may be established at a high level at the beginning of the scene, but will fade to a lower level so that the actors' voices can be heard. During the scene, however, the storm may become more noticeable and so the sound levels rise again. Since the same effect is playing throughout, it is unnecessary, and potentially confusing, to give each change of level a new sound cue number. Instead a letter is added. The sequence described above may be cued like this:

Sound Q3	Storm at beginning of scene
Sound Q3A	Storm fades down to lower level
Sound Q3B	Storm increases to a louder level, but actors can still be heard
Sound Q3C	Storm fades down to lower level
Sound Q3D	Storm fades out completely
Sound Q4	Tolling bell

In some instances, particularly when live mixing takes place in musicals, the sound operators will work from the auditorium itself. The Deputy Stage Manager may not be required to cue the sound at all. Operators listen to the sound coming from the stage and listen to sound cues as well. If sound cues are required, cue lights (rather than headsets) may be the preferred method of communication.

If cues are added at a later stage, usually at the technical rehearsal or after a dress run, the original cues are not renumbered. New cues can be identified with letters: LX Q2A, 2B and 2C, would follow LX Q2, but would come before LX Q3.

Alternatively point numbers can be used: Sound Q3.5, 3.6 and 3.7 would come after Sound Q3 but before Sound Q4.

Standby Cues

Once all of the cues for each department have

been added to the prompt copy, **standby cues** must be shown. These provide warnings to the relevant technicians and operators that a cue is coming up and that they should be ready. The standby cue is inserted roughly half a page of standard text or at least 30 seconds before the 'Go' is required. Long standbys of over a minute in duration can be counterproductive.

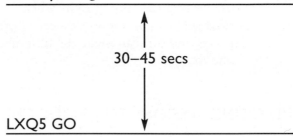

Standby LXQ5

30–45 secs

LXQ5 GO

With more complicated cueing sequences, standbys are grouped together for convenience and clarity. For example, three lighting cues that occur over a period of 20 seconds, would be given as a single standby:

Standby LXQs 19, 20 & 21.

Standby and go cues should not be interspersed. A clear and logical system is required, so that operators are not confused by a mixture of standby and go cues.

Consider this sequence of cues that occur close together during a production:

Sound Q5 GO
LX Q 8 GO
LX Q9 GO
Sound Q5A GO
LX Q10 GO
LX Q11 GO
LX Q12 GO
LX Q13, Sound Q6, and Flys Q3 GO
LX Q14 GO

Where should the standby cues be? Mixing standbys amongst a series of go cues would increase the likelihood of operators becoming confused and performing cues on the standby instead of on the 'Go'.

In the above example, it would be necessary to give a standby for the full run of cues, if they occur relatively soon after each other. In this case, the standby would be inserted in the text at least 30 to 45 seconds before Sound Q5 is required, and would read:

Standby LX Qs 8–14, Sound Qs 5, 5A & 6, and Fly Q3

No further standbys are required until this complicated sequence has been concluded by LX Q14.

If there is a sufficient time lapse between individual cues in this sequence, the Deputy Stage Manager would deal with the sequence in two or more parts. For example, if there was a 2 minute gap between LX Q10 and LX Q11, with no cues between, the Deputy Stage Manager might opt to give one standby for the first group of cues:

Standby LX Qs 8, 9 & 10, and Sound Qs 5 & 5A

This would be followed by the sequence of cues, given in the appropriate places.

The second group of standby cues would be:

Standby LX Qs 11–14, Sound Q6, and Fly Q3

Again, this would be followed by the sequence of cues in the right places.

Cueing Technique

The key to accurate cueing is anticipation and a familiarity with the on-stage action and cue sequences. Prior to the technical rehearsal, it is a good idea to run through the standby and go cues.

Cueing can be very demanding. There is a considerable weight of responsibility to get the cues exactly right. However, when the cues are given correctly and a performance runs smoothly, the satisfaction can be enormous.

To ensure that each cue is given at exactly the correct time it is necessary to anticipate the cue word so that the 'Go' is heard at the same time as the boxed cue word is said by the actor.

TASK

Practise cueing from a prompt copy in a small group. Take turns to cue while the others read out loud the lines of the script as they would occur on stage. If there are enough people in the group, you could also nominate lighting and sound operators, who will acknowledge their standby cues.

Working from the prompt copy, say the standby and cue information aloud as the lines are spoken. Try and anticipate the cue word so that 'Go' is said at exactly the same time as the 'actor' speaks the cue word in the line. Where sequences are difficult, stop your colleagues and ask them to repeat the section of the text. Make sure that you go back to a line *before* the standby cues for the particular sequence. Run the sequence again until you are confident that you can get it right every time.

Make sure that your instructions are always clear and precise. You need to sound confident, even if you don't feel it! A hesitant cue will make the rest of the crew feel uneasy.

CONTROL ROOM AND COMMUNICATION SYSTEM ETIQUETTE

The Deputy Stage Manager is responsible for ensuring that the crew behave in a professional manner. Conduct in the control room, behaviour and use of the communication system during technical and performance work should be closely monitored.

There should never be unnecessary talk on 'cans' or headsets and, except in an emergency, no one should speak once a standby cue has been given.

The crew should acknowledge cues and/or cue lights by replying with, 'Standing by'.

Other points of etiquette regarding the use of the communications system are:

- No eating or chewing gum.
- No heavy breathing.
- Microphones should always be switched off before headsets are removed to avoid a loud bang and/or a high-pitched screech being relayed to other users.

There should be no visual or aural distractions in the vicinity of the control room or near the operators. People who are not involved in the cueing or technical operation of the show should not be allowed in the control room during a technical or dress rehearsal, or during a performance. This includes the director.

PREPARATION FOR THE TECHNICAL REHEARSAL

Before the technical rehearsal the Deputy Stage Manager studies the prompt copy to ensure that they understand all of the new cue information and that it is clearly written. They should also ensure that each cue has a standby cue and that these standby cues are expressed in a logical and appropriate way.

It is important to be familiar with the technical controls in the venue and control box and these should be checked prior to performance. You may well be asked as part of the pre-show routine to check that ventilation systems are off or switched to a particular setting.

Checklist for the Technical Rehearsal

Is the cueing position set up and ready?
Are all of the following provided?

– a chair or stool

– a pencil
– a rubber
– a note pad or blank paper
– a stopwatch
– the prompt copy
Is there a clear view of the stage?
Are the communication headsets working?
Is the show relay working?
Is it loud enough for you to hear the stage?
Is the backstage calls system working?
Can calls and the show relay be heard in the dressing rooms and green room?
If there is a video monitor, can you see a picture of the stage? Is the camera on?
If there is a cue light system, is it working?
Do all of the out stations work properly?
Are all of the switches that you need to use labelled correctly?

PRACTISING CUES IN THE TECHNICAL REHEARSAL

The technical rehearsal is the only opportunity for the Deputy Stage Manager and crew to rehearse the cueing sequences and is also the only occasion when they are allowed to get a cue wrong! If the show is one where there are large sections of script without cues or changes on stage, it may be appropriate to run a cue-to-cue technical rehearsal. This involves jumping the parts of the script where there are no cues.

If cues do not run smoothly, as intended when they were plotted, it will be necessary to repeat each sequence until the desired effect is achieved. Actors may need to be redirected, the timing or level of technical cues adjusted, or cueing points altered in the prompt copy. Sometimes additional cues may need to be added to the prompt copy. The technical rehearsal is discussed in more detail on page 90.

PREPARING FOR THE DRESS REHEARSAL

Once all of the cues have been established and they are unlikely to be adjusted further, it is common practice to overwrite the standby cues in red ink and the go cues in green ink. Narrow felt-tips are ideal for this. The coloured ink corresponds to the colours of the cue lights. It also provides an added visual guide in the cues column. Other information, such as front of house and backstage calls may be inked in black.

It is wise not to erase pencilled cues before inking in, as there is a danger of losing vital information.

The final preparation for the dress rehearsal involves adding in all of the pre-show calls (see below) and obtaining some blank copies of the **show report** (see page 91). A separate report is filled in for each performance. The dress rehearsal should be run exactly as if it were the first performance under strict performance conditions.

Adding Pre-Show and Front of House Calls

On a clean page at the beginning of the prompt copy, the following pre-show calls for the cast and crew are added:

35 minutes before performance	Half hour call
20 minutes before performance	15 minute call
10 minutes before performance	5 minute call
5 minutes before performance	Beginners' call

The Deputy Stage Manager is also usually responsible for giving front of house calls to inform the audience that the performance is about to begin. There may be a P.A. system for announcements, or there may be a series of pre-recorded announcements to be replayed. Alternatively there may be a coded system of bell calls. Whatever the method, the front of house calls should be noted in detail.

Front of house calls are usually given as follows:

5 minutes before performance
3 minutes before performance
2 minutes before performance
1 minute before 'curtain up' – the final call.

TASK

It is advisable to write down every word of a front of house call. It is easy to get tongue tied once the microphone is 'live'. Write some calls and practise to make them sound clear and spontaneous, not as if they are being read from your prompt copy!

Pre-show checklist

For a performance beginning at 7.30 pm, the pre-show calls and routine would occur as follows. This checklist would also be used at the dress rehearsal.

- 6.55 pm   **Backstage: Half hour call**
Good evening Ladies and gentlemen. This is your half hour call. Half an hour, please. Thank you.'
- Check with the Stage Manager that:
  1   The cast and crew have signed in
  2   The stage is set, masking and props are ready
  3   The auditorium is clear
  4   The cast and/or musicians are in position if they are needed on stage prior to the audience entering the space
  5   The preset lighting is on, house lights are up, fluorescent lights are off, working lights are on, the control box lighting is dimmed.
  6   The pre-show sound is running.
  7   The house can be opened.
- 7.00 pm   **Front of house: House open bell** (one long bell to signal that the house can be opened).
Backstage: House open call
'Ladies and gentlemen of the cast and crew, the house is now open. The house is now open. Thank you.'
In addition a warning may be given about noise levels or there may be a reminder that the stage cannot be crossed if the audience are in full view.)
- 7.10 pm   **Backstage: 15 minute call (the Quarter)**
'Ladies and gentlemen, this is you 15 minute call. 15 minutes, please. Thank you.'
- 7.20 pm   **Backstage: 5 minute call**
'Ladies and gentlemen, this is your 5 minute call. 5 minutes, please. Thank you.'

- Check all technical personnel are in position and on cans.
- 7.25 pm   **Front of house: Welcome call**
'Good evening ladies and gentlemen. Welcome to [venue] for tonight's performance of [title] by [Company]. The performance will commence in 5 minutes. Thank you.'
- 7.25 pm   **Backstage: Beginners' call**
'Ladies and gentlemen, Beginners, Act One please.
Miss Watson
Miss Woods
Mr Andrews
Mr Cowen
Mr Turton, this is your beginners' call. Thank you.'
- This call is repeated.
- 7.27 pm   **Front of house: 3 bells and/or 3 minute call**
'Ladies and gentlemen, will you kindly take your seats as the performance will begin in 3 minutes. Thank you.'
- This call is repeated.
- 7.28 pm   **Front of house: 2 bells and/or 2 minute call**
'Ladies and gentlemen, will you please take your seats as the performance will begin in 2 minutes. Thank you.'
- This call is repeated.
- 7.29 pm   **Front of house: 1 bell and/or final call**
'Ladies and gentlemen, will you please take your seats as the performance is about to begin. Ladies and gentlemen, this is the final call, will you please take your seats as the performance is about to begin. Thank you.'
- Check beginners are in place.
- Put crew and cast on standby for first sequence of cues.
- 7.30 pm   Wait for front of house clearance to start the show.
- When front of house clearance is received from the House Manager:

On Cans: 'We now have front of house clearance ... LX Q1 and houselights GO.'
- The performance has begun.

- As soon as the first sequence of cues has been given: **backstage call** 'Curtain up, Act One.'

The Get-in and Fit-up

PREPARING THE VENUE

Moving into the venue is a major step and marks the beginning of the production week. If there is not a Production Manager or Technical Manager, the Stage Manager will plan the order in which things should be done. The Stage Manager may, in any case, find themselves supervising the fit-up of the stage and co-ordinating the various production departments, so it is important that they have an overview of the planned schedule.

On arrival at the venue, the Stage Manager should ensure that they are familiar with the building and its facilities. They should also introduce themselves to key members of the resident staff.

The Stage
The Stage Manager assists the stage crew to bring the production scenery and equipment into the venue, and locating the setting on the stage. The stage management team sweep the stage and mark out the set from the ground plan, so that key items of set can be quickly located and the build can begin. Marking out is covered on pages 48–54.

Throughout the fit-up, technical and dress rehearsals the stage management team are responsible for keeping the stage area clean, so that it is a safe environment for the crew to work in. During the fit-up this means regularly sweeping and mopping the stage. Some stage floors (e.g. dance flooring) may need special treatment.

Safety Checklist
These things should be considered before the cast use the stage:

- Is the stage swept and clean?
- Are the edges of raised staging and treads marked with white or fluorescent tape?
- Are all tools, nails, ladders and technical equipment put away?
- Is there sufficient illumination? Are the backstage working lights on?
- Are all exits clear?
- Are braces, weights, scenic items, booms, stands and lanterns at floor level marked with white tape?
- Are sightlines marked on the floor (so that the actors know when they cannot be seen from the auditorium)?
- Are corridors around the stage area free from obstacles?
- Is all flooring secured? Taped down? Check for frayed carpets or other tripping hazards on stage or off stage.
- Post 'Quiet Please' notices on backstage doors leading to the stage.

Masking
Masking refers to using drapes or scenic flats on the stage wings to prevent the audience from seeing off stage.

Masking is usually directed by the Stage Manager from the auditorium, since the correct positions will depend on sightlines from the seats at the extremities of the auditorium. Borders, legs and tormentors may be used in the traditional proscenium setting; tabs and drapes are employed in other venues to mask offstage activities. Masking may be rigged at an early stage in the fit-up, but will not be finalised until all of the scenery has been built and the lighting is in place. It is essential however, that the masking is in place before the lights are focused.

Dressing Rooms

Before the cast arrive at the venue, it is the Stage Manager's task to allocate dressing rooms. The Deputy Stage Manager will have a good idea about who gets on with whom, and who doesn't! A provisional list should have been prepared in advance, and discussed with the Director and wardrobe department. Some contracts may specify precedence for certain cast members which should be reflected in which actor is allocated which dressing room. Special costume requirements and quick changes may also have a bearing. Labels should be posted on dressing room doors before the cast arrive, and a list of the occupants of each room should be circulated to the stage door personnel, the wardrobe department, as well as being posted on the company notice board.

Members of the company are expected to sign themselves in once they have entered the building, and the list will be checked for any absences at the half hour call. If the venue has a stage door keeper, it may be appropriate to leave the register there. Once members of the company have signed in, they should not leave the building without notification.

ARRIVAL OF THE CAST

Arrange a convenient time to walk the cast through the set, show them the entrances and exits, and to indicate any potential hazards or unusual variations in the staging.

SCENE CHANGES

The actual method of scene changes can be very complex. Scenic items may move vertically (flying, drops, rollers, traps, lifts) or laterally (revolves, trucks, shutters, tracks, etc.) Sophisticated computer controlled hydraulic mechanisms can perform several functions at once. Even the simplest combination of scene changes will need good coordination to get it right.

The Setting Plot or List

Throughout rehearsals a series of **Setting Lists** (maps or lists showing the set layout for each scene) will have been created. Precision is important, since this information needs to be followed exactly to set the stage for each performance. Both on stage and off stage locations of props should be included on the setting plot, see Figure 3.17.

Running Lists

Running lists are cue sheets for the Assistant Stage Managers and on-stage crew. These detail which items need to be changed and in which order throughout a performance. The running lists may also give an indication of the speed of the scene change, see Figure 3.18.

If there is sufficient time in the schedule, it is a good idea to practice each scene change.

THE LIGHTING SESSION

A lighting session is required to finalise the lighting plot. At least one Assistant Stage Manager should be available to 'walk' for the lighting. This means that they make some of the actors' moves, so that the lighting designer can see the intensity of the light against the skin and check whether the actors' faces will be evenly lit.

Figure 3.17   *An example of a setting list*

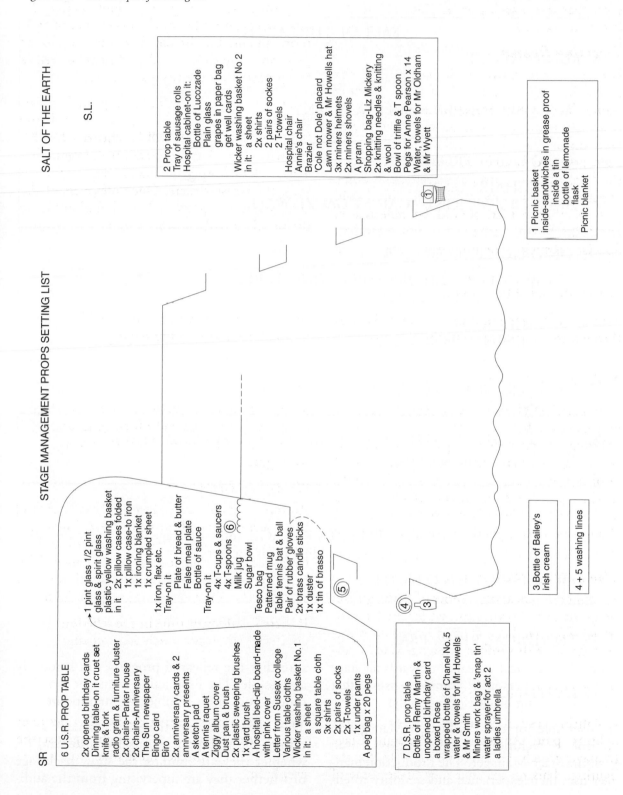

SALT OF THE EARTH

STAGE MANAGEMENT PROPS SETTING LIST

SR

S.L.

6 U.S.R. PROP TABLE

2x opened birthday cards
Dinning table-on it cruet set
knife & fork
radio gram & furniture duster
2x chairs-Parker house
2x chairs-Anniversary
The Sun newspaper
Bingo card
Biro
2x anniversary cards & 2
anniversary presents
A sketch pad
A tennis raquet
Ziggy album cover
Dust pan & brush
2x plastic sweeping brushes
1x yard brush
A hospital bed-clip board-made
with pink cover
Letter from Sussex college
Various table cloths
Wicker washing basket No.1
in it: a sheet
         a square table cloth
         3x shirts
         2x pairs of socks
         2x T-towels
         1x under pants
A peg bag x 20 pegs

1 pint glass 1/2 pint
glass & spirit glass
plastic yellow washing basket
in it 2x pillow cases folded
         1x pillow case-to iron
         1x ironing blanket
         1x crumpled sheet
1x iron, flex etc.
Tray-on it
         Plate of bread & butter
         False meal plate
         Bottle of sauce
Tray-on it
         4x T-cups & saucers
         4x T-spoons ⑥
         Milk jug
         Sugar bowl
Tesco bag
Patterned mug
Table tennis bat & ball
Pair of rubber gloves
2x brass candle sticks
1x duster
1x tin of brasso

7 D.S.R. prop table
Bottle of Remy Martin &
unopened birthday card
a boxed Rose
wrapped bottle of Chanel No.5
water & towels for Mr Howells
& Mr Smith
Miners work bag & 'snap tin'
water sprayer-for act 2
a ladies umbrella

2 Prop table
Tray of sausage rolls
Hospital cabinet-on it:
         Bottle of Lucozade
         Plain glass
         grapes in paper bag
         get well cards
Wicker washing basket No 2
in it: a sheet
         2x shirts
         2 pairs of sockes
         2 T-towels
Hospital chair
Annie's chair
Brazier
'Cole not Dole' placard
Lawn mower & Mr Howells hat
3x miners helmets
2x miners shovels
A pram
Shopping bag-Liz Mickery
2x knitting needles & knitting
& wool
Bowl of triffle & T spoon
Pegs for Anne Pearson x 14
Water, towels for Mr Oldham
& Mr Wyett

1 Picnic basket
inside-sandwiches in grease proof
         inside a tin
         bottle of lemonade
         flask
Picnic blanket

3 Bottle of Bailey's
irish cream

4 + 5 washing lines

Figure 3.18   *An example of a running list*

SALT OF THE EARTH

S.M RUNNING LIST.

ACT 1

p1.   ACT 1 BEGINNERS = FULL COMPANY

- -

p6.   ON Q LIGHT FROM U.S.R

SET 2 CHAIRS U.S.R
SET GRAMOPHONE AGAINST GAUZE WALL.

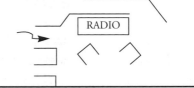

---

p11.   ON Q LIGHT FROM U.S.R

SET BETWEEN 2 CHAIRS THE DINING TABLE
ON IT 50'S TABLE CLOTH

CRUET SET
KNIFE & FORK.

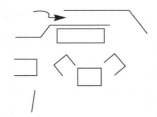

ON Q LIGHT S.R. PUT WIND MACHINE ON.

---

p21.   ON Q LIGHT U.S.R. PUT ON SMOKE U.S.C. FOR 'ZIGGY STARDUST'.
2 or 3 blasts then get off stage.

---

p23.   ON Q LIGHT U.S.R

STRIKE 2 CHAIRS & THE TABLE OFF STAGE. (once off stage re-set the table with
The Sun, Bingo Card, Pen, 2 Silver wedding cards for Act 2).

BLACKS OUT ON Q LIGHT.

THE TECHNICAL REHEARSAL

From the technical rehearsal onwards all stage management personnel should ensure that they are wearing black clothing only!

It is sensible for the Production Manager to control the technical rehearsal in close liaison with the Stage Manager. The Production manager uses their experience and seniority to en-

sure that the rehearsal progresses as smoothly as possible. The Production Manager can view proceedings from an objective standpoint.

The precise nature of the Stage Manager's role during the technical rehearsal will depend on whether they are running the show backstage or whether they are supervising from the auditorium, in place of the Production Manager. If it is necessary to stop the rehearsal for some reason, the Stage Manager should inform the Production Manager and the Director. Once cast and crew are ready to continue, the Stage Manager should tell the Deputy Stage Manager where to restart. If the Director stops the technical rehearsal, the Stage Manager should always appear on stage to find out why the run was interrupted and to assist if required.

Directors should be briefed not to stop the technical rehearsal for the direction of the actors, unless this has a direct bearing on the interaction of setting, costume, props, lighting or sound!

The technical rehearsal can be a long and protracted process and may last a couple of days for complicated shows. It is important that concentration is maintained by both cast, crew and technical operators throughout the process. The Stage Manager should ensure that the stage management team and other members of the company take their allocated breaks.

BAND CALL

There will be a band call, if the show involves live music. This is often arranged after the technical rehearsal, due to the additional cost of keeping musicians on call. The band call provides an opportunity for the sound operator to balance levels, and to check cues.

THE DRESS REHEARSAL

The dress rehearsal should be treated in exactly the same way as a performance. The run should not be stopped except in an emergency.

Many of the pointers for a real performance are, therefore, relevant here (see Chapter 4).

AFTER THE SHOW

Show Report

From the first dress rehearsal onwards, the Deputy Stage Manager on the book will also be responsible for filling in a show report after each performance. This document provides a snapshot of the progress of each performance, the timings of scenes, Acts and intervals and details of any problems or unusual occurrences. Where mistakes have occurred, these should be noted and the reason why should be given. Notes on the audience size and response can also be useful to place the performance in context. The names of the operators running the show should be recorded. The show report is signed by the Deputy Stage Manager and countersigned by the Stage Manager. It should then be duplicated and given to the Director as soon after the performance as possible. A second copy should be given to the Production and/or the Technical Manager, who will want to investigate any problems that relate to the staging of the show and make sure that they are resolved before the next performance.

Notes Sessions

Notes sessions occur after the dress rehearsal and after the first performances. The stage management team should be present at every notes session. Any action required should be minuted. The Deputy Stage Manager should attend with the prompt book, to clarify queries associated with actor's moves, lines and technical cues.

On some occasions it may be appropriate to ask the director to give a separate notes session

Figure 3.19   *Example of a show report*

Bolton Octagon Theatre
Show Report 'TWO"

| Date | 3.10.98 | Performance Number 10 | | Capacity (%) 74 |

DSM on the book	A. Van Den Berg	Lighting operator	A. Gent
Duty Stage manager	S. McDonald	Sound operator	A. Gent
Duty FOH manager	S. Galligan	Wardrobe	A. Bateson
Act One Up	7.30pm	Act One Down	8.14pm
Act One Duration	44 mins	Interval Duration	21 mins
Act Two Up	8.35pm	Act Two Down	9.23 mins
Act Two Duration	48 mins		
Total Running Time	1 hr 47 mins	Total Playing Time	1 hr 27 mins

NOTES

1) Act 1 went up late due to a hold up at box office.
2) The show relay feeding the cans went down during scene 1. Mr Gent managed to replace the battery a short time later.
3) Ms Kerr's entrance as Maudie was late. Mr Howell's speech as Moth went quicker not allowing Ms Kerr time to change.
4) The SR captain's chair is very squeaky.
5) A mobile phone went off during a landlord/lady scene in the second half. The customer answered the phone and talked for two/three minutes. An usher eventually went to ask the gentleman to turn it off.
6) A member of the audience made a paper aeroplane and sent it onto the stage. Mr Howells managed to take it off stage during the Fred and Alice scene.
7) LXQ 34 went early (Going out of the Fred and Alice into the Landlord/lady) Mr Gent did not wait for his go. Operator error.
8) The toilet system (underneath the fixed seating) seems to make a loud noise every night during Mr Howell's final speech. It is very distracting to both actors. Is there anything that can be done to prevent this?
9) There was one extra call

Thank you

Andrina

for stage management, technical and design related areas.

Bear in mind that this is not a forum for blame, but should be seen as another way of getting things right.

The Performance

THE FIRST NIGHT

In theory, the first performance should run even better than the last dress rehearsal. However, the presence of a live audience makes a huge difference to performers, stage management personnel and technicians alike. Actors may be especially nervous and will need the team to be supportive and calm.

All members of the company will experience increased levels of adrenalin as the performance time approaches. It is important to be aware of this: people can do strange things under pressure. This is when the amount of pre-show planning and preparation should pay off. Even though everyone will be feeling nervous, they should be reassured by the detail of the pre-show planning. The lists and diagrams which were prepared during the rehearsal and production process should ensure that everything proceeds as planned.

All backstage staff should be aware of a number of theatrical superstitions, which are often adhered to by performers. You should never, therefore, wish a performer 'Good Luck'. Instead, you should use the phrase 'Break a leg!'.

There are other superstitions thought to bring bad luck. *Macbeth* is never mentioned in theatre buildings. The play is referred to in theatre circles as 'the Scottish play' since it has a history of major misfortunes. Whistling used to be a signal for fly operators to drop scenery on stage and, as a consequence, is considered unlucky if heard either on stage or backstage!

HOUSE MANAGEMENT

System for Front of House Clearance

During the hours leading up to performance, the Stage Manager has control of the space. At the half an hour call, the Deputy Stage Manager will check with the Stage Manager that the stage is set, auditorium cleared and that everything is ready for the audience. Once this has been established, and pre-show lighting and sound are in place, the control of the space is effectively handed over to the Front of House Manager, who will have their own pre-show checks to undertake. Once the house has been opened, and the audience have entered the auditorium, any backstage or technical work should take place out of sight.

The Front of House Manager will need to know the following information:

- running time of the show
- number and timing of intervals
- any cast changes
- any special circumstances – do actors enter or exit through the foyer areas; do actors perform in the foyer before, during, or after the show?
- is a strobe light used?
- any other Health and Safety issues
- pre-set details: are actors pre-set on stage before the audience enter; are tabs in or out; any pre-show music or lighting?

You should also discuss the venue's policy on late admissions. The Director will also have a view on this matter. Will the performance be severely interrupted by latecomers, or can appropriate points be identified when latecomers could be admitted without major disruption?

Once the house has been opened, the Deputy Stage Manager, lighting operator and, if pre-show sound is playing, the sound operator, should not leave the control positions.

Once all of the audience have entered the auditorium, the control of the house passes back to the stage management team.

PREPARING FOR THE PERFORMANCE

Pre-Show Checklists

Each member of the stage management team should have a pre-show routine to carry out in exactly the same way before each performance. It is helpful to have lists that can be followed precisely and ticked off as each task is accomplished.

Pre-show checklists are essential. For the stage management team, they should detail every item of set and all props, but will also include points relating to the infrastructure of the building, e.g. heating, lighting, ventilation, doors.

The pre-show checklist can be a fairly extensive document or it may take the form of several documents. Certainly, it will include a props setting diagram and layout plan of the stage. For shows destined for a long run pre-show checklists can be laminated and ticked with felt pen or chinagraph pencil. This can be erased afterwards and the list used again for subsequent performances.

Example Pre-Show Checklist

1 Check cast and crew register.
2 Inform appropriate staff of any absences.
3 Prepare an announcement for the Front of House Manager if an understudy is to be substituted.
4 Ensure heating and ventilation settings are correct.
5 Check working lights are out and backstage lights are on.
6 Check control room working lights are on.
7 Backstage checks.
8 Lighting checks.
9 Sound checks.
10 Check show relay is on.
11 Check speakers in dressing rooms are on.
12 Check prompt desk.
13 Check all cue lights are working.
14 Check communications system and all headsets.
15 Check that the stage is set for performance.
16 Ensure the edges of the stage and treads are marked with white or fluorescent tape.
17 Check that props are set on stage and off.
18 Ensure masking is in place.
19 Check the auditorium is clear.
20 Check the house lights are on.
21 Check the tabs are in (if required).
22 Ensure the pre-show lighting and sound are running.

THE DEPUTY STAGE MANAGER IN PERFORMANCE

The highlight of the Deputy Stage Manager's role is to run the show in performance. The Deputy Stage Manager is responsible for cueing all of the technical elements on stage from the moment the Front of House Manager gives clearance. It can be a very unnerving, but ultimately very exhilarating experience. The method of cueing can make or break a performance and the Deputy Stage Manager should not be distracted at any stage during the performance. The Deputy Stage Manager may have to do any or all of these things at once:

- **watching**
  - the positioning and movement of actors on the stage
  - the changing scenic elements
  - the actors' use of props
  - the lighting states on stage
  - cue light signals
- **listening to**
  - the lines that are spoken
  - sound cues and music replayed
  - responses to and acknowledgements of standbys
- **reading**
  - the script
  - the cues column
  - the calls column
- **as well as**
  - giving appropriate verbal cues
  - giving front of house and backstage calls
  - switching on appropriate cue lights
  - noting the timing of individual scenes, acts and intervals
  - filling in the show report as the performance progresses.

As well as keeping a track of all of the above elements, the Deputy Stage Manager also plays a crucial role in maintaining discipline and concentration amongst all of the technical operators throughout the performance.

Dealing with Mishaps

Even the best Deputy Stage Manager can miss a cue or mess one up. It is important not to get upset, since this reaction is likely to compound the error. The situation could develop into a downward spiral of panic! Try and forget about any errors and, instead, concentrate extra hard on getting the next sequence of cues right.

Even major mishaps can go unnoticed by an audience, so it is important to keep any error in perspective. In any case, nothing can be

done immediately to put right what has gone wrong in a performance, so it is best to make a brief note in the show report and wait until after the show to analyse what went wrong. Hopefully, it will be possible to identify the reason for the mistake and to work out what action to take to prevent the error happening again.

Calling and Cueing

Keep to the same routine for every performance, so that cast and crew are not unnecessarily confused. Call actors at the same point in the play. Other members of the cast or crew may use the call to prepare for a cue.

In a studio situation in close proximity to the audience, it is necessary to cue quietly. Other members of the crew may need to turn up the volume on their headsets to compensate and they should also whisper if they need to communicate.

Cue Lights

If there is no masterswitch on the prompt desk, use a ruler to move groups of switches to the 'on' position.

The Deputy Stage Manager should always keep their finger on the green 'Go' buttons, so that they can switch them off once the cue has occurred. This will prevent the green lights being left on by mistake and operators thinking that they've been given the 'Go' for the next cue!

Prompting the Actors

It is rare to have to prompt the actors during a performance. Most directors expect that cast members should have the skills to be able to extricate themselves from problems on stage. Often when this happens, the event goes unnoticed by the audience. This would not be true of a loudly whispered prompt from the wings. Historically, prompts were necessary only when actors in repertory theatre were playing a different part each night and, consequently, struggled to remember the lines. In modern productions the Deputy Stage Manager can only prompt if they are located at a prompt desk in the wings, and even then it is usually as a last resort. Many Deputy Stage Managers cue from a control room at the rear of the auditorium, so prompting is not possible.

THE STAGE MANAGER IN PERFORMANCE

As has already been noted, in an ideal situation the Stage Manager should be kept free from any routine performance duties, so that they can deal with any emergencies and cover for any member of the team if required. This also allows the Stage Manager to monitor the performance from the front.

Maintaining the Performance during the run

During an extended run of a play, after the Director has moved on or is directing the next show in the repertoire, it is the Stage Manager who is responsible for maintaining the quality of the production. It is very easy for a show to become stale during a long run.

The Stage Manager, therefore, needs to develop a critical eye, to observe the performance from an objective point of view. The Stage Manager should examine scenery, props, costumes and be aware of discrepancies in the lighting and sound plots. Running repairs, cleaning, repainting and other maintenance will be required to keep the show looking fresh.

Maintaining the standard of the performers' work is, perhaps, the most difficult aspect of the Stage Manager's job.

The Stage Manager is responsible for sorting out any problems in their area, highlighted in the show report. In a repertory situation the areas will usually be confined to stage management issues: cueing, scene changing, props and setting. On a tour, where the Stage Manager takes on a wider production or company management role, all areas of the show report will fall within their jurisdiction.

Understudy Rehearsals

Details of these rehearsals should be posted on the Company notice board as soon as they are known. Understudies will need to be rehearsed on stage during the day throughout a long run of a play. It is the Stage Manager's responsibility to run understudy rehearsals, but the Director may want to be involved.

THE ASSISTANT STAGE MANAGER IN PERFORMANCE

The Assistant Stage Manager will be involved mainly in running the props, setting and scene changing. They may also be required to do other tasks, such as assisting cast members with quick costume changes, operating smoke machines, etc.

THE LAST PERFORMANCE

Beware Jokers!

The stage management team should be particularly alert during the period leading up to the last performance of a show. Actors have developed the habit of creating practical jokes on the last night of a performance, which the crew often join in or embellish. This should be regarded as unprofessional, since it does not serve the purpose of the production. Attempt to dissuade actors and crew from this practice as the jokes, if noticed, are rarely funny to an audience. Be particularly vigilant once 'the half' has been called and double check your own props and the stage settings to make sure that you are not a victim of someone else's idea of fun!

After the last Performance

The stage management team should co-ordinate the get-out, particularly for items associated with settings and props. The stage and backstage areas are priorities and a plan for the striking (taking down) and packing of items should have been worked out in advance.

Particularly valuable, fragile or potentially dangerous items should be removed from the stage area at once and stored in a safe location. Make sure that props are sorted into boxes for storing or returns, so that they are easy to distinguish after the get-out has been completed. All props used during the show should be carefully retrieved, to prevent souvenir collecting by members of the cast.

Ensure that the prompt copy and all accompanying documentation is filed in the production office for future reference. Collect lighting, sound and fly cue sheets, plans and computer disks together with all of the stage management material to comprise a complete record of the production.

Returns

The speedy return of properties that have been lent or loaned to the production is an essential, but often neglected, area of theatre practice. Props that have been hired should be returned quickly, to avoid excess charges. Borrowed items should also be taken back as soon as possible, before they go missing or get damaged. Remember to ring ahead in advance to check when it will be convenient for you to return the items you have borrowed. If you have already agreed a date and time to return props, then make sure that you stick to it.

When making returns, it is polite to take spare copies of the programme with you. The owner of the prop may wish to see that a proper acknowledgement has been made.

POST MORTEM OR PRODUCTION EVALUATION

After a day or so, try and find time to analyse the stage management contribution to the production. Senior members of the team will also be asked to join a wider evaluation of the production.

Here are some general questions to consider at this point:

- How well did the team work together?
- Could communication systems be improved in future?

- What were the main difficulties during the process?
- Could these have been foreseen? By whom?
- Was time used as efficiently as possible?
- What worked particularly well?
- How could the stage management contribution be improved in future?
- What have the team learnt as a direct result of working on this project?

chapter four
LIGHTING

Introduction

Lighting the stage involves a combination of skills: a thorough grasp of the technology, a practical ability and a creative vision. Simple illumination of a stage space is relatively straightforward, but does not contribute artistically to a performance, other than allowing the audience to see the action. The creative use of light as an integral part of performance developed in the early 1500s when experiments in Renaissance Italy created extravagant spectaculars that amazed audiences. The dramatic use of light in performance gained increased significance once theatres moved from outdoor spaces, lit by sunlight, to indoor halls, where artificial light became an essential element.

The Lighting Designer is a relatively modern phenomenon. In British theatre the term was largely unknown until the 1960s, when lighting was still controlled by the Stage Manager or Director. However, the rapid development of technology, increasingly sophisticated lanterns and control systems and the realisation that lighting has a contribution to make to performance, has lead to the need for a dedicated lighting designer.

This section of the book attempts to deal with the two, apparently contrasting aspects of stage lighting – the technology and the dramatic potential of light in performance. The first part looks at the technical equipment used in lighting a performance. The role of lighting design is then discussed, together with practical strategies and a method of approach for lighting a production.

THE LIGHTING TEAM

The lighting team will vary in number depending upon the size of the venue and the type of work that is produced. A large-scale rock concert requires an enormous number of riggers and technicians to prepare the lights in a relatively short space of time. A small performance space may only have one resident technician who fills in as lighting and sound operator, as well as stage management!

A typical repertory theatre company would contain:

a Chief Electrician
a Deputy Electrician
two Assistant Electricians
a pool of six or more casual staff.

ROLES AND RESPONSIBILITIES

The Lighting Designer
The Designer should provide an appropriate, creative use of light in a production. This requires a mixture of practical, technical and conceptual skills, and the ability to translate a mental image of light into a reality on

stage. Weeks of preliminary work with the Director and other members of the artistic team are required to formulate a coherent lighting style that will contribute imaginatively to a production. Extensive preparatory work will be undertaken in order to convert original ideas into a workable lighting scheme on stage. The Designer must draw up a rig plan, specify equipment types, co-ordinate the colour, direction, focus, and intensity of individual lights. Timings of changes to the lighting will be set precisely and a series of 'lighting states' will be created, to provide suitable moods and a shifting atmosphere throughout the show.

Lighting Designers usually work as freelancers, employed by a company to work on a single production at a time. For some productions, particularly in venues which produce their own work, the resident Chief Electrician may be asked to design the lighting.

Designers need to be able to respond imaginatively to a play text or brief, have excellent communication skills to explain this response to other members of the team and have great organisational skills to be able to implement the scheme in the theatre. An ability to stay calm, think quickly and to modify design ideas when necessary are also important, since the Lighting Designer is usually working under extreme pressure of time.

The Chief Electrician (Chief LX)

The Chief LX runs the electrics department, which looks after the stage and electrical maintenance of the theatre. This usually involves electrical supervision and maintenance of all areas of the building, not simply the stage and the auditorium! The Chief Electrician determines the day-to-day allocation of tasks within the electrics team and co-ordinates the lighting process of every production, working closely with the visiting Lighting Designer. The Chief LX must maintain an adequate stock of spares, be aware of lighting industry developments and ensure that lighting equipment in the venue is stored and maintained correctly.

A good relationship with visiting freelance Designers is essential if the production process is to be as smooth as possible. The resident team can assist the Designer, since they know the building inside out and can give advice on relevant technical matters. It is important that the Chief Electrician understands the fundamentals of lighting design and the likely requirements of different dramatic genres, especially since they may be required to fulfil the role of Lighting Designer on some productions. On a practical level the Chief LX supervises all of the lighting work from the fit-up to the get-out, but may not be directly involved in the performance work itself. The operation of the lighting control board is often delegated to other members of the team, but the Chief LX will be able to step in at any time.

The Deputy Chief Electrician (Deputy LX)

The Deputy LX may take on some of the responsibilities of the Chief LX, such as co-ordinating the repair and maintenance schedule for lighting equipment or assisting a designer who is unfamiliar with the venue. The Deputy LX should have an advanced knowledge of electricity, electrical installations, lighting control systems and plotting techniques. A working knowledge of computers and electronics is useful, as is the ability to design and build props and special effects. The Deputy LX must be able to work well with the Designer and the junior members of the electrics team and will probably take responsibility for the plotting of complex shows during the lighting session. The Deputy LX may also get opportunities to develop design skills, particularly if the venue has a studio theatre, or stages occasional amateur productions.

Assistant Electrician (Assistant LX)

This is the most junior of the permanent staff employed in the lighting team. The Assistant

Figure 4.1   *The process of lighting design*

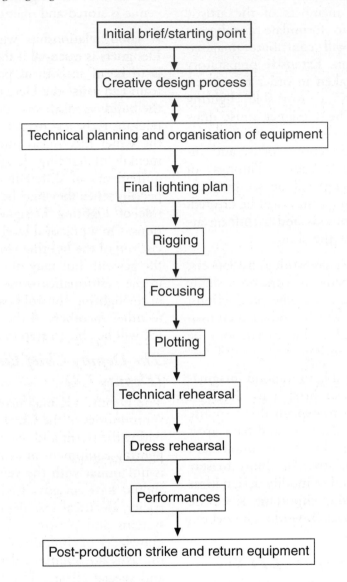

LX undertakes the majority of the rigging and focusing of the lighting design, typically working at height, in dark, cramped spaces, with hot and temperamental equipment! The Assistant LX often runs the show from the lighting control board or undertakes on-stage electrics work during the performance. Junior members of the LX team need to be fit, organised, technically competent and able to work safely at speed and under pressure.

Casual Staff

Casual staff are usually employed to assist with get-ins, fit-ups and get-outs, as well as production work such as operating follow spotlights and on-stage electrics, such as smoke machines. Experience in a casual role is usually an essential preliminary step to gaining employment as an Assistant LX.

THE LIGHTING PROCESS

Initial Brief

The lighting design brief is usually acquired through detailed discussion with the Director and/or other members of the design team. A style and period for the production will be established, as well as the role and function of the lighting.

Creative Design Process

There is a period when design ideas are developed through immersion in the project, attending rehearsals, research and further discussions with the Director and Designers. Experimentation with ideas will take place on paper and in practice.

Technical Planning and Organisation

This involves the translation of the conceptual response to the script in terms of light, to a lighting plan and other accompanying documentation that can be understood by members of the electrics team.

Rigging

Rigging is the process of placing every lantern in a rig, according to the lighting plan. This process occurs as part of the fit-up of a production. Each lantern is plugged in to a dimmer to create a circuit.

Focusing

The orientation and beam characteristics of each lantern are set. As well as the precise positioning of each lantern in relation to the stage, the beam may be altered in size, shape, texture or colour.

Plotting

The lighting is created by setting the level of intensity of each lantern to build up individual stage pictures of light or 'lighting states'. Each state is then plotted (recorded precisely) so that it can be replayed accurately in performance.

Technical Rehearsal

As we have discussed this is the run through of the performance with the cast and all of the technical cues in place. This is the time for the Lighting Designer to check for timing, light levels, colour, positioning of cues and whether what has been plotted is technically feasible in performance. Minor changes are often made to the lighting plot at this stage.

Dress Rehearsal

This non-stop run-through of the play under performance conditions gives the first uninterrupted view of the lighting. Fade times, intensity and visual impact of the lighting on the stage are monitored.

Performance

Lighting should be replayed exactly as it has been plotted. Freelance lighting designers usually leave the show after the opening night, to begin work on another project.

Post-Production

At the get-out all equipment is derigged and hire equipment is returned. The lighting team may be involved in post-production evaluations.

The Lighting System

The lighting system in a theatre consists of the following elements:

- **A mains power supply** – this provides the electrical power to the dimmers.

- **Mains fuses and RCD trip switches** – these limit the amount of power that can be used and also protect the equipment from electrical overload. **RCDs** (residual current circuit devices) make electrical shocks to humans less likely by monitoring the mains current for evidence of an imbalance. If a piece of equipment is faulty or if someone touches a live contact, the RCD 'trips' and disconnects the circuit. Fuses and trip switches are found in the dimmer and also in the distribution box. This distribution box should have a switch or lever to enable the power to the lighting system to be isolated.

- **Dimmers** – these are electrical devices that allow individual lamps in each lantern to be dimmed smoothly. Most portable dimmers are grouped in sets of six dimmers within one pack. Each individual dimmer will have its own separate fuse and may have two sockets to allow two lanterns to be connected to it at the same time. If lanterns are paired like this, each dimmer pack can control 12 lanterns. Professional theatre dimmers are large items of equipment and are permanently installed, often a considerable distance from the stage and the control room. This form of dimmer is 'hard-wired' (see below), is fitted inside a cabinet and does not have front-mounted sockets. Lanterns are connected to the dimmers directly, once they are plugged in on the rig.

- **Cabling** – this links the lanterns to the dimmers. The lanterns may be rigged a considerable distance from the dimmers, so cabling can be quite elaborate. It may involve different types of connectors and methods of connecting lanterns to the dimmers. A **patch panel** provides flexibility in a lighting installation, since it allows any lantern on the rig to be connected (patched) to any dimmer circuit. A patch panel allows the designer or technician to assign lanterns to specific dimmers,

so that they may be organised into logical groups and be controlled more easily from the board. Other systems are said to be 'hard wired', which means that if a lantern on a rig is plugged into socket number 5, it will be powered by dimmer number 5 and operated by fader number 5.

- **Lanterns** – or 'luminaires' are specialist lighting fixtures for theatre. Most are between five to 20 times more powerful than a 100 watt domestic light bulb. There are a number of different types of lanterns which are designed for specific purposes.

- **A control board** – or 'desk' is linked to the dimmers by control leads. The control board allows very precise operation of lanterns by the movement of faders, by a keypad, or often a combination of both. On a manual control desk, each fader corresponds to a dimmer and this is termed a **circuit** or **channel**. Fader 1 operates dimmer 1 and the lantern or lanterns connected to it. This is known as Circuit 1. The control board itself either receives its power from the dimmers or from its own separate supply via a 13 amp socket. Control boards often have a 'pre-set' facility which allows the complex cues for a lighting state to be set up in advance.

- **Computer control board** – more advanced systems store lighting cue information in a computer memory and allow sophisticated and accurate control of changes in light intensity. Several cues can be performed at the same time and complex effects can be achieved. Computer control boards usually require a display monitor, which also needs a separate power supply. The monitor allows the operator to view the levels of all of the circuits at any one time and will also display cue, patch and other information as required. Computer systems working with conventional analogue dimmers need one or more **demultiplexers** or 'demux units' (see page 132.)

Figure 4.2   *This diagram shows how a lantern is connected to a dimmer and controlled in a typical lighting system*

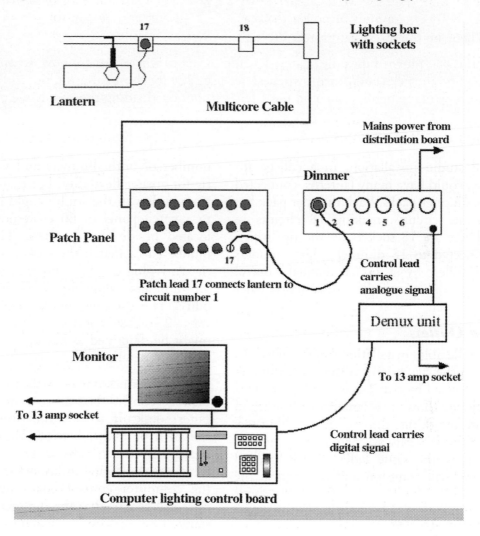

Theatre lighting installations vary considerably according to the size and type of venue, the amount of power available and the equipment that was specified when installation took place.

Older systems tend to be smaller and less flexible. Some may even be dangerous if the writing or fusing has not been upgraded.

A SIMPLE LIGHTING SET-UP

A simple set-up might involve four lanterns on a stand, connected to a single dimmer pack, which has been plugged into a conventional 13 amp socket. Some dimmers have faders mounted on a front panel to enable the lights to be operated without a separate control board. Alternatively, a simple control board can be linked to the dimmer pack by a control lead.

TASK

Where are the fuses that protect this lighting system?

If this was plugged into the nearest 13 amp socket to where you are now, where would you find the fuses and/or trip switches? See page 224 for the answer to this task. To find out how many lights you could use safely without overloading the supply see p. 136.

STUDIO INSTALLATIONS

A small studio installation, in a college for example, could have many lanterns, connected to three dimmer packs. Each dimmer pack has six separate circuits, making 18 circuits in total. There are 18 sockets on the rig, which are connected to 18 dimmers. The dimmers are controlled by a preset manual control board with 18 circuit faders and a master fader for each preset.

Paired Outlets

A more flexible installation might have 36 sockets in the rig, paired so that each dimmer can be accessed by two sockets in the rig. This arrangement allows two lanterns on the rig to be connected to one dimmer at any one time. Because the lanterns are paired, they will be operated by the same fader on the control board and will come on and fade out at the same time.

Patchable System

A larger studio installation may have a larger number of both dimmers and sockets in the rig for greater flexibility. For example, 60 separate outlets in the studio could be connected to a patch panel of 60 corresponding plugs, located beside the dimmers. The plugs are numbered to match the socket outlets on the rig. Any plug can be connected to any one of 48 dimmers, allowing for maximum flexibility. The dimmers are controlled by a 48 way, 2 preset control board. This studio might be described as having 48 circuits with a 60 way patch.

The same studio may wish to upgrade the manual control board to a memory (computer) desk. If so a demux (demultiplexer) unit will be added between the new control board and the dimmers. The demultiplexer translates the digital information generated by the computer control board into analogue, electrical signals that the dimmers can understand.

LIGHTING INSTALLATION IN A LARGE VENUE

A larger theatre installation may have 144 sockets in the rig which are hard-wired to a corresponding number of digital dimmers. These dimmer racks do not require a demux unit, since they are designed to work from digital information supplied by a computer control board. The control board is likely to be very sophisticated and will include software that, amongst other things, allows the dimmers to be renumbered so that dimmer number 15 can be controlled as circuit 1 if desired. (This is known as soft patching.)

RIGGING AND HANGING POSITIONS

Lanterns are usually connected to a rigging position by a **yoke** and **'G' clamp** which hooks over a metal lighting bar or **barrel**. The clamp is secured tightly to the bar by a large wing nut. The yoke (also known as a **fork** or **trunnion bar**) suspends the lantern underneath the hook clamp and allows the lantern to be positioned precisely by **panning** (moving from side to side in the horizontal plane) or by **tilting** (moving it up or down in the vertical plane). A control knob allows the direction of the lantern to be locked to prevent it from moving once it has been set.

A secondary suspension method, such as a **safety chain** must be used. This should pass over the lighting bar and under the yoke. Most modern lanterns have a suspension point on the lantern housing to which one end of the chain should be secured.

Lanterns can also be rigged on floor stands (see Figure 4.4). They can be hung on barrels with 'G' clamps, or the clamp can be removed and the yoke screwed directly onto a 'T' bar with appropriate holes in it. Spigots connect the barrel or the 'T' bar to the lighting stand itself.

Lanterns can be mounted singly on a stand, e.g. a follow spot. The yoke may need to be taken off and reversed for this to work. A

Figure 4.3 *A lantern rigged correctly and plugged into a socket on an internally wired bar (IWB)*

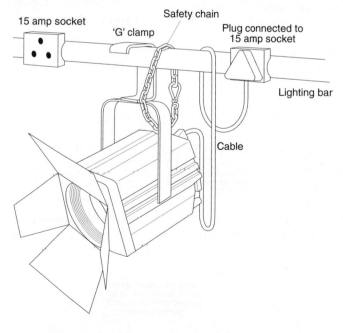

Figure 4.4   *Using a spigot to rig a lantern on a stand*

spigot can be connected directly to the yoke and then inserted into the top of the stand.

Make sure that the lantern is mounted the correct way up.

Alternatively, it is possible to make a low floor stands from two pieces of wood, drilled with a 10 mm hole. The reversed lantern yoke can then be screwed directly through the wood.

Some telescopic stands can provide lighting positions over 4 m above the stage. Particular care must be taken when rigging and focusing these.

Safety Note

Make sure that stands cannot tip over and that lanterns and T bars are firmly locked in place. If possible, attach a safety chain from the top of the stand to a fixed point and secure the feet of the stand with stage weights. Cables should not be too taut and should be tidied out of the way. Where cables run along the floor, they should be taped down to avoid causing a tripping hazard. Ideally, professional cable channels, ramps, or rubber mats should be used to protect all electrical cables on the floor.

Figure 4.5   *Rigging a lantern – clamp and yoke detail*

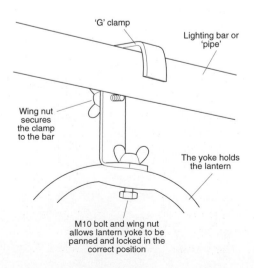

Figure 4.6 *Booms provide vertical rigging positions*

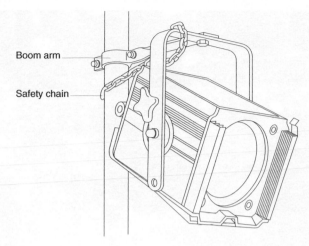

Boom arm

Safety chain

Booms

Vertical bars are known as booms and these provide rigging positions at the sides of the stage. Although some smaller and lightweight lanterns can be rigged directly onto the booms using 'G' clamps, it is better to use boom arms which allow larger and heavier lanterns to be rigged. The boom arm is connected to the boom by nuts and bolts, which need to be secured tightly by spanners or ratchets. Lighting ladders are similar fixtures, usually suspended or fixed to the wall of a venue to allow side lighting.

Trussing

Trussing is a relatively modern system for creating temporary lighting rigs, and is used extensively in rock tours and in venues with insufficient permanent lighting positions. Sections of aluminium or steel truss are bolted together and then either suspended or supported by legs, also constructed from trussing. This provides a versatile and portable lighting rig which can be assembled quickly. Lanterns are fixed to the truss bars with hook clamps in the same way as for a conventional lighting bar.

Cabling

Some lighting bars are installed with the necessary cabling and sockets already connected to the bar itself. These are known as **IWB**s (internally wired bars) and they reduce the need for massive amounts of temporary extension cables (see Figure 4.3).

Other rigging positions can be provided by 50 mm aluminium or steel scaffold bars. Lanterns rigged on these will need temporary extension cables running from a nearby power supply.

When several cables are run in this way onto the same bar, they are often taped together with PVC tape for neatness. This is often known in the industry as 'tripe'!

A more sophisticated means of providing additional sockets in a rig involves the use of socapex cable and connectors. Socapex is an 18 core cable which is terminated in 19 pin round connectors. The socapex connectors themselves can be adapted to 15 amp plugs and sockets at each end of the cable, so that lanterns can be plugged to the dimmers. These are industry standard electrical cables, which allow six separate circuits to be supplied along one larger cable. Socapex is used extensively in temporary lighting installations, such as rock concerts, since it makes cabling lanterns much quicker and the result is far neater. Socapex is also commonly used in studio theatres that do not have sufficient permanent socket outlets in the venue or to provide additional temporary outlets, at floor level, for example.

Figure 4.7   *Trussing is used to create temporary lighting rigs*

THE QUARRY THEATRE, WEST YORKSHIRE PLAYHOUSE

In a modern theatre such as the Quarry Theatre there are a number of options for rigging positions.

Front of house lighting, to illuminate the performers in the downstage area of the stage, is supplied from lighting bridges concealed in the ceiling of the auditorium. The majority of the other bars are situated above the stage and suspended in the fly tower. These are lowered to stage level during the get-in for the rigging to take place. Additional rigging positions are found on upstage bridges, on bars along the fly floor and from ladders and perch positions against the walls of the auditorium. In addition, booms and ladders can be added in the wings to provide sidelight. Several modern theatres have towers which control the width of the proscenium opening and mask wings, and also have lighting positions within them.

Of course, older proscenium theatres, built before the advent of electric lighting, are unlikely to have ideal lighting rigging positions. These may be restricted to bars flown over the stage and to a bar fixed to the front of the dress circle. Additional positions may be added to the sides and roof of the auditorium.

Figure 4.8   *Quarry Theatre, West Yorkshire Playhouse*

BASIC SAFETY

- Always disconnect the power before rigging or patching lights.
- Never connect or remove a plug with your fingers near the pins. Hold the body of the plug only.
- Never undertake an internal inspection of equipment, unless you are qualified to do so.
- Never work alone.
- Wear rubber-soled shoes when working with electrical equipment.
- Always alert others when you are turning out lights. Shout 'Going to black'.
- Never attempt to move about in a black-out.
- Be aware of where CO_2 fire extinguishers (for electrical fires) are located.

Lanterns

INTRODUCTION TO LANTERNS

Theatre lanterns, sometimes called 'luminaires' are metal boxes that contain a light source (known as a lamp). The precise size and construction of the metal box or 'housing' is re-

Figure 4.9   *Parts of a typical lantern*

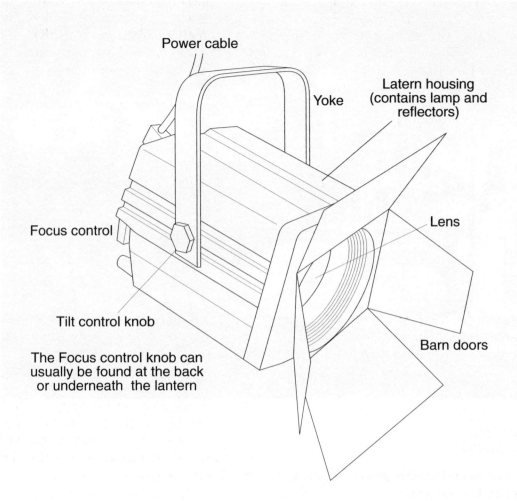

lated to the amount and quality of light that can be projected onto the stage.

Generally speaking, the larger the lantern housing, the more powerful the light. Within the housing there is a reflector, for maximising the amount of light that is emitted. Depending on the type of lantern, the housing may also contain one or more lenses which enable the light beam to be **modified** (or **focused**).

Basic Focusing

The lantern housing is suspended by a yoke which allows the lantern to be pointed in any direction (see Figure 4.3). By loosening the wing nut which joins the yoke to the 'G' clamp, the lantern may be 'panned' (moved from side to side). By loosening the knob at the side of the yoke, the lantern can be 'tilted' (raised or lowered). These two controls allow the projected light beam to be positioned where it is needed on stage. The process of positioning individual light beams in relation to the stage is called '**focusing**'. The two controls for panning and tilting should be tightened again once the lantern has been positioned correctly.

The quality and size of the beam, as well as the

direction, can be adjusted in most types of lanterns. The light can be coloured by placing filters or 'gels' in a frame which slides into a slot at the front of each lantern. Different sizes of gel are cut to fit the different lantern sizes. Take care when cutting gel. When using a scalpel, use a metal safety rule and cutting board or mat. A good tip is to make templates for each size of frame to make gel cutting easier.

Lanterns are described in terms of their beam characteristics and are also rated according to the amount of electricity that they use. As a general rule, the higher the wattage, the more powerful the light.

- A modest lantern for a small studio space is likely to contain a 500 Watt lamp. This is often known as a ½kW lantern. (Sometimes abbreviated to ½K).
- A typical lantern in a medium-size theatre would be twice as powerful at 1000 Watts (i.e., 1kW or 1K).
- Lanterns in larger performance venues can be 2000 Watts (2kW) or greater.

The more powerful lights are more expensive and tend to be larger, heavier and consequently more difficult to rig.

TYPES OF LANTERN

There are five main types of lanterns used in performance work. Each is designed for a specific purpose and is constructed differently:

1 floodlights
2 par cans and beamlights
3 fresnel spotlights
4 PC spotlights
5 profile spotlights.

You need to be able to recognise each of the five types and to understand how they might be used to light a performance.

Each type of lantern has its own universal lighting symbol which is used as a shorthand guide when drawing up a rough lighting plan. Examples of more specific symbols which identify precise details on a plan are shown in Figure 4.32.

Floodlight

- Gives a very wide, soft-edged beam.
- The simplest and oldest types of theatre light
- Consists of lamp and reflector mounted in the lantern housing.
- The beam angle is wide and there is little control.

- There is no lens.
- The shape and size of the beam cannot be changed.
- Focus is only by panning and tilting.
- Use is limited.
- They are ideal for lighting backcloths and cycloramas as floods can cover large expanses easily and blend together well.
- Can also be used as house lights for lighting the auditorium.

Floods are often mounted together in a single unit and can be placed upstage, at stage level (**groundrows**) or rigged in rows above the stage (**battens**).

Figure 4.10 *Universal lighting symbol for a floodlight*

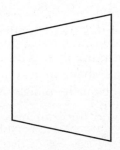

Figure 4.11   *Universal lighting symbol for a compartment floodlight*

There are two types of floodlight. A flood which is required to light an area evenly from a distance will have a symmetrical or even beam spread. Floods that are designed to light backcloths and cycloramas from a relatively short distance have a modified reflector, which creates an asymmetric beam spread.

Figure 4.12 a&b   *There are two types of floodlight with different beam characteristics*

Lighting a backcloth evenly from above with an asymmetric reflector floodlight

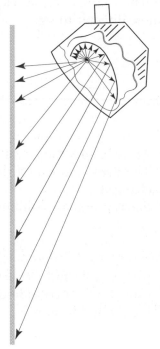

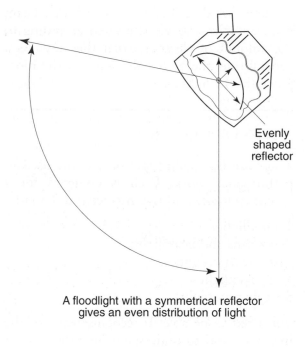

Evenly shaped reflector

A floodlight with a symmetrical reflector gives an even distribution of light

TASK

1. Experiment with a range of floodlights and throw distances observing:

    • the size of area lit
    • the shape of area lit
    • the quality of light when illuminating a cloth, wall or other large piece of scenery.

2. Try and find out how to light a wall or cloth evenly in washes of two or more colours.

Par Cans and Beamlights

The Par Can

- Has a soft-edged ellipsoidal (oval) beam.
- Was developed from aircraft landing lights for the music industry in the late 1970s.
- Consists of a lamp, reflector and lens in a single 'sealed beam unit' (like a car headlight), which is positioned at the end of a metal tube (the can).
- Common types are: 500W PAR 56 and 1kW PAR 64.
- The beam angle depends on the lamp type and can be adjusted by fitting a different lamp unit.
- The size of the beam cannot be changed by focusing.
- Focus is by panning and tilting. The lamp can also be rotated.
- Use is limited.
- It is idea for splashes of colour, strong shafts of light, colour washes, backlighting, music and variety shows.
- A parallel beam can be dramatically enhanced by smoke effects.

Like the floodlight, it is not possible to focus the beam of the par can, but there are a variety of lamp types available which can be substituted to achieve particular effects.

Lamps for the PAR 64 come in four forms:

- very narrow beam
- narrow beam
- medium flood
- wide flood.

Despite their limitations, par cans have become popular, since they are cheap, simple in design, and easy to rig and focus. They provide strong pools of light and if used in moderation are a useful addition to traditional theatre luminaires, particularly in musicals and dance where saturated (intensely coloured) beams of light are often required.

Birdies

Miniature lanterns of this type are called Par 16 mini cans and are often known as 'birdies'. They are used where rigging space is limited, such as inside scenic pieces and at the front of the stage. Because birdies run at 12 volts, they have to be wired to a transformer before being plugged to an electrical supply. They use a MR16 lamp (see p. 126)

The Beamlight

Beamlights are a similar type of lantern to the par can, but instead of containing a sealed beam unit, they use a conventional lamp and a parabolic reflector without a lens. This gives a

Figure 4.13 *A Par 64 lantern*

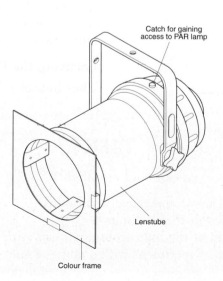

Catch for gaining
access to PAR lamp

Lenstube

Colour frame

Figure 4.14 *Universal lighting symbol for a par can*

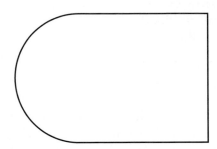

very narrow and intense shaft of light, similar to a searchlight. The parallel beam has the same spread of light whatever the throw distance and is easily visible since it picks up dust and moisture particles in the air. Many beamlights are fitted with spill rings at the front of the lantern which gives them a distinctive appearance.

Beamlights are relatively expensive but have recently regained popularity as follow spots used closer to the stage than the conventional fol-

Figure 4.15 *Universal lighting symbol for a beamlight*

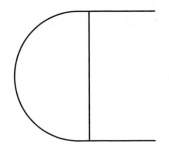

lowspot. Smaller beamlights can also be used together in a batten, which is particularly effective in providing steep intense shafts of backlight.

Fresnel Spotlight
- This is a soft-edged spotlight.
- The lens was designed in the early nineteenth century for use in lighthouses.
- Consists of a lamp, reflector and stepped lens.
- The beam angle is variable – from intense spot to a wider wash.
- Focused by moving lamp and reflector.
- Barn door fittings help to control unwanted spill and give shape to the beam.
- They are very versatile.
- Ideal for lighting acting areas as their beams blend together well.

The fresnel (pronounced 'fra-nell') spotlight is easily recognised by its distinctive lens which is stepped or grooved, to allow a greater intensity of light to reach the stage.

The fresnel's soft-edged beam is easier to control than the floodlight and so it is ideal for creating a wash of light over the performance area. Several fresnels are used together to create an even 'general cover' of light so that performers' faces can be seen clearly. However, due to spillage and therefore reduced levels of light intensity, fresnels are rarely used at any great distance away from the stage.

Focusing the Fresnel
The fresnel's beam is focused by moving

TASK

Experiment with a range of par cans and beamlights.

- Compare the quality, shape and size of the beams.
- Experiment with different throw distances.
- Compare the intensity of the light from a par can with other types of lanterns of the same power rating. Experiment with a range of colour filters.

Figure 4.16   *This diagram shows how the beam size changes when the lamp and reflector are moved during focusing*

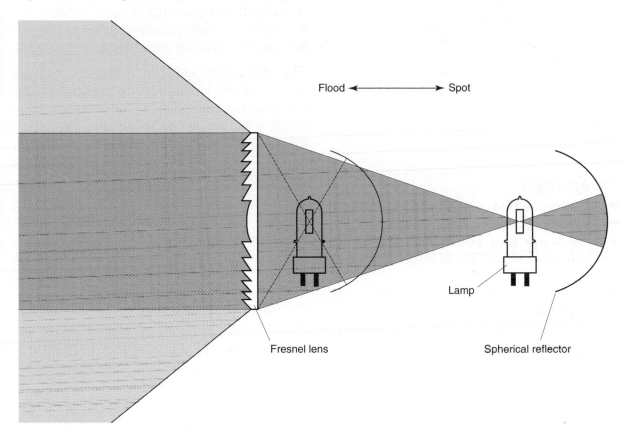

Flood ← → Spot

Lamp

Fresnel lens

Spherical reflector

the lamp tray, with lamp and reflector, in relation to the lens which remains static. The widest beam angles are achieved when the lamp is nearest the lens, the narrowest beam angle when the lamp is as far back as possible.

On smaller lanterns the focus knob is found underneath the lantern. This is unscrewed to allow the lamp tray to move. It should be tightened again, once the beam angle is set. An alternative mechanism on larger lanterns employs a focus knob at the front or rear of the lantern which is turned to move the lamp tray towards or away from the lens.

TASK

1   Practise focusing a fresnel lantern. Note the range of beam sizes, quality and intensity of light.
2   Practise using barn doors to shape the beam and control light spillage.
3   Study the edges of the beam when the lantern is fully spotted and set at widest flood.
4   Find out the beam angles of the different types of fresnels in your theatre space.

Figure 4.17 *Universal lighting symbol for a fresnel spotlight*

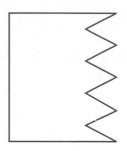

PC Spotlight

- This is a soft-edged spotlight.
- A modern variation of the fresnel.
- Has better light output than the fresnel with less spillage, but it doesn't blend so well.
- Consists of a lamp, reflector and prism convex lens.
- The beam angle is variable, with a greater range than a fresnel.
- Focused by moving the lamp and reflector.

- Barn door fittings help to control unwanted spill and shape the beam.
- These are very versatile with many uses.
- Ideal for lighting acting areas.

The PC (plano-convex, pebble-convex, or prism convex) is identical in construction to the fresnel, except that a plano-convex lens, which is frosted or pebbled, is used instead of the grooved fresnel lens.

The PC is designed for the same purpose as the fresnel, although the beam has a harder edge and the lens allows a higher proportion of light to reach the stage. Although the PC has a wider beam angle range than the fresnel and is able to produce a tight narrow spot through to a flood, the beam does not blend quite as well. It is a versatile lantern and can be used as an alternative to a defocused (softened) profile spotlight, e.g. for front of house cover.

Focusing the PC is identical to focusing the fresnel (see below).

Figure 4.18 *Focusing a PC spotlight*

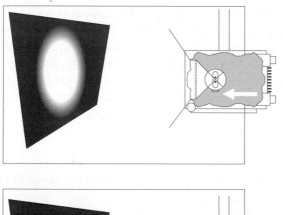

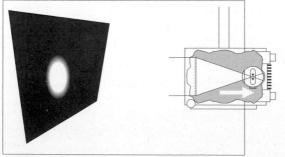

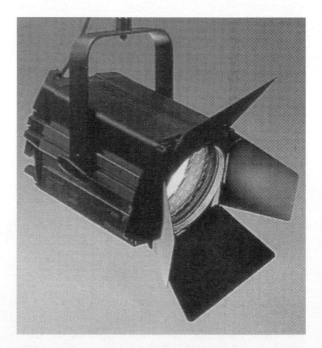

TASK

1 Compare the range of beam sizes, quality and intensity of light from a fresnel and a PC of the same power rating.
2 Compare beam quality and light spillage between fresnels and PCs of different sizes, power ratings and manufacturers.
3 Analyse the differences in the edges of shadows, an object or person when adjusting the focus of the beam.
4 Find out the beam angle range of types of PCs in your theatre space. How do they differ from the equivalent types of fresnel lanterns?

Figure 4.19 *Universal lighting symbol for a PC spotlight*

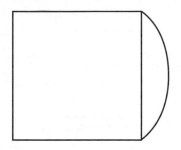

Profile Spotlight

- This is a hard-edged spotlight.
- It consists of a lamp, reflector and one or more 'plano convex' lens.
- It is the most complicated and expensive type of conventional lantern.
- The beam angle is variable, depending on the position of the lenses.
- Some profiles allow interchange of lenses.
- Focuses by moving one or more lenses.
- Shutters shape the beam.
- Gobos can be inserted in the 'gate' to project images (see below).
- Irises can be inserted to make the beam smaller.
- Very versatile with many uses.
- Ideal for defining precise areas on stage.

- Can be used with animation disks to create moving effects.
- Ideal for lighting acting areas from front of house positions.
- Also known as Lekos and ellipsoidal spotlights in the USA.

There are two basic types of profile lantern:

1. Single lens profiles have a fixed beam angle.
2. Zoom profiles are very versatile and contain two or more lenses which allow a variety of beam sizes.

Focusing Profiles

Unlike the fresnel and PC where the lens remains static and the lamp and reflector move, the profile is focused by moving a lens or lenses in relation to a static lamp and reflector. When focusing a zoom profile, both of the lenses are moved independently to determine both the size of the beam and the degree of sharpness at the edge of the beam.

Most profiles also have a field adjuster at the back of the lantern which allows the lamp to be set for a bright-centre 'peaky' beam, or a flat, even-intensity beam. The profile's beam can be shaped by shutters or made smaller by introducing an iris into the gate.

Gobos

A patterned metal disc, known as a 'gobo', can be placed in the gate of the profile to project an image onto the stage or scenery. Common uses of gobos include windows, trees, clouds, leaves and the projection of abstract patterns.

Figure 4.20 a&b   *Universal lighting symbol for a) a profile spotlight, b) a followspot*

Figure 4.21   *Cutaway diagram of a Source 4 fixed lens profile lantern*

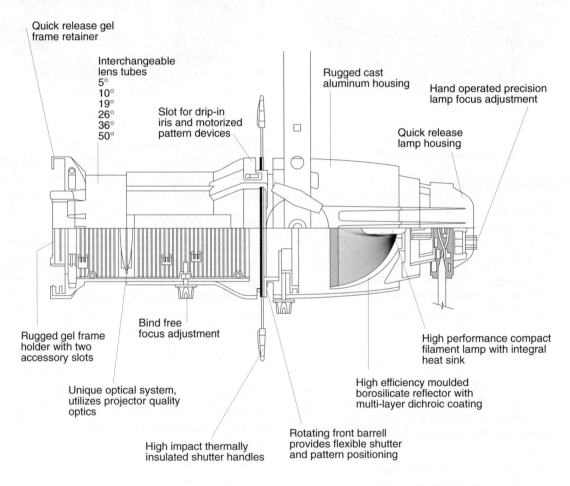

Quick release gel
frame retainer

Interchangeable
lens tubes
5°
10°
19°
26°
36°
50°

Slot for drip-in
iris and motorized
pattern devices

Rugged cast
aluminum housing

Hand operated precision
lamp focus adjustment

Quick release
lamp housing

Rugged gel frame
holder with two
accessory slots

Bind free
focus adjustment

High performance compact
filament lamp with integral
heat sink

Unique optical system,
utilizes projector quality
optics

High efficiency moulded
borosilicate reflector with
multi-layer dichroic coating

High impact thermally
insulated shutter handles

Rotating front barrel
provides flexible shutter
and pattern positioning

Figure 4.22 *A gobo can be used to project an image onto the stage or scenery*

TASKS

1 Practise focusing a single lens profile and a variable focus zoom profile. Compare the range of beam sizes, quality and intensity of light.
2 Observe the beam variations possible with a zoom profile and note the quality and softness of the edge of the beam. Add an iris and see what difference it makes.
3 Practise using shutters to shape the beam. Note how the shutters affect the beam. Try and create:
   - a square beam of light
   - a rectangular doorway
   - a triangle.
4 Study the effect of adjusting the beam field adjuster from 'flat' to 'peaky'.
5 Experiment with a range of gobos, altering the focus to achieve a variety of designs from a sharp image to a blurred textured effect.
6 Find out the beam sizes and ranges of the profiles in your theatre space. Why are there so many variations?

TASK

Followspot Technique
Practise lining up the followspot with a target. If possible, use features of scenery or an architectural aspect as a reference point to help you to line up.
Practise following a person as they move on stage. Find out how to fade the light, change the colour of the beam, make the beam size smaller.

LANTERNS: A QUICK IDENTIFICATION GUIDE

No lens = floodlight (or beamlight if housing is 'can' shaped)
Clear lens = profile spotlight

Grooved lens = fresnel spotlight
Prism lens = PC spotlight

Moving Lights

FOLLOWSPOTS

The largest and most powerful profile lanterns are used as **Followspots** (these are spotlights which track the performers). They are usually rigged and operated a considerable distance from the stage. The best effects are achieved if they are positioned with a steep vertical lighting angle of between 30 and 60 degrees.

Followspots also known as 'limes', (short for limelight), are worked manually by a member of the crew. Whilst some followspots are dimmable and controlled from the lighting board, most contain a high output discharge lamp which cannot be dimmed electrically.

Operating a Followspot

Operating a followspot is a demanding task, which will not be noticed when done correctly but everyone knows when you get it wrong. Because of the intensity of the light and the distance the light is projected, the smallest movement from the operator is magnified on stage. Practise is required to follow a performer smoothly and to be able to adjust the beam size, focus, change the colour and fade the light out subtly.

The followspot must be able to hit a particular target and pick up a performer in a black out. The best technique is to aim the followspot at the target and then open the iris smoothly when the light is needed.

The followspot is often used to cover the entire figure of a performer. It is important to make sure that their head and feet stay within the beam of light at all times.

Followspots are also used in less obvious ways to provide subtle highlights in dramatic productions. The beam is usually softened either by being out of focus or by introducing a light frost filter in the colour frame.

Figure 4.23 *a) a stage lit by Vari*lite intelligent lights*
b) a VL5™ wash light

INTELLIGENT LIGHTS

Great advances have been made in the area of remote controlled lighting or intelligent lighting. Developed almost exclusively by the rock industry, moving lights have allowed increasingly spectacular lighting.

In recent years, there has been extensive devel-opment of intelligent luminaires by a wide range of manufacturers.

There are two main types:

1 moving mirror
2 moving yoke.

In the moving mirror type the lantern fixture remains static and the light beam is moved by mirrors. Examples are:

Cameleon Telescan range
Clay Paky Golden Scan range
Martin Professional Roboscan range
High End Systems Technobeam range

With the moving yoke fixtures the motors allow the entire luminaire to pan and tilt. Examples are:

Vari*lites
High End Systems Studio range
Clay Paky Stage Light series
Martin Professional MAC series
Strand PALS and Pirouette systems

The development of intelligent moving lights had direct implications for control systems. These now have to be able to operate a whole range of functions. Control over a single intelligent lantern can take up a large number of faders on a standard, DMX512 compatible control board. A Martin MAC 500 luminaire, for example, will take up 16 channels on a control desk (pan, tilt, intensity, colour, etc).

Some intelligent lights use an internal colour wheel to switch and mix colour. More sophisticated luminaires employ a dichroic colour system, which allows the light to be coloured in hundreds of hues and for the colour changes to be blended live.

Remote control of these parameters creates vast design possibilities. However, each effect takes a considerable time to programme, and many conventional theatre boards are unsuited to the task. Although new and larger theatre lighting control boards are designed to be able to cope with intelligent lights, dedicated lighting boards are often used alongside conventional theatre boards to control the moving lighting only.

There are a number of concerns which have, so far, prevented intelligent lights from being widely adopted for use in theatres:

- *Cost.*
- *Technological concerns* – intelligent lights are highly complex units which require regular servicing and technical support. They also need dedicated lighting control desks.
- *Practical concerns* – most intelligent lanterns are still large, heavy and noisy. Motors and fans create noise which is distracting to an audience.
- *Aesthetic concerns* – The intense light generated by the lamps which are used by the majority of moving lights are perfect for creating powerful beams of saturated colour in the rock industry and on TV, but are not as suitable in other performance contexts.

The future?

There is little doubt that, as technology advances and prices fall, intelligent lights will become increasingly common in performance venues and will be used for theatre, as well as the more spectacular music-based shows.

Lamps and Reflectors

Types of lamps

Lamps convert electrical energy into light. Many variations of lamps are used in theatre lanterns but there are two main types:

1 tungsten-halogen filament lamps
2 discharge lamps

Filament lamps convert only 8% of energy into light, 92% or more is lost in heat. Theatre lanterns, their reflectors and lens systems attempt to maximise the light output of the 8% and are also designed to redistribute the heat safely.

There are many types of lamps available for theatre lanterns. Lamps vary in construction according to their type and the manufacturer. It is important to be able to select the appropriate replacement lamp for a lantern, since there are many variations. Lamps vary in the following ways:

- wattage
- voltage
- shape
- size
- base type
- base size
- filament type.

Tungsten-Halogen Filament Lamps

Conventional incandescent theatre lamps, which can be dimmed, consist of a glass envelope, containing a **tungsten** metal wire coil – the filament. The glass envelope is filled with an inert gas, such as Halogen, to prevent the filament coming into contact with oxygen in the air and burning out. The glass is joined to a metal or ceramic base, which contains the lamp's electrical connections and enables the lamp to be fitted securely inside the theatre lantern.

Electric current passes through the filament which glows producing light heat.

Figure 4.24   *A typical tungsten halogen lamp found in most theatre spotlights*

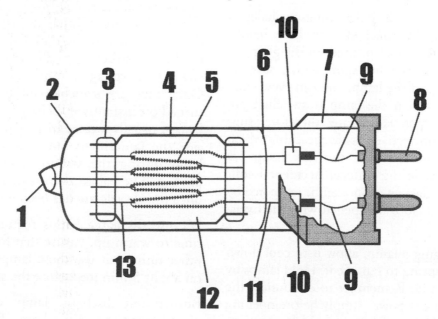

1 Tip Off	8 Type GY9.5 Cap pins
2 Quartz glass envelope	9 Fuse
3 Bridge assembly	10 Seals
4 Tungsten bridge support	11 Current lead
5 Coiled-coil grid filament	12 Halogen gas filling
6 Pinch seal	13 Filament hook supports
7 Ceramic base (cutaway to show inner detail)	

Although older tungsten lamps are still available (e.g. the T1 and T3 which fit Patt 23 and 123 lanterns), the majority of professional theatre lanterns have been fitted with more modern tungsten-halogen lamps.

Care of Lamps

Despite the fact that tungsten-halogen lamps have many advantages, they are less robust than the older type. When lit, tungsten-halogen lamps are far more vulnerable to sudden movements (e.g. when focusing) and to rapid increases in light intensity, particularly when first switched on. The filaments can break if the lantern gets knocked. Treat lanterns and their lamps gently; they are expensive.

Lamps should be warmed gently for a few minutes before turning them up to full power. Lamp life can also be prolonged by remembering to burn lamps at full for a few minutes at the end of the day.

Unlike domestic light bulbs, tungsten-halogen lamps cannot be touched with bare hands, since grease may be deposited on the glass envelope. This causes hot-spots which severely reduce the life of the lamp, and can even cause an explosion when the lamp is switched on. Tungsten-halogen lamps are, therefore, supplied with a protective plastic sheathing which should be removed once the new lamp has been fixed inside the lantern. Accidental contact with the glass envelope can be remedied by wiping with a cloth dampened with methylated spirit.

When changing a lamp, allow it to cool down before attempting to remove it. Hold lamps by their bases only. Remember to disconnect the lantern from the power supply before opening the casing. Always dispose of old lamps carefully.

New Generation Efficient Lamps

Recently a new, lower wattage lamp has been developed for 'cool beam' profiles and has also been adapted for other lantern types. These 575 W or 600 W lamps are a compact-filament halogen/krypton gas lamp, with a base that includes an integral heat sink. The lamps are designed to burn horizontally and to be combined with reflectors and lenses which diffuse the heat efficiently, whilst maximising the light output. The improvement in efficiency means that a 575 W lamp is able to generate more light than a conventional 1 kW or 1.2 kW lamp.

Discharge Lamps or Arc Lamps

These are extremely bright lamps, commonly used in followspots, moving lights and in professional projection equipment. They produce four times the amount of visible light than conventional tungsten-halogen lamps, but they cannot be dimmed electrically. Fading must be achieved by mechanical means, such as shutters or irises.

Discharge lamps work by creating an intense arc of plasma across a small gap between electrodes which are sealed in a gas-filled glass envelope. The arc is often described as 'a continuous miniature bolt of lightning'. Lamps need to be 'struck up' – a process which generates a high voltage impulse to create the arc. Once they are switched on they cannot be turned off instantly. Discharge lamps require a ballast, usually located in a separate unit alongside the lantern, to limit the current to the lamp during the striking and warming up process. The ballast then regulates the voltage once the electric arc has been established.

Because discharge lamps require a period of time to warm up, ensure that followspots and other units that use these lamps are switched on about 5 minutes before the show.

Burned out discharge lamps cannot be replaced until they have been allowed to cool down. This is a job for a trained technician.

Types of Discharge Lamps

There is a range of discharge lamps which use different gases within the glass envelope. Some common examples are:

HMI   Hydrargyrum-medium iodide (Osram)
CSI   Compact Source Iodide (Thorn UK)
CID   Compact Iodide Daylight (Thorn UK)

MSR   Medium Source Rare Earth (Phillips)
XBO   Xenon (Osram).

LAMP CLASSIFICATION

It is important that the correct type of lamp is fitted to each type of lantern. The precise location of the filament in the lamp is critical if the light output is to be optimised by the reflector and lenses of the lantern. Lamps generate substantial amounts of heat and must be located correctly within the lantern housing.

If a lamp is burned at an angle for which it was not designed it can cause a fire hazard, may work inefficiently, or have a shorter life.

Lamps can be classified according to their shape and type, their filament construction, their burning position, their base type and their wattage.

Lamps are classified according to shape and type:

A   arbitrary (used in projection equipment)
C   cone shape
G   globular
PS   pear shape
PAR   Parabolic Aluminized Reflector
R   reflector
T   tubular
TH   tungsten-halogen.

They can be classified according to filament construction:

C   single coil
CC   coiled coil

MP   monoplane grid
B1   biplane grid.

Lamps are also classified according to burning position:

P   horizontal
S   vertical
SE   lamp may be tilted
H   burns upside down.

Lamp classification according to base types:

- *Bayonet base* – a round base with two pins of different sizes to provide correct orientation of the lamp.
- *Bipost base* – two-pronged base with slightly different sized pins to ensure correct alignment. Commonly used with spotlights and projectors.
- *Mogul End Prong* – (Mog EP) Two flat-pronged connectors, common in PAR lamps.
- *Prefocus base* – medium prefocus (Med pf) bases are used in spotlights to ensure correct alignment of the filament in relation to the lenses and reflectors.
- *RSC base* – stands for recessed single contact.
- *Screw base* – Larger versions of the domestic edison screw (ES) base are commonly found in older spotlights and floodlights.

TASK

Study a theatre lamp catalogue to establish which lamps are required for which lanterns. Pay particular attention to the lamp base types and the wattage. How are these lamps classified? How much will it cost to order a spare lamp for each of the lanterns in your theatre venue?

REFLECTORS

There are three main types of reflector used in theatre lanterns to improve the amount of light that passes through the lens system.

- **Spherical reflector** – this type is used extensively in fresnel and PC lanterns to increase the amount of light projected through the lens. The reflector is mounted on a tray with the lamp so that a constant distance is maintained between the two and the filament is aligned correctly with the focal point (centre) of the sphere. Spherical reflectors are also used in some floodlights to focus the beam and to provide a wide distribution of light.
- **Ellipsoidal reflector** – this is used extensively in profile spotlights (ellipsoidal spotlights) and is also found in some types of floodlight. It is the most efficient type of reflector, since it has two focal points. When the light source is directed at the primary focal point (within the reflector) the light will be reflected through the conjugate focal point. This is found beyond the gate in a profile spotlight and enables the lens system to focus and magnify the beam of light to project clear and sharply defined images.
- **Parabolic reflector** – this reflects light in parallel beams to produce narrow, intense beams of light that create strong, sharp-edged shadows. They are fitted to beamlights and incorporated into a single sealed beam unit in a par can.

Combination Lamps and Reflectors

Par Lamps

Originally known as birdseye lamps after their inventor Clarence Birdseye, PAR is an acronym for the parabolic aluminised reflector which is incorporated in a single unit with the filament and a glass lens. Its construction is similar to a car headlight and provides a very efficient light output. Because it is a sealed unit, it cannot be focused, although beam sizes can be changed by using different lamp types.

Recent innovations have led to the development of the **Par Plus lamp** which does allow the beam to be focused.

Standard PAR lamps are available in a range of sizes. Common types are:

PAR 38   4¾ inch diameter
PAR 46   5¾ inch diameter
PAR 56   7 inch diameter
PAR 64   8 inch diameter

MR 16 lamps or Mirrored Reflector Lamps

These are small, 50 mm diameter, low wattage and low voltage lamps which incorporate a small tungsten-halogen lamp within a dichroic reflector. Lamps are manufactured with a variety of beam angles from very narrow to flood. They are commonly used in display lighting and have been adapted for theatre use. The lamps are fitted inside miniature lanterns and are very useful since they provide surprising amounts of light from a fixture that can be hidden easily on stage. However, because these lamps operate at 12 volts, a suitable transformer compatible with dimmers has to be used to reduce the input voltage to the lamp.

Specialist units such as the **howie batten** use several of these lamps mounted together in a single unit to achieve dramatic directional lighting.

LANTERN MAINTENANCE

A regular maintenance programme should be undertaken to ensure that lanterns are safe to use and that light output and mechanical performance is optimised. An electrical inspection should be undertaken at least every year.

- Clean lantern housing externally.
- Clean internal components, especially lenses, lamp and reflector. (Use methylated spirits and a lint free cloth, or specialist anti-static cleaners. Avoid touching surfaces by hand.)
- Check hook clamp, safety chain and gel frame.
- Check the suspension system.
- Check panning and tilting mechanisms.
- Check yoke, wing nuts, bolts and clamps.
- Check focus mechanisms.
- Check for any loose parts.
- Check that the safety shield is intact.

Profiles

- Are shutter systems complete?
- Do shutters move freely?
- Does the peak/field adjuster work?
- Do lens tubes and lens carriers move freely?
- Do focus knobs lock easily?

Fresnels

- Does the lamp try move freely?
- Does the focus mechanism lock in position?

- Do barn doors move freely and stay in the desired position?
- Do they rotate easily?
- Do they have locking devices?

Electrical Inspection

- Carry out a visual inspection of plugs and wiring, including glands and anchorage points, and frayed, worn or loose cable.
- Undertake a PAT continuity test of plugs and connectors, lamp holder and terminal blocks, and earthing.
- Log the inspection or repair on the appropriate sheet. Sign and date.
- Repair or remove from stock any equipment which does not meet safety requirements.

Final Beam Check

Bring up lantern to full power.
Check focusing mechanisms by projecting on to a screen.
Check for unwanted light spill.
Check profiles for flat field.
Log details on an appropriate lantern job sheet.

Rigging and Access Equipment

Preparing a venue such as a theatre for a performance is a dangerous activity. Work often needs to take place quickly, at height and with heavy items of equipment. During the fit-up, the theatre building is full of potential hazards. Both lighting and sound installation involves extensive work with electricity.

Safety considerations must be of paramount importance when undertaking technical production work. A senior member of staff will be responsible for safeguarding the Health and Safety of everyone working in the venue, as well as members of the audience who enter the premises.

There will be safety rules and codes of practice in any venue, designed to protect employees and member of the public. Protective headgear (e.g. hard hats) may have to be worn when working on stage during the production week, for example. Any safety requirements should be followed at all times.

Additional regulations are imposed on venues by local licensing authorities and national legislation. Variations in local licensing requirements will determine exactly what is allowed within a performance space: the maximum number of audience members; the number and location of fire exits; whether lanterns can be rigged at floor height near the audience and so on. It is important, therefore, to establish what the local requirements are for each venue. It is essential that all such regulations are complied with, or the production may be closed down.

TASK

Familiarise yourself with a performance space.

1. Establish which authorities are responsible for licensing the performance space. How do local requirements affect technical and design plans? What restrictions are there?

2. Find out about:

- how the working lights are turned off and on
- where the main isolating switch is for the lighting installation
- how to isolate the power in an emergency
- the types of access equipment and their safe operating heights
- the location of fire exits, fire alarm points, first aid boxes and details of the accident reporting procedure
- the location, types and suitability of fire extinguishers
- the location and operation of emergency lighting.

WORKING AT HEIGHT

Most theatre lanterns are rigged overhead, which means that ladders and other access equipment are used to rig and focus each light. The common forms of access equipment are:

- *Extendible ladder* – these are often fitted with hooks to fit over lighting bars to give extra stability. Particular care needs to be taken when manoeuvring long ladders.
- *Step ladder or 'A' frame ladder* – beware since taller versions are unsuitable and can easily topple over. Some manufacturers provide an extending ladder which works in conjunction with a sturdy 'A' frame (e.g. Zarges). Step ladders should only be used when fully open and should have metal braces to prevent the ladder from collapsing when in use. Ladders should be supported to prevent them slipping or tip-

ping over to the side. They should never be used close to the edge of the stage.

- *Tower* – this is a structure built from scaffolding pieces to provide a high level platform. These structures are usually mobile, fitted with wheels and can be dismantled and stored flat after use. The Zip-up tower is a commonly used type. There are additional safety issues associated with using wheeled access equipment (see below).
- *Tallescope* – this is a specialist, extendible ladder with a metal box or 'cage' at the top which provides a small enclosed platform for one person to work from.

Safety Rules for Working at Height

1 Never work alone.
2 Understand how to use equipment correctly and safely.

3 In some venues a compulsory hard hat policy is in force. Make sure that everyone on stage complies with this requirement whilst rigging is in progress.

4 Outriggers should be fitted to towers and tallescopes at all times.

5 Make sure that there is adequate visibility when working at height. Usually, you should ensure that the working lights are on before moving or climbing access equipment. Rigging of equipment should always take place with working lights on.

6 Make sure that your pockets are empty of tools, keys, coins and other loose items before working at height.

7 If you drop anything from a height, shout the warning 'heads' as quickly as possible. This emergency alert is universally understood. If you are on the stage when 'heads' is shouted, do not look up! Instead, move away from the source. The same warning is used when equipment is about to be flown in or lowered near workers at stage level.

8 Never leave tools on the top of a ladder, or on a platform at height, since they can easily be knocked off and cause severe injuries to workers underneath. Make sure all tools are secure. Ideally, they should be clipped onto a belt or kept in a dedicated pocket. It is a good idea to put a large tool pouch at the top of the tower or tallescope to hold objects such as tape, tools, nuts and bolts, etc.

9 Never overreach. Reaching out beyond the ladder, tallescope or platform can tip the equipment over.

10 Keep quiet. A reasonably quiet environment is important when people are working at height. Music should not be allowed during such work since it prevents technicians from hearing each other easily.

Ladder Safety Rules

1 Ladders should only be used at the correct angle.

2 When climbing ladders, you should al-

ways maintain three points of contact – e.g. two feet and a hand.

3 Always have a colleague present to support the foot of the ladder.

4 Metal ladders should have rubber feet.

5 Extreme care should be taken when ladders are used near the edge of a stage.

6 When focusing, ensure that you can reach all of the lantern's controls comfortably.

7 Step ladders and 'A' frame ladders should be fully opened and locked in place by metal support arms.

8 Position ladders carefully on a level surface, away from the edge of the stage and as close to the rigging position as is comfortable to avoid overreaching.

9 Do not stand on the top two rungs of the ladder.

10 Take care when moving ladders. Make sure that extendible ladders are fully retracted.

Safety Rules for Mobile Access Towers and Tallescopes

1 Refer to the manufacturer's safety guidelines.

2 Ensure that the structure has been assembled correctly, with the appropriate number of braces locked in place.

3 Make sure that outriggers are attached and positioned correctly.

4 Kickboards should be installed around any platform over 2 m.

5 Never climb up the outside of a tower. There should be an internal access ladder with a trapdoor onto the working platform.

6 Use the brakes on each wheel to lock the tower or tallescope in place.

7 Always pull, never push mobile access platforms. There should be at least two technicians to move towers and tallescopes.

8 Particular care should be taken near the edge of the stage and on stages with different levels.

Raked Stages

Working from mobile access platforms on a raked stage is particularly hazardous. Although the wheels of towers and tallescopes can be adjusted to compensate for the rake, this should only be done with professional supervision. Many serious accidents have occurred through the incorrect use of access equipment on raked stages.

RIGGING LIGHTS

First, make sure that the power supply to the dimmers is switched off before rigging begins.

Rigging lanterns over the stage in a theatre with a fly tower is relatively straightforward, since the lighting bars can be lowered and lanterns can be rigged and cabled up by technicians standing on the stage. Colour filters are also added before the lighting bar is flown out to its correct position. In most other cases, lanterns have to be hoisted from floor level to a rigger working at height, so that the lantern can be attached in the appropriate place.

Before offering up a lantern to be rigged, at the very least, undertake a brief visual inspection (see page 127). It is worth testing the lantern to make sure that it is working. To do this use a 13 amp to 15 amp cable and connect it to a 13 amp switched mains socket.

Lanterns should be lifted in the vertical position, having made sure that the plug, cable and any accessories, (barn doors, colour frames, etc.) are secure and will not drop out. Beware of plugs on swinging cables! If you are using a rope to raise and lower lanterns from the rig, the rope should pass under the yoke. It is not safe to simply loop the rope under the tip of the 'G' clamp. A rope and pulley block attached to a spare 'G' clamp can be used to lift equipment from the stage to workers on the platform. The weight can be taken by technicians at stage level as they pull the lantern up to the rigger.

If the rigging height is below 3m, lanterns can easily be passed up by hand.

Rigging Procedure

1 Rig each lantern as close as possible to the position indicated on the lighting plan, checking that it is a safe distance away from scenery, drapes and tabs.
2 Tighten the 'G' clamp so that it will not move on the bar.
3 Attach the safety chain to connect the lantern housing to the bar.
4 Angle the lantern in the approximate direction that it will be required. If you are unsure, point it straight ahead at an angle of 45 degrees.
5 Tighten the wing nut on the yoke to make sure the lantern stays pointing in the right direction.
6 Open the barn doors, or shutters fully, if they are fitted.
7 Fit the colour gel and frame if these have been supplied.
8 Check that all fixtures are secured.
9 Plug the lantern into the nominated socket, making sure that there is no strain on the cable.
10 Extension cables should not dangle from the rig, as they get in the way of beams of light from other lanterns and will distract the audience. They should *not* be coiled tightly around the bar, but coiled neatly and taped to the top of a bar out of view.
11 *Never* use Gaffa tape on lanterns or on cables in the rig. It melts and creates a sticky mess when heated.

'Flashing Out'

Once the lights have been rigged, cabled up and 'patched-in' (connected to the dimmers), it is time to check that each circuit works. This process is known as 'flashing out'. This procedure is described below:

1 Switch on the power supply to the dimmers and the control desk.
2 Slowly bring up the fader on the desk to around 40%. Switching on too quickly may cause some lamps to blow.
3 If you are lucky, all of the lanterns on the rig will work perfectly. Often, especially on larger rigs, problems arise. The lighting technician must establish what the problem is as quickly as possible and get the light working again. This should be achieved by a logical process of elimination (see the checklist below).
4 Make sure that the circuit is not live when you are unplugging and plugging up lanterns. Whenever possible, work with the power switched off.

Problem-Solving Checklist

If no lights are working:

- Is there power to the dimmers?
- Has the main fuse blown?
- Is the mains isolator switch on?
- Is the control cable connected to the dimmers and the control board?
- If the control leads pass through a demux (De-multiplexer) box, is it switched on?
- Is there power to the control desk?
- Is it switched on?
- Is there a blackout switch? Is it in the correct position?
- Are the master faders up?
- Are the correct preset master faders up?
- If it is a memory board, is the software configured correctly?

If some lights are working, but a large group of lights will not come on:

- Check that each dimmer has power. Some dimmer packs have control lights – is each control light on?
- If not, has a mains fuse blown?

- Has a RCD tripped because of a fault?
- Is the dimmer physically connected to a power supply?
- Has a control lead become disconnected?
- Are all demux units switched on and connected properly to the relevant dimmers?
- Are the master and preset master faders up on the control board?
- If using a memory control board, is the software configured correctly?

If two lights come on when a single fader is up:

Both plugs have been connected to the same dimmer, either on the rig or at the patch panel. (In more advanced systems they may have been linked together by the computer control board).

If an individual light does not work:

The fault will be one or more of the following:

- The barn doors have not been opened.
- The shutters have not been pulled out.
- The lantern has not been plugged in on the rig.
- The extension cable is faulty.
- The lantern has been incorrectly patched at the dimmer. Does the socket number on the rig match the patch lead number?
- The dimmer is not working. Has the individual dimmer fuse blown?
- There is a problem between the control board and the dimmer pack. Is the correct numbered circuit fader for the dimmer up on the control desk? Is local control on the dimmer overriding control board information? Is the correct preset fader up?
- The lamp has blown.
- The cable is loose. Some lanterns have detachable cables which can work loose. Check that the connector is pushed firmly into the base of the lantern.
- The internal wiring of the lantern, connecting cable, socket or patch lead is faulty.
- There is an internal electrical fault with the control board, dimmer or demultiplex unit.

Fault Tracing

The quickest way to establish why a lantern is not working is to cross plug it to a circuit that you know to be working (e.g. temporarily plug the lantern into a nearby socket on the bar that is connected to a working lantern). This will tell you if the lantern works or whether the problem lies with the lantern, its lamp or its wiring. Remember to re-plug both lanterns back to their correct sockets once you have rectified the fault!

If the lantern works once you have cross plugged it, the fault must lie in the cabling, patching, dimming or control system associated with the circuit it was originally plugged into. A further process of gradual elimination should pinpoint the problem!

Once all of the lanterns are working, the electrics team are ready to begin positioning each lantern precisely and to focus the beams on stage. Complete darkness is required for the focus session.

Lighting Control

Precise control over the intensity of light is an essential aspect of any lighting design. This control is achieved with dimmers which regulate the power to individual lanterns and a lighting control desk or 'board', which is operated by a technician.

DIMMERS

Dimmers are complex electrical devices that control the intensity of individual lanterns or circuits by regulating the amount of power sent to the lamp. Dimmers receive and respond to signals from a control board allowing individual lanterns to be controlled precisely.

Several dimmers are located in units called packs, banks or racks. Whilst professional theatres have several large racks containing many dimmers, smaller studio theatres tend to have compact or portable dimmer packs which usually contain multiples of six dimmers within one pack.

There are two types of dimmer:

1 analogue dimmers
2 digital dimmers.

Analogue Dimmers

The analogue dimmer supplies power to a stage lantern in proportion to the control voltage generated by the control desk. The control voltage is usually very low and is typically on a scale of 0 V to 10 V. As the control voltage is varied by a fader on the desk, the dimmer responds by smoothly increasing or decreasing the light on stage.

Digital Dimmers

Digital dimmers were introduced in 1990 and have replaced analogue dimmers in larger theatres and in new installations. Digital dimmers use numbers in place of voltages to control the intensity of a light. Electronic information is given as a series of binary digits in 8 pulses or 'bits'. The microprocessor in the dimmer is able to distinguish between zero (off) and 255 which means on at full. Digital dimmers are more accurate than their analogue counterparts since they work with exact numbers rather than imprecise voltage levels.

Multiplex control

Because it would be unwieldy to send a separate signal to each dimmer, the information is multiplexed. The dimmers are linked together and given an address or reference number. The multiplexed signal is transmitted from the control desk and each dimmer responds to the precise information that follows its unique address code. Most manufacturers have agreed a worldwide standard for transmitting control data in this year. The protocol is known as DMX 512.

LIGHTING CONTROL BOARDS

The lighting control board or 'desk', allows the operator to have precise control of each lantern on the rig. In the past, control was achieved by directly controlling the dimmer, but since the advent of electronic dimmers, the control board can be located anywhere in a theatre venue with a small cable linking it to the dimmers.

There are two types of lighting control boards:

1 manual control boards
2 memory systems.

Manual control boards have a fader for every lighting circuit, two or more presets with corresponding numbers of faders, and master faders which control the overall output from the desk to the dimmers. Extensive written information is required to operate even the simplest shows correctly.

Memory systems may also have a number of manual faders, but are able to store lighting level information in computer memories. Typically computer lighting desks have a display monitor and a single button to execute each cue. Very smooth fades of a long duration can easily be achieved.

There are also some combination systems which combine attributes of both manual and memory systems.

TASK

Investigate the range of control boards which are currently available from lighting manufacturers. Can you identify their intended markets and use?

What features would you consider essential if you were to select a new lighting board for your performance space? Which board matches this specification? Why? How much does it retail for?

Electricity and Theatre Lighting

Electricity is dangerous. A basic understanding of electricity and electrical safety is therefore essential for anyone considering working in a theatre environment. If you are unqualified or unsure you should always seek specialist assistance.

The amount of power that is available in a venue is often the greatest constraint on a lighting design, since it will affect how large the rig can be and the brightness of the lights. It is vital that both designers and technicians understand how much power can be used safely.

ELECTRICAL THEORY AND SOME BASIC TERMINOLOGY

Volts, Watts and Amps

In an electric circuit, electrons flow from a power source, along a wire, through an appliance (in this case a lamp), and back to the source along a separate wire. This flow of electrons is called a **current**, the size of which is determined by the **wattage** of the lamp.

For the current to flow there must be a pressure difference between the outgoing and incoming wires of the power source. The pressure in electrical circuits is called the **voltage**. If there is no difference between two wires then no current will flow. In a mains electrical circuit in the UK, the source voltage is 240 volts (240 V). The voltage is high enough to force an electric current through a person and cause a shock. Such shocks can kill.

Since 240 V is a high pressure, it causes a large current to flow through the wires of a circuit.

Every electrical appliance offers a high resistance to the flow of current and this limits the amount of power the supply has to provide. Electrical appliances are measured in **watts**. The higher the **wattage**, the more current is taken. Appliances have two wires which are rated for the amount of power which the appliance requires. Thin or 'light duty' wire, which is suitable for a tape recorder, will not be able to carry the high current that an electric kettle demands. However, the heavy wire supplied with a kettle would be able to carry the smaller current required by a tape recorder or a hair dryer.

1000 watts is also known as 1 kilowatt or 1 kW.

Figure 4.25   *It is vital to wire plugs correctly. This is a 13 amp plug*

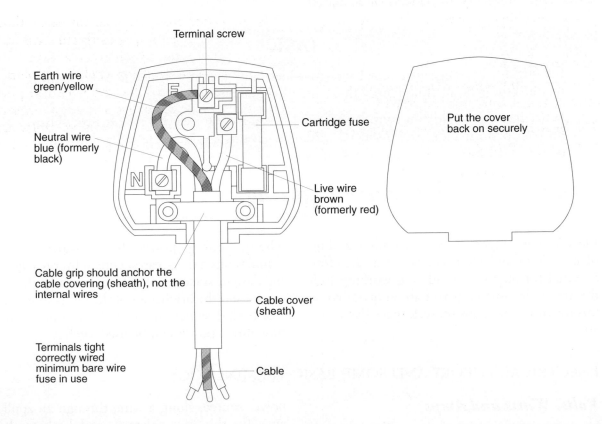

The measure of current carrying capacity is called the **Amp**, or Ampere.

There is a rule known as **Ohm's Law**, which connects amps, watts and volts.

$$\frac{\text{Wattage}}{\text{Voltage}} = \text{Amps}$$

Fuses

Fuses are used to prevent possible problems from occurring. A fuse is introduced into an electrical circuit and is connected to the wire which comes from the power source. This is called the **live** wire. If more than the safe amount of current tries to flow (usually because a fault develops or someone connects an appliance that needs too much power), the fuse breaks and disconnects the circuit.

Fuses are essentially quick-melting wires and are commonly rated at 3, 5, and 13 amps for domestic use. The higher the wattage of an appliance, the higher the value of fuse that has to be fitted.

Wiring a plug

The **green and yellow** striped wire is connected to the **Earth** terminal, marked **E**.

The **brown** wire is connected to the **Live** terminal, marked **L**.

The **blue** wire is connected to the **Neutral** terminal, marked **N**.

The terminal screws should be tight and hold the wire firmly.

There should be little or no bare wire protruding from the terminals.

The cable's outer insulation (not the wires themselves) should be held firmly by the cable sheath grip so that the connections inside the plug are not put under stress.

Visual checks on cable tails should be undertaken regularly to identify splits or breaks.

Damaged cables should never be used.

Most professional theatre lighting is based on 15 amp, round pin plugs and sockets. Some older theatre lighting installations (particularly those in schools) are based on a smaller, 5 amp, round pin system to restrict the amount of power that can be used.

You will notice from the diagram below that, unlike domestic, 13 amp, square-pin plugs, the 15 amp plug does not contain a fuse. The reason for this is simple: it would be impractical and complicated to locate a particular plug on a rig in order to change a fuse, particularly since a large number of extension cables are often used! All theatre lighting circuits are

Figure 4.26   *Wiring a 15 amp plug*

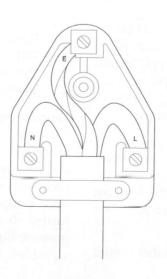

fused at the dimmer with specialist 'quick blow' fuses. This allows faults to be traced quickly.

In many organisations, writing inside plugs and sockets can only be carried out by qualified technicians.

PUTTING THEORY INTO PRACTICE

Calculating Current

It is essential that you are able to calculate the amount of current a device, such as a theatre lantern, uses. This knowledge is important so that:

- you can ensure that the cable feeding the device is able to take the necessary load
- you can be sure that the electricity supply is capable of feeding the lantern with the required power.

Cables

As theatre lighting rigs tend to be temporary, many extension cables may be used to connect lanterns to their dimmers. These cables must not carry more than their recommended load, otherwise overheating could easily occur. This could result in either a fuse blowing or a fire. Always check cable sizes and establish their current-carrying capabilities. (This may be marked on the cable, but can also be established by referring to the IEE Regulations.) For standard theatre use, with each circuit pulling no more than 2.4 kW, 1.5 mm cable is commonly used.

The lantern loading for each cable can be established by using Ohm's Law. For example, a 1000 watt lantern on a 240 volt supply would require a current of just over 4 amps:

$$\frac{1000 \text{ (watts)}}{240 \text{ (volts)}} = 4.166 \text{ (amps)}$$

Thus, the cable required to supply power safely to this lantern would have a minimum capacity of about 5 amps. Since theatre lanterns are often paired together, higher rated cables are used for safety.

Many school theatres and some smaller venues are fitted with cables, plugs and sockets rated at 5 amps. By rearranging Ohm's Law we can establish that the maximum safe loading on these cables is:

$$\frac{\text{watts}}{\text{volts}} = \text{amps}$$

$$\text{volts} \times \text{amps} = \text{watts}$$

$$240 \text{ volts} \times 5 \text{ amps} = 1200 \text{ watts}$$

Although most professional venues use 15 amp plugs and sockets to connect lights in an installation, cable rated at 10 amps is commonly used. This is known as TRS cable meaning tough rubber sheathed cable. So, although the connectors are rated at 15 amps, the cable restricts the maximum safe loading to:

240 volts × 10 amps = 2400 watts or 2.4 kW

In fact, most theatre dimmers are also rated at 10 amps per circuit. So, the maximum safe loading on each circuit is also 2400 watts (2.4 kW).

In other words, with a circuit fused at 10 amps we could connect any of these possibilities:

1 × 2000 W (2 kW) lantern
2 × 1200 W (1.2 kW) lanterns
3 × 650 W lanterns
4 × 500 W lanterns
6 × 300 W lanterns.

Despite the fact that individual dimmer circuits are rated at 10 amps, we also need to check that sufficient power is available to run the full lighting system. Six dimmer packs, each with six circuits rated at 10 amps, would need a supply of 360 amps if they were fully loaded (6 × 6 × 10 = 360 amps). In most purpose built theatre spaces this would not be a problem. Many spaces have been adapted for performance work and may not have a suitable supply to run the dimmers at full capacity.

So, we need to check the amount of power going to each individual dimmer pack, as well as calculating the overall capacity of the lighting system.

Calculating Loading and Supply

Ohm's Law can be used to calculate the maximum number of lanterns that can be fed from a particular mains supply. It is essential to establish the type of supply (or capacity) for every lighting installation that you are intending to use. This information can be found on the main switchgear for the dimmer racks. The switchgear should have an isolating switch, as well as a number of individual RCD trip switches, depending upon the way the supply is distributed to the dimmer racks. These should be clearly labelled to indicate their rating in amperes. Phases should also be indicated in a three phase installation (see below).

So, if the mains supply is, for example, 240 volts at 60 amps, the following is true:

mains capacity (watts)
= 240 volts × 60 amps = 14,4000 watts

So, this mains supply could run a **maximum** of: 14 1000 watt lanterns, **or** 28 500 watt lanterns **or** 22 650 watt lanterns.

Of course, a mixture of different rated lanterns can be used and 2.4 kW can still be supplied from any single individual dimmer, **but the overall mains capacity must not be exceeded**.

Using Ohm's Law, we can also establish that the mains supply from a 13 amp socket will allow a **maximum** load of 3120 watts (i.e. six 500 watt lanterns):

240 volts × 13 amps = 3120 watts

TASK

Here are some values for common mains supplies at 240 volts. Calculate the maximum safe wattage for each example.

32 amps
63 amps
100 amps
150 amps
200 amps
300 amps.

Calculating Voltages Abroad

Voltages vary from country to country and although the formula for calculating loadings remains the same, there will be significant differences in the results. In USA the voltage is 120 V. In Europe 220 V is common.

Recently in the UK, electricity companies have been allowed to vary the electrical supply from between 220 and 240 volts. Calculations

might be better, therefore, if they are based on an average of 230 volts.

Three Phase Electrical Supply

Because of the way in which electricity is generated at power stations, it is normally distributed to large buildings in three separate supplies or phases. These are indicated by primary colours: red phase, blue phase and yellow phase.

Many studio and professional theatre venues require substantial electrical supplies and the lighting system may have an electrical supply which is provided on three phases. This trebles the amount of power that is available.

So a three phase 60 amp supply at 240 V would allow:

$$240 \text{ (volts)} \times 60 \text{ (amps)} \times 3$$
$$= 43{,}200 \text{ (watts)} = 43.2 \text{ kW}$$

TASK

Calculate the maximum safe wattage for each of these three phase supplies:

32 amps
63 amps
100 amps.

Danger!

Three phase electrical supplies are separated by 415 volts and must not come into contact with each other in a lighting installation. A shock of 415 volts is usually lethal.

In large theatre venues safety is maintained by distributing the three phases of electricity to separate parts of the theatre. Red phase electricity supplies circuits over the stage for example, yellow phase is used at floor level and blue phase supplies all of the front of house rigging positions. The only place where the three phases will be present in close proximity to each other is at the dimmers.

Many theatre lighting plans indicate the location and phasing of sockets, so that the Designer and Electrician can work out the circuiting in advance. When circuiting a plan, the Electrician will try to achieve a rough balance across the three phases.

In smaller studio theatres, however, there may not be such a neat separation of phases and the use of temporary cables may mean that two adjacent lanterns on a rig are powered from different electrical phases. Detailed planning will help to avoid this, but during a production week the lighting rig may be altered. Even the best planning may not be able to achieve an adequate phase separation. Extra care should always be taken when working with a three phase supply and if you are in any doubt you should consult a qualified electrician.

TASK

Find out what the supply is for a theatre lighting installation that you know and calculate the available capacity in terms of watts.

MAINTENANCE

All electrical equipment must be checked regularly by law. Adequate records must be kept and portable items, such as lanterns, must be tested by a qualified person. All stage lanterns should be serviced regularly to check for electrical safety. In addition, lenses and reflectors should be cleaned and shutters, focusing controls and other attachments checked to ensure that they work smoothly. Cables, dimmers and sockets on the rig also need to be checked regularly.

General Safety Precautions

1 **Make sure that you know how to isolate the electrical supply in an emergency.**

2 Isolate the power before rigging and de-rigging lanterns. It is not sufficient just to switch the lighting board off as voltage will still be present until the dimmers are turned off.

3 Always isolate (switch off and disconnect) an electrical device before attending to it.

4 Conduct a visual inspection of every lantern before rigging it (see page 127).

5 Ensure that the mains supply is not exceeded by the number and type of lanterns. Use Ohm's Law to calculate the overall load as well as the load on individual dimmers and groups of dimmers.

6 Make sure that you know where to find an appropriate fire extinguisher and First Aid.

7 Do not plug a lantern into a live circuit.

8 Do not switch dimmers on or off unless all lanterns are faded to 'off'.

9 Do not allow food or drink near the control boards, dimmers, or patch panels.

10 Never work alone.

11 If you are at all unsure, seek advice from a qualified electrician or technician.

12 Additional help and support is always available from specialist (often local) theatre equipment suppliers.

Understanding Light and Colour

LIGHT

Light is a form of **electromagnetic radiation** which is visible to the human eye. It travels in waves at a speed of about 186,000 miles (300,000 km) per second.

Different colour sensations are created by light vibrating at different frequencies. What we perceive as white light is actually a combination of visible wavelengths in the spectrum.

Figure 4.27   *a. Wavelengths of light in the visible spectrum b. Effects of mixing primary colours of light*

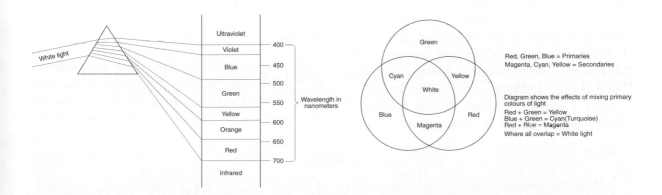

Wavelengths of light are measured in units called Angstrom or nanometres (nm).

Surfaces both reflect and absorb light. Different surfaces absorb more of some frequencies than others and this determines their precise colour. Black surfaces absorb nearly all light, whilst white surfaces scatter light of all wavelengths equally and absorb little.

We can only see an object if light strikes it, either directly or indirectly. It is only possible to see an object properly if it is lit by light containing some of that object's colour – if not, it will not reflect the light and will appear black.

TASK

Test this by lighting a red object with green light and observing the results. Change the filter to create a red light. Note your observations. How can you explain the results?

Some Properties of Light

Refraction – a change in light direction caused by it passing from one medium to another e.g. air to glass in a lens.

Diffraction – spreading of light waves as they pass through a barrier.

Reflection – bouncing of light waves from a highly polished surface, e.g. a mirror.

Shadow – an unlit area created by an object which blocks the path of light and which absorbs and/or reflects all of the light.

Light and Colour Temperature

Each light source has a distinctive colour of light. This is known as **colour temperature** and it is measured in degrees on the Kelvin temperature scale. However, colour temperatures are rarely static. Light from the sun varies according to many factors: the time of day, weather conditions, latitude, altitude, atmospheric conditions and time of year. Even with identical circumstances sunlight changes from 2000 K to 4500 K within 2 hours of sunrise. When theatre lights are dimmed to lower intensities a warmer (redder) light is produced, which has a lower colour temperature.

Light Colour Temperatures in Degrees K

20,000 K	Bright clear sunlight
13,700	Blue sky with thin clouds
7000	Uniform overcast sky, 'daylight'
6400	Xenon arc
5740	Average noon summer sunlight
5600	HMI, MSR lamps
5500	Sunlight
5070	Average noon winter sunlight
5000	Daylight photographic lamp
4500	Camera flashlight
4100	Sunlight reflected from the moon
4000	CSI
3500	Sun one hour after sunrise
3200	CP class lamp
3000	1 kW tungsten-halogen lamp
2800	Domestic light bulb
2700	Low wattage lamp, e.g. in a torch
2500	TH lamp at 50% intensity
2000	Sunlight at sunrise
1900	Candle flame

Other factors influence the colour temperature of light that we perceive. Sunlight, when it is filtered by clouds, has little of the red end of the spectrum and proportionately more blues.

TASK

Watch a sunrise or sunset and make notes as the light changes. What colours are visible in the sky? Try and plot changes in the light on a graph, using a lighting colour swatch book as a reference.

On an overcast day, the light appears greyer. Under trees a lot of light is reflected by the foliage. The leaves create shadows beneath but also absorb the red wavelengths of light, casting a greenish tint on the ground below.

Our perception of the world around us changes with light. Human eyes see best in light from the middle part of the spectrum: the yellow and green wavelengths. At night, our sense of distance and colour is impaired because blue wavelengths predominate.

Colour Temperature and Artificial Lighting

As we have discovered, artificial light in the theatre is created by using electricity to heat combinations of gases and metals contained in glass envelopes (lamps). The precise nature of this light depends upon the intensity, the colour temperature of the lamp and how the light is distributed by the lantern's lenses and reflectors.

As we have already noted, the colour temperature of artificial lighting varies according to the lamp style. Fluorescent light differs greatly from a domestic light bulb. Stage lanterns tend to use tungsten-halogen lamps which are designed to work at around 3000 K at full intensity, but this figure is altered as soon as filters are used to colour the light.

As a lantern is dimmed, its colour temperature decreases, which causes the perceived colour to change from white to red. The light on stage will, therefore, appear warmer and far less like daylight.

Lanterns with tungsten-halogen lamps can be made to match the colour temperature of daylight by using appropriate colour correction filters. Other filters can be used to give effects such as candlelight.

Designing with Light

The Lighting Designer has control over a number of different parameters which influence the way in which the light is realised on stage. The four main elements of theatre lighting are:

1 intensity
2 distribution
3 colour
4 movement.

The Designer can use these elements of light to enhance the stage environment and to communicate meaning. On a practical level, using combinations of these elements allows the Designer to define individual areas of the stage, and to highlight certain parts of the action and/or individual characters. Light is the most subtle way to direct the audience's attention to concentrate on specific aspects of the dramatic action. The ability of light to create a focus in this way is known as '**selective visibility**', since the human eye is naturally, but unconsciously, drawn to the brightest object on the stage. The Lighting Designer can use this principle to guide the audience's attention through a performance.

A follow spot is probably the most obvious application of this principle and, in addition to the brightness of the light, also attracts the eye because it moves.

INTENSITY

The Designer can alter the relative intensities of all of the lanterns in a rig by making adjustments at the control board. The maximum possible intensity of light will depend, not only on the type and size of lantern, its lamp type, electrical and optical systems, but also how far away it is positioned in relation to the stage.

The intensity of the source is measured in **candelas** or **lux**. There is also a law which describes the intensity of light. When the measurement in candelas or lux is divided by the square of the distance the light travels, it provides the **inverse square law** of illumination. This law tells us that light spreads in all directions, so if the distance between a light source and its subject is doubled, the beam of light will be able to light an area four times the size, but its intensity will be reduced by one quarter. So, the further away from a stage a lantern is placed, the greater the area it will be able to light, but at a significantly lower intensity.

Inverse square law

$$\text{illumination} = \frac{\text{intensity}}{\text{distance}}$$

or

$$\text{lux} = \frac{\text{candelas}}{\text{metre square}}$$

So, a particular Profile lantern fitted with a 650 W lamp has a maximum peak candela of 13,000 with a flat field focus.

This figure can be used to estimate the maximum illumination from a specific distance, say 5 m.

$$\frac{13000}{5 \times 5} = 520 \text{ lux}$$

Note that spotlights should only be compared with each other using the same beam angles.

Some Common Measurements of Light Intensity

Foot-candle (f.c.) – the brightness of a 1 foot square surface, when lit by a specific type of candle from a distance of one foot.

Candela – a modern measurement of luminous intensity, that is generated by a more specific and accurate source than a candle, (in reality this is a very similar measurement to a foot-candle).

Lumen (1 m) – a measurement of the quantity of light falling on 1 square foot of screen from a distance of 1 foot by a single candela.

Lambert – a larger, metric unit of light measurement describing 1 lumen per cm² (or 2.054 candelas per square inch)

Lux – this is the conversion of a lumen to a metric scale. It describes the amount of light from 1 candela onto a surface of 1 m² from 1 m away. Typical light levels in a cinema are around 50 lux. Office or classroom lighting ranges between 300 and 500 lux. Average stage lighting is around 500 lux, whilst the light for a professional production might reach levels of around 2500 lux.

Peak candela – this is the maximum level of brightness, in the centre of the beam. This figure when divided by the square of the throw distance will give the output in terms of lux.

Beam Angles and Field Angles

It is worth noting that lanterns rarely provide the maximum peak candela due to dust and dirt on the reflector and lenses, differences in lamp output, and the fact that lanterns are rarely used at their narrowest (and hence brightest) beams. Profile lanterns can be adjusted to provide an even flat field of light, which will give a lower peak intensity.

The data relating to lamps and lanterns often give a figure for **beam angle** (B/A) and **field angle** (F/A). The beam angle relates to the size of the beam measured to a point where the light is reduced to 50% of maximum intensity. The field angle is a wider measurement, to a point where the light output is measured at 10% of the maximum intensity.

DISTRIBUTION

The shape and direction of light will determine how the audience perceives the stage environment in three dimensions. The angle of light and the amount of shadow created are important for the revelation of form on stage. The Lighting Designer can create soft, apparently shadowless, even light or stark directional shafts of light. Light can be arranged so that it appears to come from a single direction, or it may be deliberately scattered around the stage.

By considering precisely where the light sources are situated, the Lighting Designer is able to control the direction and distribution of light across a stage. Changes in the direction of light can be used to great dramatic effect, either discreetly or in an overt way.

Lighting from the Front

Frontlight

This angle of lighting is used to achieve the best visibility. It is ideal for lighting the face, eyes and the mouth of the actor – essential for any speech-based performance. A person who cannot be seen properly on stage, also cannot be heard easily.

Frontlight is ideally angled at 45 degrees above and 45 degrees to the side of the actor. The 45 degree angle is idea since it mimics the dominant direction of sunlight and, consequently, shadows fall on the stage floor. In older, proscenium theatres, however, the classic angle may not be possible to achieve because of the location of rigging positions.

Extreme Frontlight

This is a flat lighting angle which hits a performer in the face and dazzles. It is often used as a fill light in film and television, alongside the camera. As the height of the lantern is reduced from the 45 degree angle, the features of the performer become flattened and the amount of shadow projected is larger. Extreme frontlight is rarely used on its own, except for

effect. It is more commonly used at a lower intensity as a fill light to help general visibility, and especially to counterbalance steep overhead lighting.

Uplight

This is light from below the level of the face, usually from floor level. Until the twentieth century this was the dominant stage lighting angle. Today, it is probably the least useful lighting angle, since it is very unflattering, making nostrils prominent and throwing strange shadows around the eyes. Uplight can be used subtly as a fill light or more commonly as a special effect, such as firelight.

Toplight or Downlight

This is a vertical beam of light, directly above the actor. It is a very dramatic lighting angle, but distorts the features of the face. The eyes and mouth can be made to disappear! It is often used in combination with other lighting angles or on its own for dramatic effect. Downlight is useful to highlight areas of the stage, individual items of furniture, and to create the impression of overhead lighting fittings.

Lighting from the Side

Topside Light

This is 45 degree lighting, from 90 degrees to the performer. It is also called high sidelight and three-quarter toplight. This lighting angle is often used above end stages for dance and theatre, balanced by a second lantern which lights the other side of the performer. Two shadows are created, one each side of the performer. At 45 degrees a single beam of light accentuates the shoulders and side of the face, just beginning to catch one eye and one side of the mouth. If the angle of light is lowered, the face is increasingly better lit.

Sidelight

This is characterised by horizontal beams of light across the stage. It is very useful for modelling and shaping performer's bodies and is, therefore, of paramount importance in dance shows. Shadows can be lost into opposite wings of a proscenium theatre, creating bands of light across the stage which are invisible until a performer breaks the beam. The modelling effect of sidelight is enhanced by lighting in contrasting colour tones from each direction. A single sidelight may prove problematic, since the performer nearest the light source will cast a shadow over anyone beyond, but this effect can also be used creatively.

Lighting from Behind

Backlight

Backlighting is the most important lighting angle after frontlighting. It helps to make the stage picture a dynamic one. When used on its own, it creates a silhouette and a halo effect around the head. It is probably the most dramatic lighting structure and can be employed to great effect if the performer's face does not need to be seen. When used with the rest of the stage lighting, it assists with the modelling of the actor by distinguishing them from their surroundings.

Backlighting is the best way to colour the stage without affecting the skin tones of the performers and is, therefore, extremely useful when the Designer wishes to change the look of a scene easily.

Side Backlight

Lighting placed behind and level with the performer, e.g. in the upstage corners of the stage, is rarely used in theatre but is fairly common in dance productions. The halo effect of backlighting is retained and extended to the full

TASK

In small groups, experiment with a range of lighting angles and observe the effect on performer's faces. Make sure that you all get to see someone standing in the beam. Note your observations for future reference – sketches may be helpful.

Light a performer with two frontlights at 45 degrees in the classic manner. Is this the best solution for lighting the face? Try varying the levels of each of these lanterns. What effect is created? Add a different colour tint to each lantern. Record your observations as you vary the intensities of each light.

Now ask a performer to wear a cap or hat with a brim and repeat your lighting experiments. What are your observations? Is 45 degrees still the best angle or does it need to be modified? Is it best to change the lighting angle entirely, or to add another lantern to provide a fill light? Where should the new rigging position be?

Light a performer with a single sidelight on the face. Note your observations. Add a second sidelight from the opposite side. Look at the nose carefully. Are there any problems in using this method of lighting? What about for use in dance? For theatre? For music?

Experiment with a combination of three contrasting lighting angles. Add a variety of colour gels and experiment with slow changes in level. Watch the effects carefully and note down your observations.

Place a light on a floor stand at a low level. Experiment with positioning this in relation to a performer. Watch the shadows carefully. Can you see possibilities for using this angle of light in a production? What might this communicate to an audience?

Figure 4.28   *Lighting the performer from different angles*

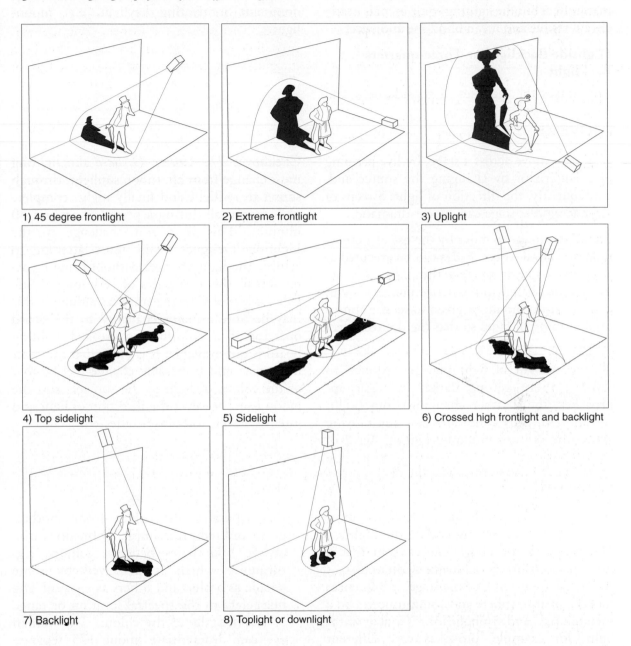

1) 45 degree frontlight

2) Extreme frontlight

3) Uplight

4) Top sidelight

5) Sidelight

6) Crossed high frontlight and backlight

7) Backlight

8) Toplight or downlight

body. Side backlighting is used for specific dramatic effect but the lighting equipment is nearly always visible and it can blind the audience!

Highside Backlight or Three-quarters Backlight

This mixes the qualities of topside light and backlight and is often used in theatre as a dominant motivating keylight, e.g. moonlight.

MOVEMENT

Light can move across a stage, by live panning of a lantern or by changing the source and, consequently, the direction of light. Sweeps of light across the stage can appear dramatic.

Light can appear to move by the use of a **cross-fade** or a **chase** effect. Fades can be executed at a variety of speeds, to make the audience aware of a tempo change in the performance. Careful consideration should be given to set the appropriate timing of fades so that the desired effect is achieved.

The movement of light may be required to show a room getting darker as night approaches, the weather changing from bright sunshine to foggy conditions, the sun moving across the sky, for example. During Act 2 of Chekhov's *The Cherry Orchard* the lighting must change from afternoon sunlight, through sunset to twilight and finally night, complete with moon, all during a period of around 30 minutes. This is a real challenge to the Lighting Designer, who must attempt to achieve the light changes without bringing attention to them. A series of very long, subtle fades are probably the answer, although this may become a major challenge to the board operator if a computer controlled lighting board is not available! It is likely that the most important and noticeable change will be that of the colour of light as the sun sets and the moon rises, however the direction of light and intensity levels will also be affected.

COLOUR

The use of coloured light is one of the most powerful tools at the disposal of the Lighting Designer and is probably the element that is most noticed by the audience. Colour shapes the visual appearance of the stage, it influences mood and atmosphere and communicates on a metaphorical and symbolic level. Cool or warm light, for example, provokes very different emotional responses from an audience. Colour may be used realistically to mimic everyday light conditions, such as light filtering through leaves, but it can also be used to represent dramatic elements such as purity, evil, royalty etc.

There are three different aspects of colour:

1 **Hue** – this is the qualitative description that separates one colour from another, green and red for example. Difficulties arise at the boundaries between colours, e.g. turquoise which is perceived by some people as a blue and others as a green! The hue refers to the spectral location or range of wavelengths of the colour. The human eye can differentiate about 175 separate colour hues.

2 **Saturation** – this is the percentage of hue in a colour or the degree of purity. The degree of whiteness or the amount of 'redness' of a red, for example.

3 **Brightness** – this is the perception of intensity or the apparent difference from black.

There is also a factor called **chroma** which is the combination of hue, saturation and brightness that produces a distinct colour. Normal vision can detect approximately 17,000 chromacities. The eye is far more sensitive to differences in the middle range of the spectrum.

Behaviour of Light

White light is a mixture of all of the wavelengths (colours) that make up the visible spectrum. Coloured light *does not* behave like pigment, when it is mixed with another colour.

Primary Colours of Light

These colours are hues that cannot be derived or created by combinations of other hues:

Red	Lee 106
Green	Lee 139
Blue	Lee 120

Note the difference with the primary colours of pigment: red, blue and yellow.

TASK

Test this by focusing three identical profile lanterns at a white wall and insert a different primary filter in each. Overlap the beams and observe the colours that you are able to create (see Figure 4.27). Experiment with altering the intensity of each colour.

Note the difference with the secondary colours of pigment: purple, green and orange.

Secondary Colours of Light

These colours are created by the mixing together of two primary light colours:

Yellow	101
Cyan	116
Magenta	113

Complementary colours

When a primary colour of light is combined with its complementary secondary colour, it produces white light:

Blue and yellow = white light
Red and cyan = white light
Green and magenta = white light

So, combinations of primary colours of light create secondaries and all three primaries together produce white light. (For this to work properly, blue may need to be at a higher level, due to the lower transmission levels of the filter).

Colour Filters

Conventional theatre lights are coloured by placing filters in front of the lantern. Many different substances have been used as filters: coloured water, silks and glass for example. Many methods were unsafe and some filters were very inefficient in transmitting light. In the past dyed gelatine sheets were used. The shorthand term 'gel' derives from this. Filters are now made of heat resistant plastics such as polyester or a polycarbonate.

Colour nomenclature has never been standardised, so identical colour names from different manufacturers do not refer to identical filters.

It is important to check filters regularly. At the end of each performance or in good time before the next performance, make sure that you look closely at the filters. Change any gels that look paler in the middle, especially the saturated colours with low transmission values. Blues, in particular, burn through quickly, even if they are high temperature versions.

How Filters Work

Filters work by allowing certain wavelengths of light to pass through. They effectively remove parts of the spectrum by absorbing them or 'filtering' them out.

Figure 4.29 *Transmission data for some commonly used colour filters. Note the variations in the wavelengths of light and the overall percentage of light allowed through each filter*

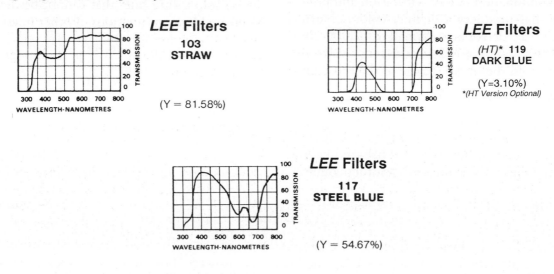

So, a deep blue filter removes all wavelengths of light, except blue. Only a small percentage of the wavelengths of white light is actually allowed to pass through (see Figure 4.28).

TASK

Study a lighting colour swatch book. These can be obtained free from manufacturers or from local theatre suppliers. Each filter gives details of transmission values: the wavelengths and the total amount of light that is transmitted through the filter.

Blue is at the left of the scale at around 425 nm, green around 525 nm and red at 650 nm. The visible spectrum ranges from 400 to 750 nm. Ultra violet and infra-red wavelengths are present to either side of the visible spectrum.

Colour Mixing on the Stage

Two lamps, each with a different filter, can combine to give a coloured light on stage. This is **additive mixing**.

Subtractive colour mixing involves placing two filters in front of the same light source. The colour is mixed at the lantern, rather than on the stage. This works like mixing pigment and is only really practical with tints as the amount of light reaching the stage is much reduced.

TASK

Try placing a primary green filter in a lantern. Now add a red filter. What is the result? Can you explain it?

If we place a Yellow (e.g. Lee 101) and a Blue-Green (e.g. 116) filter together in front of a light beam, the resulting light will be a shade of green. This is because the filters only transmit *common* wavelengths of light. A subtractive mix is shown as a *minus sign* on a lighting plan or list, e.g. 101 – 116.

Split Gels

A number of interesting effects can be achieved using a split gel, a single filter with two or more contrasting colours. For maximum effect the centre of the beam should pass through the join between the colours.

TASK

Experiment with split gels using a profile lantern and a range of gobos. Alter the focus of the lantern to create a range of effects. Note how the colour behaves as you change the focus. Try the same or similar split gels in other lanterns. Observe the results. Can you explain why there are differences?

Changing Colours

There are a few alternative methods of changing the colour of light from lanterns. A range of technology has been developed to allow the remote control of colour. Colour wheels, semaphore changers, and scrollers can allow up to 12 separate colour choices to be selected for the same lantern during a show. This saves rigging several lanterns, one for each different colour.

Dichroic filters also allow one lantern to provide several colours of light. Dichroics are expensive glass filters covered by chemicals which reflect light at different wavelengths, depending on the angle at which the light hits them. Combinations of dichroics are used inside intelligent lights, such as Vari*lites, to create pure mixes of any colour.

Some glass gobos allow the beam of light from profiles to be patterned and coloured at the same time.

USE OF COLOUR IN DESIGN

There is little scientific knowledge about the human response to colour and most decisions taken by the Designer are intuitive. Human reaction to colour is subjective and individually variable. Each member of the audience will, therefore, have a different psychological and symbolic response to a particular colour. However, we can make general assumptions – warm colours excite and stimulate, cool colours calm and depress. Traditionally, therefore, warm colours have been used for comedy and cool colours for tragedy.

Using Colour to Communicate Meaning

Colours can communicate symbolic and metaphoric meanings. Why is the evil witch in pantomime so often lit in green?

Red: death, blood, devil, anger, fear, danger, love, attraction
Blue: night, depression, calm, cold
Green: evil, jealousy, calm, hope, rural or pastoral
Yellow: warmth, sunlight
Purple: associated with royalty

TASK

In a small group, consider what other meanings different colours can communicate.

Colour choice

The Designer should not rely heavily on highly saturated colours or pure primaries unless the dramatic material calls for it. Over use of strong colours can produce a gaudy and garish stage. Similarly, using pale pastels and tints to the exclusion of saturated colours will result in a lifeless design. The Designer must let the colour choice fit the need of the piece. It is important to develop a knowledge of how different colours work together. A poor choice of colour will ruin the stage environment and can result in the colour information from settings and costumes being destroyed. The Designer must, therefore, take the time to experiment with colour combinations at different intensities and to study the likely effects of these choices on the stage. Tints such as No Colour Pink, Daylight Blue, Straw, Bastard Amber and Lavender can be used to light the acting area (they are ideal colours to complement the skin tone), and a bolder choice of colour can

TASK

Try some of these experiments with coloured light and note your responses. What relevance might the experiments have to a Lighting Designer?

1 Find a large image which contains saturated colour, e.g. a painting. Project saturated coloured light onto a white wall and concentrate on this for a while. Now look at the large image under white light. You should notice that complementary colours cancel each other out and appear grey.
2 Experiment by projecting alternate primary colours of light onto the image. Record how you perceive the colour information. Try the same experiment with complementary colours and other saturated colours.
3 Stare at a spot of red light projected onto a wall for a minute or so. Turn the red light off and replace immediately with a yellow light. What colour do you see? Check how quickly your eye readjusts to perceive yellow. Is this the same for everyone in your group?
4 Project a bright yellow light onto a white wall. After a while it seems to gain a greenish tint before returning to yellow. Now look at a white light. Does it contain a tint?
5 Place three squares of grey paper against white, grey, and black backgrounds. Light in sequence with a red-tinted light and describe the tint of the grey squares against each background.
6 Light an object such as a chair from three lanterns. If the object is on or near a white surface the resulting effect will be clearer. Place a different primary filter in each lantern and observe the colour of the shadows. Can you work out why this happens?
7 Project an intense white light at a wall. Lower to a very low intensity and add a multi-coloured image. The colours should become more saturated over time. Do all colours emerge at the same rate?

be used as toplight, sidelight and backlight. In this way, the stage can be transformed radically without the skintones being affected.

Remember that using combinations of different lanterns can sometimes cause problems, since larger wattage lamps have higher colour temperatures and may not balance with lower wattage fixtures. Choice of colour filters should, therefore, be made carefully and the likely equipment and levels of light taken into account. Experimentation is the key to successful lighting design.

Just as our eyes adapt to changing levels of intensity, they also compensate for exposure to colour over a period of time by becoming less sensitive to colour information. **Colour fatigue** leads the eye to become confused after being exposed for long periods to a single dominant colour. An after image effect can result and it takes a few moments for our eyes to readjust. Staring at a colour for a period of time causes the colour to appear whiter, i.e. desaturated. When a new colour is introduced, our eyes become confused and the colour information is misinterpreted. Using coloured light on the stage can create similar effects and our perception of pigment colour alters when viewed in coloured light.

LIGHTING DESIGN AND STYLE

The Designer makes some key decisions about the style of the lighting, the precise role of light and the dramatic potential of light in the production.

A production of Shakespeare's *A Midsummer Night's Dream*, for example, requires a minimum of two lighting states to represent the two locations of the play: the Athenian court and the forest. The forest is the most important location, since it is the setting for all of the action in Acts 2, 3 and 4. Most of the forest scenes are played at night, which demands another response from the Designer. Moonlight, if not a visible moon, is required for the beginning of Act 2; '*Ill met by moonlight proud Titania*'

The Lighting Designer may also wish to address the two worlds of the play, the human and the fairy worlds, in the lighting concept. Furthermore, the Designer may want to emphasise specific moments, help to accentuate the confusion in the forest, and/or to highlight the inner struggles of the main characters, by their choice of lighting states.

TASK

Light can be used dramatically in a number of different styles. From plays that you know and productions that you have seen, consider the different roles that light can have on the stage.

1 Consider how light can be used symbolically. Can you think of an example?
2 How might the lighting contribution differ for these types of dramas?

a comedy like Wilde's *The Importance of Being Earnest*
a Greek tragedy like Sophocles' *Oedipus*
an absurd drama like Beckett's *Waiting for Godot*
An expressionist play like Wedekind's *Spring Awakening*
A twentieth century play with distinct shifts in time and mood, or flashback sequences,
    like Miller's '*Death of a Salesman*'.

Figure 4.30 *Backlighting from a production of Jesus Christ Superstar*

CREATING EFFECTS

Naturalistic Lighting

The Lighting Designer must start from the situation of a play and will consider place, time and direction of light. For any production that is remotely 'realistic', the Designer will need to consider the likely source or sources of light for each scene. Sources can be defined in two ways:

1 motivating light
2 motivated light.

Motivating Light

Motivating light is a light source (or sources) which is actually visible on stage and, therefore, *motivates* the actions of the characters. The source is often the key to the look of a scene and should influence the actor's movements; crossing the stage towards a lamp to read a letter, for example. Common motivating light sources include:

a candle
an oil lamp
an electric light
a fire
the moon and stars.

Luckily, the need to actually see the sun on stage is rare. It is virtually impossible to recreate, however, the setting sun may be realised as a projected effect.

Motivated Light

Motivated light is a cheat to create the illusion that light is coming from a particular source. Usually this source is the sun located offstage but may be a candle or electric light, for example. Stage lighting may be required to cheat the effect so that the audience believe that the light on stage is coming from the visible source. Motivated light is the most dominant light on stage and often referred to as the **keylight**.

Creating a Night Time Scene in a Room with a Window

1 Shafts of moonlight (motivated, since the moon is not seen) flood through window USL.

2 Character enters room from doorway USR, faint light (motivated, source not seen) seen from beyond

3 Character crosses the room and switches on a lamp (motivating) on a table

4 Character closes the curtain. Room is lit entirely by the lamp (probably cheated) and therefore motivated.

TASK

Select some large colour photographs from a book or magazine. Study each image in detail. Try to ascertain the following information:

Is there a motivated light source? Where?
Is there a motivating light? Where?
What is the direction of light – how can you describe it in theatre terms? Where exactly is the main source of light positioned?
Can you describe the quality of light?
What does the light tell you about the precise time of day, location, season or weather?
Does the light communicate anything else? Mood? Atmosphere?
How might you recreate this image on the stage?
Exchange a photograph with a colleague and repeat the exercise. Compare your observations. Were there disagreements? Why?

TASK

Study the opening scene from *Macbeth*. Plan the lighting for it. Consider what will be an appropriate style. What motivating or motivated light sources have you chosen? Is your lighting scheme purely 'realistic' or does it suggest other ideas? If so what are they? Justify your approach to others. Why is yours the most appropriate solution in your opinion?

DESIGNING THE GENERAL COVER

In the vast majority of scenarios, at least one general acting area lighting state will be required to ensure that faces are visible from the auditorium. The 'general cover' should not be specifically noticed as a design element by an audience, but should light all areas of the stage adequately and evenly. A poorly designed or focused cover will create very bright 'hot spots' in some areas of the stage, whilst others may be underlit. If actors in a realistic drama are suddenly plunged into dark areas of the stage as they move across or up and down stage, this will be immediately apparent to an audience who will be reminded that they are watching a performance and become momentarily disengaged from the piece.

So the general cover will provide an even illuminated stage at head height. Although it may not contribute much on a creative level, it will give you confidence that you can light a performer on the stage wherever they are standing! The general cover need not be used at full of course, and may indeed work better as a barely noticeable fill light.

The cover should be planned by dividing the stage area into manageable segments, each of which should be lit from two sides at around 45 degrees. Calculating lighting sections will provide the correct positioning for these lanterns and allow beam angles to be checked. This ensures that the lights will be able to cover the area that you are requiring them to (see page 158). Careful positioning of lanterns on the plan will provide a good horizontal and vertical overlap of beams across the stage.

Sometimes you will need to design more than one cover of the stage, e.g. for plays with interior and exterior scenes or for daytime and nighttime scenes. The warm coloured light for the daylight will look completely wrong for the night scenes. If you have plenty of lanterns and circuits available then a double cover may well be the best solution. Alternatively, you might aim to select a colour that works for both daytime or night, such as Surprise pink (L194). However, the classic stage lighting technique involves using one lantern with a cool gel and one with a warm gel focused on each acting area from either side. When used at equal intensity the colour will appear relatively neutral, but variations in the intensity of circuits allows the warm lanterns to be accentuated for daylight and the cool lanterns emphasised for the night scenes.

Once the general cover has been planned you can now concentrate on more creative lighting design, knowing that you have achieved the first aim of the lighting designer – that of visibility.

Keylighting

Some designers prefer to establish the keylighting, before progressing to the designing of the acting area lighting. Keylight will help with the visibility of a scene, but more importantly it will provide a motivated light that gives a distinct emphasis to the scene. Keylight direction, colour and intensity will probably change throughout the piece and so will need to work in conjunction with the general cover.

Using Other Directions of Light

The addition of side light, top light and backlighting will also enhance the stage picture, helping to create a dynamic look through its sculptural effect on performers and setting alike. Such lighting angles are often an ideal way to add saturated colours to a scene, without adversely affecting facial tones and, when used alone, can create highly dramatic images.

Specials

A special is any single lantern rigged to fulfil a specific function, e.g. to light a doorway, to isolate a character or to project a gobo. Specials can also be used to subtly highlight principle areas of action such as a sofa, or a throne. Often a steep angle is used to pick out the area from the surrounding 'cover'.

Motivating light sources should not be ignored. A 100 watt domestic light bulb hanging in the centre of the stage will need a circuit, and one or more lanterns may also be required to cheat the effect – to provide light as if it is coming from the visible bulb.

A Lighting Design Chronology

The lighting design process has been discussed throughout this book. It is given in summary here with cross references to relevant sections. This example is based on the design process for a dramatic play text, and it is important to note that the lighting design process for other performance types such as music, dance and devised pieces may differ significantly, due to the way in which they are developed through work in rehearsals.

EARLY DESIGN IDEAS

1 The role of the Designer has been discussed and a number of strategies were suggested for developing design ideas, (see pages 27–31).
2 The Lighting Designer will draw upon a wide range of stimuli, including the play text itself, in order to develop a design concept. As has already been noted, it is useful for the Lighting Designer to build up a scrapbook of interesting visual material over a period of time which will often spark creative thought and stimulate new design ideas (see page 28).
3 From initial readings of the text and other preliminary research the Lighting Designer creates Initial Lighting Scene Synopsis which lists all of the essential lighting changes in the play.
4 The Lighting Designer will prepare sketches of the early lighting ideas in preparation for the next stage (see below). Charcoal or pencil drawings can give an indication of light direction. Watercolour washes may help to show direction, pattern and colour of light. Using coloured chalk, pastels or coloured pencils on black paper can give an overall impression of the lighting. A series of images like this will form a storyboard of the play's main lighting states or key moments

THE DESIGN OR PRE-PRODUCTION MEETING

This is the forum in which the Lighting Designer communicates ideas to the Director and other Designers (see pages 21 and 30).

DEVELOPING THE DESIGN SCHEME

1 Once a set model has been produced, the Lighting Designer can plan how to realise lighting ideas on the stage in detail. Detailed discussions with the set and costume designers will continue at this stage.
2 It is important to check where the available rigging positions are. Is there sufficient space available to light the stage or are some areas of the stage difficult or impossible to light?
3 Consideration is given to scenery at this point: if scenic elements are to be flown, have sufficient bars been left for the rigging of lights? Do individual scenic components make lighting difficult or impossible? Some scenic items may require lighting to make them work as intended (windows, etc.)
4 Practical restrictions on lighting design include time, people, equipment and money.
5 Some Designers use 'blob and arrow' drawings to express light colour and direction at this stage. The drawings are fairly rough and are really just a chance to experiment with ideas. To do this redraw a plan of the set in miniature and copy it a number of times. Use one drawing for each major lighting cue or state. Use colour pencils or

felt pens to indicate the colour of the light with an appropriate 'blob' and the direction of the light with an arrow. These rough 'shorthand' drawings for each lighting state provide a representation of the storyboard images in plan form.

6 At this point the Lighting Designer amends the original lighting scene synopsis and produces a more detailed breakdown of cues. Information may now include colours, direction, and estimated fade times of each intended cue throughout the play.

THE REHEARSAL PERIOD

1 The Lighting Designer will amend and consolidate the lighting design ideas through regular visits to rehearsals.
2 During the rehearsal period the Lighting Designer should receive regular communications from the stage management team in the form of rehearsal notes (see page 64). These will keep everyone informed of progress in rehearsals on a daily basis. Rehearsal Notes will detail any new lighting requirements or changes the Director may be requesting from what has previously been suggested or agreed.
3 Throughout the rehearsal period the Lighting Director should also be attending regular production meetings (see page 47).

FINALISING DESIGN IDEAS

1 The Lighting Designer assimilates all of the information collected previously and attempts to imagine how the lighting is going to look throughout the play.
2 Lighting plans become more specific. The key areas to consider are direction, intensity, colour and movement of light (see pages 143–149). It is time to make decisions about the mood and atmosphere, the texture of light, visibility, and the timing of individual fades.
3 At this stage the Lighting Designer may experiment with a small model box of the stage. A torch, such as a Maglite, can be manoeuvred to try out a variety of possible lighting angles. Strips of gel can be held in front of torches to give a rough idea of colour combinations. More sophisticated set-ups may use 500W lanterns or small low voltage lanterns such as birdies (see Figure 4.31). Although it is valuable to experiment with colour, it is worth noting that because of the difference in the lamp colour temperatures, the torches and low-voltage lanterns will not replicate the exact effect of colour from theatre lanterns.

DRAWING UP THE LIGHTING PLAN

1 The Lighting Designer must commit the lighting ideas to paper in the form of a lighting rig plan which will identify the precise type, location and orientation of each lantern. It will also indicate the appropriate patch and circuit number, any pairing, colour information and any other accessories which need to be added to the lantern, e.g. colour wheels, gobos, irises, barn doors, etc.
2 Individual lighting symbols indicate the particular type of lantern, its positioning on the rig and its orientation. The universal lighting symbols (see pages 111–118), are not sufficient for use on a professional lighting plan. Instead, specialist graphic symbols are

Figure 4.31   *Experimenting with light on a model box*

used to represent specific lanterns at the correct scale (see Figure 4.32). These symbols differentiate between manufacturers, ranges of lanterns, model and lens types, etc. Each lantern, therefore, has its own individual symbol which will be shown in a key at the side of the plan. Stencils are available from the major manufacturers of lighting equipment and from lighting supply companies. Increasingly, lighting plans are drawn with the aid of computer software which can include a vast array of symbols from many different manufacturers.

3 The method for calculating the positioning of an individual lantern is shown below.

How to establish where to rig lanterns

We have already examined what types of lanterns are useful to achieve particular effects but we also need to establish precisely where a lantern should be rigged to achieve the effect that is desired. The Lighting Designer calculates the optimum rigging position for each lantern, although once the rigging distance away from the stage has been established for an angle of 45 degrees, other lighting positions can often be approximated. In recent years, sophisticated computer software drawing programmes have become available which undertake all of this work and are able to calculate a range of information including the beam angles from specific lanterns.

Calculating Lighting Angles for Acting Area Light

Designing the acting area light is usually the first step of any design scheme, since it will ensure visibility. Once the calculation has been undertaken, the data will be used to establish the rigging positions of other lights on the plan.

1 Divide the stage area into manageable segments for lighting. These will depend upon the size of the stage and the number of separate acting areas that are required. A simple nine area stage (see page 15) may be sufficient. However, the stage may not divide so easily and it may not be appropriate to divide it equally. A composite set, for example, is likely to require a series of unequal areas for lighting. The appropriate area size will also depend upon the throw distance and the type of equipment, that is available. 2 kW lanterns are designed to project light from a considerable distance from the stage, but are expensive and the further away a lantern is rigged, the larger the area that will be lit on stage. 500 W lanterns would generally be inappropriate for large distances, due to lower light levels. Appropriate lanterns will have a field area at least as big as the acting segment.

As a rough guide, acting segments should be around 2 to 3 m^2. Larger stages may need to be lit in areas up to 4 m^2. For a general cover of acting area light aim to achieve an overlap of around 30% between lanterns. The field angles will overlap and blend to give an even wash of illumination for actor's faces.

2 Draw a section of the stage with an actor placed in the centre of the segment. Decide on a suitable level at which to light. For drama, aim to light faces, not feet. So, this level should usually be around 1 m 60 cm above the stage height.

3 Draw a horizontal line on the section to represent this plane. This is the level to light.

4 Draw in the grid height or a vertical line to represent the height of available hanging positions. For proscenium theatres you will need to establish the bar and bridge heights and locations of other front of house hanging positions. Over stage hanging positions are likely to be flexible, but check whether heights have already been set for the bars which are to hold scenic items. These could interfere with the light.

Figure 4.32   *Detail from a lighting plan*

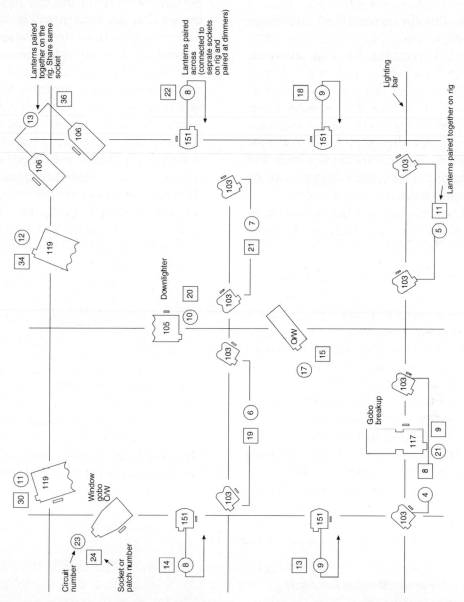

5 Measure 45 degrees and draw a line from the actor (at the lighting plane) to the grid or hanging height.

6 Measure the distance from the centre of the segment to where the line intersects the grid height. This provides you with the ideal lighting angle of 45 degrees and the required rigging distance away from your subject. (Whenever you are using the 45 degree angle this distance will always be

the same – the lighting plane minus the distance to the grid, so a simple calculation will save you from drawing a section!)

If there is not a suitable rigging position at this distance away from the stage, it will be necessary to either rig a bar to accommodate the lantern or select an alternative rigging position nearby. If the lantern is primarily giving acting area light, it is best to place it slightly further away. This is preferable to a steeper top light.

7 Draw lines to the upstage and downstage sides of this acting segment, to the same grid point, to discover the angle at which the light will hit the actor when standing at the back or front of this segment. This calculation will also show the necessary beam angle required to cover the segment from a lighting position directly infront. A simple check against the manufacturer's data will show whether a particular lantern will be able to achieve this particular angle.

8 Repeat this exercise for other segments to provide an idealised section through the centre line. It is likely that the beam angles will need to be slightly wider than calculated to ensure adequate overlap between segments.

9 The above exercise is really only useful for finding rigging positions for individual lanterns and establishing the measurement on the plan that will achieve a 45 degree angle.

For general cover of lighting acting areas, two lanterns should be used at 45 degrees *to each side* of actor. Since the lantern now has to light a wider area (diagonally across the square segment) and it is physically closer to the acting area segment (because it

has moved 45 degrees to the side), it is important to establish the real beam angle to ensure that our lantern will be able to light the entire area from that position.

10 Instead of a 2 m width beam, a 2.8 m beam spread is required to cover the diagonal distance from corner to corner of the acting area square. Redrawing the section from the new (closer) position of the lantern, will show the actual beam angle required and also the large amount of overlap into neighbouring acting areas. This spill will assist greatly with the blending and toning both up and down, and across the stage, and should result in an even general cover of illumination, which is not noticed specifically by an audience.

The method detailed above provides a way of lighting acting areas with two frontlights at 45 degrees to achieve an even wash of light. This can be supplemented by the addition of backlight, sidelight, toplight, etc. and specials.

Bear in mind that, where the audience is arranged around the acting area, what is frontlight to some will be sidelight or even backlight to others. Steeper lighting angles, therefore, are usually employed to light productions staged in-the-round, and on thrust and traverse stages.

TASK

Consider the difficulties and advantages of lighting an arena stage. Usually, three or four lanterns are used for each part of the acting area. Draw up a simple plan to explore how you might light an arena stage using three lanterns for each of nine acting segments.

Computer Software

There are a number of lighting software packages, which calculate the throw distances and demonstrate the beam angles of lanterns in the position in which you place them. These allow Designers to experiment on screen and the computer makes all of the calculations for them!

Conventions for Representing Lanterns on a Plan

The Lighting Designer selects a lighting symbol for each type and model of lantern that will be used. These are indicated in a key at the bottom or side of the lighting plan.

If there is not an exact match with a particular lantern an alternative but appropriate outline is chosen. It is important not to pick a fresnel outline to represent a profile, for example.

The bars, grid and other hanging positions are then drawn in pencil, if they are not already marked on the plan. The correct positioning of each lantern on the plan is indicated by adding the appropriate lantern outline. When the positions are finalised, each lantern is redrawn with a fine-tipped felt tip or graphic ink pen. Although the symbol can indicate the positioning and orientation of each lantern, it is, of course, impossible to show the degree of tilt. Those lanterns providing toplight are, however, indicated by writing D/L for 'downlight' next to the lantern on the plan (see Figure 4.32).

Once each lantern has been indicated on the plan, the colour number is added. These are usually indicated on the plan inside the lantern outline. The number of the gel corresponds to the manufacture's filter number. If no colour is to be used in a lantern, the outline is marked O/W for 'open white'.

If profiles are to be fitted with Gobos or Irises this is also indicated inside the outline of the lantern. Where lanterns are to be fitted with barn doors, the rough positioning is indicated. Lanterns rigged on floor stands are drawn with the appropriate symbol. Lanterns rigged on booms can be shown alongside the plan in elevation. The precise positioning of the boom is indicated.

Once all the lanterns have been drawn onto the plan, they must be allocated circuit numbers. The Chief Electrician often helps to do this, to ensure that the plugging up is as practical as possible.

Circuit numbers are indicated in a circle behind each lantern. If the theatre has a patch system, the socket number should also be shown on the plan (in a square). Pairing of lanterns is shown by joining them together with lines (see Figure 4.32).

SIMPLIFYING THE DESIGN

1 The Lighting Designer works on the plan until all of the design ideas are represented. Usually, more lanterns are specified than is practicable for the scale of the project. This is the point to consider a rationalisation of the design, to turn it into a workable scheme. It is always better to work from the ideal and then to make compromises.

2 Common problems:
   - Not enough lanterns or an insufficient budget to hire in extra equipment
   - Not enough of the right type of lanterns
   - Not enough circuits
   - Not enough power.

3 Finding a way to simplify the design scheme without making too many compromises can be a difficult task. The Designer looks at each lantern to ascertain how important it is within the design scheme as a whole. The aim is to achieve a balance between the general cover and more visually stimulating design ideas.

4 Once the Lighting Designer is happy with the design and is confident that the lanterns on the plan will achieve the intended visual effects within the practical constraints, they will decide whether it may be necessary to pair lanterns together.
   - Only pair lanterns which are supposed to come on and go out together!
   - Only pair lanterns that are doing the same task.
   - Try not to pair lanterns lighting different sections of the acting area, in case of later decisions to isolate the two areas.

81). The board operator notes the technical details of each cue.

6 If similar light states are required, valuable time can be saved by recalling an earlier lighting state, modifying it as necessary and then re-recording it as a separate cue.

PLOTTING AND CUE SHEETS

1 The lighting states will be established by the Designer and Director at the lighting session when they will be 'plotted'.

2 It is likely that changes will still need to be made after the plotting session. Cues are often modified at the technical rehearsal or at the dress rehearsal stage.

3 It is essential that a clear uniform system is used when plotting lighting levels and changes on cue sheets. A logical, neatly laid out cue sheet will enable the lighting operator to reproduce accurately, in the correct order, all of the lighting changes during the performance.

4 If the show has a Deputy State Manager to cue it, then the operator is freed from locating the precise place in a script where a cue should occur and the cue sheet need only contain the cue number as a reference.

5 A cue sheet needs to contain at least the following information:
- number of the cue
- the time that the cue should be operated in (fade duration)
- what needs to be done by the operator as part of the cue
- notes about the lighting state and other important information for the operator. Additional information will also be required depending on the type of control board and specific details of the type of fade required.

Using Pre-set Sheets

As mentioned previously, manual control boards allow the operator to set up the next lighting state in advance. This is called a pre-set. Pre-set sheets are, therefore, used in conjunction with cue sheets. The preset sheets contain the channel or circuit information for each lighting state so that the preset faders can be set up in advance.

Pre-set sheets should be identified clearly, so that it is clear in which order they should be used. Make sure that all of the cue information is recorded accurately. A lot of time, effort and creativity has been invested in plotting the lighting – it needs to be replayed as accurately as possible.

TECHNICAL REHEARSAL

1 This is the first run through of the lighting states in sequence with the actors. The technical rehearsal will ensure that the lighting is cued and operated correctly and allows members of the cast to familiarise themselves with the stage under performance conditions.

2 The rehearsal may be conducted as a cue to cue run, where parts of the show that do not involve technical changes of any kind are skipped.

3 It is particularly important when a manual control board is being used, to check that re-sets are physically possible to achieve in the time between one cue finishing and the next standby being given.

DRESS REHEARSAL

1 There should be a written sequence of pre-show checks as part of a routine to prepare for performance work. One of the most important of these checks is the procedure known as 'flashing out' (see page 130). The positioning and colour of each light beam should also be checked.

2 If the technical rehearsal has been conducted properly, there should be few problems at this stage that cannot be identified as minor cueing or operating errors. The dress rehearsal is the first opportunity to view the lighting under performance conditions as a continually changing design element.

3 The Designer should make notes to communicate with the board operator and/or Deputy Stage Manager after the run through.

4 There will usually be a notes session with the Director following the dress rehearsal.

5 The Production Manager and the Lighting Designer may well wish to hold additional meetings to resolve other technical or design problems not mentioned by the Director.

TASK

Make a list of pre-show checks that you would expect to undertake as a lighting board operator. Think about what equipment you will need to switch on or off to prepare the auditorium, stage and control box for a performance.

PERFORMANCE

1 By the time of the opening performance, there should be little for the Lighting Designer to do, except to watch the show, check the lighting and note any amendments and minor adjustments that need to be made.

2 The lighting technicians should concentrate on maintaining a high quality of work throughout the run of performances, adhering strictly to the cue sheets as they were plotted.

3 After the show, another notes session may be called to refine the lighting plot.

GET-OUT

Following the last performance the theatre should be returned to a black box stage. Usually this involves de-rigging all of the lanterns on the rig. Precise arrangements should be made before the last performance, so that the de-rig can be planned logically.

De-rigging Procedure

● Dimmers should be switched off.

● Control equipment is switched off.
● Lanterns should be unplugged.
● Safety chains are removed.
● Barn doors are folded in and shutters inserted fully.
● Each lantern should be panned and tilted down, so that it hangs vertically under the yoke.
● The 'G' clamp is removed from the bar.

- The lantern is lowered to stage level.
- Temporary cable and any PVC tape are removed from the lighting bar.
- Cable is coiled and taped.
- At stage level, colour frames, irises, gobos, cables, etc. should be removed, sorted and returned to store.
- Lanterns are stored by type.
- Hired equipment is identified and returned promptly to avoid excess charges.

POST-PRODUCTION

1 All equipment should be stored appropriately and any repairs undertaken.
2 Equipment that has been hired or borrowed should be returned promptly.
3 Cue sheets, lighting plans and other documentation should be filed with the prompt copy for future reference.
4 Lighting team members may be involved in a post show evaluation of the production.

TASK

Draw up an agenda for a post-show discussion to evaluate the lighting. What worked well and why? What was less successful and why? Consider the overall intention of the lighting design. Was the style appropriate? What technical problems were there and why did they occur? Can you ascertain how to prevent these problems reoccurring without putting the blame on individuals?

chapter five
SOUND

An Introduction to Sound

SOUND DESIGN

Sound design is the newest area of creative contribution to performance. Great technological advances since the mid 1970s have enabled high quality, complex sounds to be created relatively easily. Recent advances in digital audio and computer-based recording and editing systems allow the creation of almost any real or imagined effect.

Sound is subjective: one individual's response to a particular sound will differ significantly from that of any other. What may seem appropriate to the Sound Designer, may not communicate the same idea to the Director, other members of the company, or to the audience. Sound has the ability to direct and reinforce the audience's emotional response to the action on stage, in the same way as music and effects condition our reactions in films.

WHAT IS SOUND?

Sound is the movement of air in the form of waves of high and low pressure. These radiate from a sound source at a speed of about 340 m per second (760 mph or 1260 km/h). Sound travels even faster in hotter and more humid air. As they travel away from the source, the waves get gradually smaller. They lose energy, just like the ripples made by a pebble dropped into a lake. Although the waves get smaller as they move away from the place where the pebble broke the water's surface, the distance between the waves remains the same. In sound terms this example would equate to a single note from a musical instrument, which gets quieter the further the sound travels. Although the sound waves diminish in amplitude ('volume'), they remain equidistant (pitch of the note).

Unlike the example of the pebble, which causes ripples only along the plane of the water's surface, sound waves radiate from the source in all directions at the same time. Sound, therefore, radiates in ever-expanding spheres of waves. The tiny differences in pressure associated with the waves are experienced as sound by the human ear. If the sound waves are regular, we hear a sound of a definable pitch or 'note', if the sound waves are random we perceive 'noise'.

Frequency

One wave, measured from a peak to a peak, (through a trough), is known as a **cycle of vibration**. The speed of the vibration determines the sound's **frequency** or **wavelength** (see Figure 5.1). The frequency is measured and expressed in cycles per second (cps) or Hertz (Hz), named after the German engineer, Heinrich Rudolf Hertz. The frequency of sound can be measured by an **oscilloscope** and displayed

Figure 5.1 *Features of sound waves a 1 cycle (1Hz), b relationship between frequency and pitch, c amplitude and pitch*

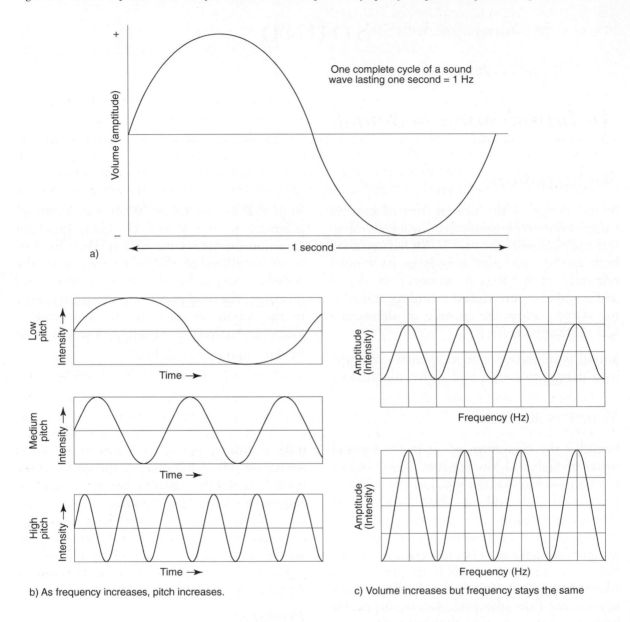

b) As frequency increases, pitch increases.

c) Volume increases but frequency stays the same

graphically. A single cycle which lasts for 1 second is known as 1 Hertz (1 Hz). Higher pitched sounds will have a higher frequency (more cycles per second) than lower pitch sounds.

Amplitude

Amplitude corresponds to the loudness or volume of a sound signal. The amplitude is the height of the wave from peak to trough. The greater the amplitude, the louder the sound. The characteristics of the way in which a sound volume varies is known as the **dynamics**.

HEARING SOUND

The human ear is capable of experiencing frequencies between about 16 and 20,000 Hz (20 kHz). This range is known as the **audio spectrum**. (Dogs can hear sounds up to 30 kHz and bats up to 1000 kHz!) It is interesting to note that this frequency range deteriorates markedly with age and sensitivity so the higher frequencies are lost first. Frequent or prolonged exposure to loud noise (including music) can cause irreparable damage to the ears and may also result in greatly reduced frequency sensitivity.

The main characteristics of sound that can be detected by the human ear are:

- **Volume** – this depends on the amplitude, or intensity, of the sound wave. The greater the amplitude, the louder the sound.
- **Pitch** – this is related to the frequency of the fundamental sound wave (the number of waves in a given time). The greater the frequency, the higher the pitch.
- **Tone** – the tone of a sound is more difficult to quantify, but the quality of sound depends on the number and kind of overtones or harmonics (see below).

Fundamentals and Harmonics

We have seen how sound vibrations are measured according to the number of vibrations per second measured in Hertz. Most sounds are actually more complex than this and create several different sets of vibrations. Only the purest sounds, sine waves, which are generated electronically, do not have these multiple sets of vibrations. An audio test signal or 'slate' is an example of pure tone which is generated at 1 kHz. The first vibration of a sound is known as the **fundamental** and subsequent vibrations are the **harmonics** which give depth to the sound.

a musical note may have a fundamental of
    100 Hz
Its second harmonic will be 200 Hz
Its third harmonic will be 300 Hz
Its fourth harmonic will be 400 Hz, and so on.

Each harmonic diminishes in intensity. The strength and quality of these successive harmonics determines the particular **timbre** or **tone** of the sound. Harmonics allow us to distinguish the difference between two instruments that are playing the same musical note. Indeed, the precise nature of each subsequent harmonic wave will allow us to differentiate between two different violins playing the same musical note. Each instrument will generate slightly different wave forms at different frequencies and levels to create a distinct timbre.

TASK

Consider why two violins will generate slightly different sound waves even playing the same note. What causes these differences?

MEASURING SOUND – THE DECIBEL dB

Sound Pressure Levels

Sound volume is measured in decibels, which is a widely misunderstood term. The decibel is a comparative measure and means nothing in isolation. If the noise output from a rock group was set at 0dB, rustling leaves would be measured as −100 dB. Therefore, 0 dB is rarely silence, but usually an *optimum* level for replaying and recording sound sources.

The **dBA Scale** (below) shows sound sources in relation to the human envelope of hearing, in this case with 0 dB representing the threshold of hearing.

200	Space Shuttle at close range
150	Jet aircraft at 50 feet, artillery fire at close range
140	Pain threshold, industrial plant
110	Rock concert
100	Large Orchestra playing at '*forte*', motorway traffic, siren on emergency vehicle
90	Underground train
80	Noisy office, theatre foyer before a performance, interior of car,
70	Conversation at 1 m
60	Suburban street, lecture
40	Quiet home, soft music
30	library, bedroom at night

20	Empty theatre, quite whisper
10	Rustling leaves
0	Inside a heavily treated room such as a professional recording studio

Threshold of pain	140 dB
Threshold of feeling	120 dB
Envelope of hearing	0−120 dB
Threshold of audibility	0 dB

UK 'A' scale

This scale shows the legal limits for exposure to continual sound. Regulations are for industry, but do not cover replay of music, since the levels are never constant.

Sound level	Maximum exposure
Under 90 dBA	no limit
90 dBA	8 hours a day
93 dBA	4 hours a day
96 dBA	2 hours a day
99 dBA	1 hour a day
102 dBA	30 minutes a day
105 dBA	15 minutes a day

Regular exposure to sound levels above 90 dBA may result in hearing loss. Exposure to levels above 130 dBA will result in immediate and permanent hearing loss.

SOUND REPRODUCTION

The principle of electronic sound reproduction is that sound pressure waves are converted into a tiny electrical signal with a pattern equivalent to the wave pattern. When this signal is amplified and fed to a loudspeaker, it causes the internal parts (the diaphragm or core) to vibrate. This reproduces the original pattern of sound pressure waves in the air which can then be detected by our ears.

Analogue and Digital Sound

We have seen how sound waves are formed and how acoustic energy can be transformed into an electrical signal, which is used by audio equipment.

Analogue sound involves a physical process, whereby the acoustic pressure waves are translated into varying electrical signals of similar magnitude and time durations. Microphones are used to generate this varying voltage which is then converted into a physical representation of the signal, either in the pattern of magnetisation on audio tape or a varying groove on a vinyl record. This physical process is less than perfect and leads to adverse noise and gradual deterioration of recordings over time. The vinyl record gets dusty and scratched, the magnetic tape may stretch or lose magnetic particles as it passes the tape heads. These imperfections are impossible to remedy once they have occurred in the analogue domain. Furthermore, the analogue signal deteriorates as it is re-recorded or copied, and the 'noise' inherent in the analogue method of sound reproduction increases.

TASK

Experiment with two cassette recorders and a number of blank cassettes. Link the player to the recorder via a stereo phono lead, connecting the output of the player to the input of the recorder (or a tape to tape machine). Use a set of headphones to monitor the sound.

Starting with a good quality recording of a short excerpt of music, record it onto a blank tape. Using this new recording (or second generation recording) re-record it onto another blank tape. Compare the results and note your findings.

Repeat the exercise to create a third generation recording and compare the resulting copy with the original. Listen carefully to the sound to detect the differences. How would you describe them? Would you consider a fourth generation copy suitable for replaying music in a performance? What happens when you amplify the sound? How many generations of recordings do you need to make before the sound breaks up and becomes unrecognisable?

Digital Sound

The advent of digital audio technology has radically altered the way in which sound can be manipulated. The Sound Designer can now easily create repetitions of sound, sophisticated loops, alter the speed and pitch of a recording and add a multitude of other effects, all without affecting the technical quality of the sound source.

Digital sound, therefore, offers many advantages over analogue signals. It has a better signal-to-noise ratio, can offer a greater dynamic range and does not suffer from the same amount of distortion or deterioration in replay or when copied. Digital sound may also be accessed more quickly and with greater precision. But storing the digital information is a far more complicated process, which involves large quantities of data. This can restrict the total amount of digital audio that can be held on a sampler or computer, although this data can be downloaded (recorded) on to other media for storage and playback.

The electrical waveform from a microphone is converted into a series of pulses or samples of information. These are essentially a series of binary digits, which represent the amplitude of the original waveform and are taken or 'sampled more than 40,000 times every second. Because the signal has been translated into a coded form of numbers rather than continually variable ones, in the case of analogue, sound recording and replay are far more accurate.

The Sound System

INTRODUCTION

We have already seen that sound can be recorded using digital or analogue means. Microphones are used for the task of converting acoustic pressure waves into equivalent electrical signals. The loudspeaker performs the opposite job to a microphone, translating electrical signals back into acoustic pressure waves, or sound.

Other items of equipment can also generate sound in the form of an electrical signal. These are known as **source equipment**. A compact disc player is a common example of this.

The passage of the electrical signal through the various pieces of equipment in a sound system can be seen as a **chain**. The links in this chain are the separate pieces of equipment which need to be joined together by appropriate audio cables to allow the signal to pass between them. In a typical hi-fi 'stack' system independent components such as a cassette recorder, radio, record player and CD player are all connected to an amplifier, which in turn is connected to the loudspeakers.

PROFESSIONAL SOUND SYSTEM COMPONENTS

The sound system can be divided into five main types of equipment, which are connected together in a chain:

1 **Source units** – which generate and transmit sound in the form of a small electrical signal. e.g. microphones, cassette players, record decks, compact disc players, keyboards.
2 **Control equipment** – these modify and process the electrical signal. The **mixing desk** is the most important unit in the chain and enables a sound engineer to control and modify the sound in very sophisticated ways. Even simple mixers allow the tone and volume of a sound to be altered and separate sound sources to be mixed together.
   Other equipment such as signal processors also fall into this category. These are dedicated units which modify the sound in a specialist way, e.g. graphic equalisers, noise gates, compressors, digital delay and reverberation units.
   Pre-amplifiers – this is usually built into mixers and/or source equipment, such as a tape deck. Pre-amps amplify the signal to a standard level which can be accepted by a mixing desk and other audio equipment. This level is known as 'line level'.
3 **Recording equipment** – allows audio signals to be stored for future use (see below).
4 **Main amplifiers** – these magnify the processed or mixed signal to a level at which a loudspeaker will respond.
5 **Loudspeakers** – these translate the variations in the electrical signal from the amplifier back onto physical vibrations (movements of the loudspeaker diaphragm). This creates acoustic pressure waves in the air that we hear as sound.

Headphones can be thought of as miniature loudspeakers which allow us to hear the sound without the need for a main amplifier and loudspeakers. Headphones can be connected to most source units and all mixing desks are used to monitor the sound once it has reached line level.

Here is a simple diagram which shows how a

Figure 5.2   *Signal path through a simple sound system*

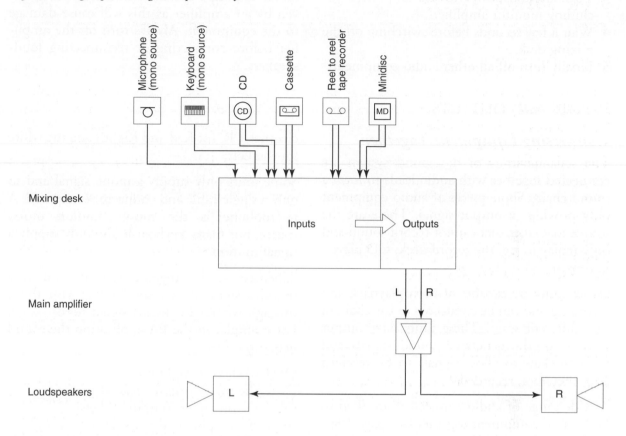

simple sound system might be set up for a live PA (public address) application.

As well as replaying sound, a sound system can also be used to capture (or record) the electrical signals for future use.

The most common form of audio recording uses magnetic tape, either in cassette format or on open reel. Increasingly, digital media such as MiniDiscs, recordable Compact Discs and computer disks are used to record and replay the audio information (see pages 180–183).

TURNING SOUND EQUIPMENT ON AND OFF

To avoid sending damaging electrical surges to the loudspeakers, the equipment in sound installations should always be turned on in this order:

1 all source equipment
2 mixing desk (with all faders down)
3 amplifiers.

When turning off the sound system at the end of a recording session or after a performance, the reverse pattern should be followed:

1 Ensure that all of the faders on the desk are down and channels are switched off.
2 Turn down the gain controls on the main amplifiers.

3 Turn off the power to the amplifiers, including monitor amplifiers.

4 Wait a few seconds before switching off the mixing desk.

5 Finally turn off all other audio equipment.

INPUTS AND OUTPUTS

Connecting Equipment Together

The separate units of the sound system are connected together with audio leads to form a sound chain. Some pieces of audio equipment only provide an output signal. These are the source machines that cannot record sound and only replay it, e.g. the record deck, CD player, keyboard, microphone.

Other units are capable of both playback and recording and can be connected to the chain in two different ways. These units have output sockets for the generated sound signals and input sockets to allow signals to be received and, therefore, recorded

A wide range of audio connectors are used to link sound equipment together (see page 196). Each type has a jack or series of pins and a socket with which it connects. These are described as male and female connectors for obvious reasons! So the phono jack plug (male) on a cable works with the phone socket (female) on the rear of a CD player for example.

Stereo, Left and Right

Where sound equipment produces a stereo sound signal there are two separate sockets for each input and output. These are for the two signals which make up the stereo sound. Therefore, a stereo lead with two connectors at each end (or two single 'mono' leads), is required to connect this equipment.

The output and inputs sockets should be marked clearly and identified as left or right. Usually, they are also coloured with the red connector always being used for the Right channel, ('R' for Red and Right!) and the white for the Left.

Some units only supply a mono signal and so only a single cable and connector is required. A microphone is the most common mono source, but many keyboards also only supply a signal in mono.

When connecting together separate units in a sound system, it is essential that you think through where the sound signal needs to go. For example, in the PA application the sound needs to travel:

OUT of the microphone
IN to the mixer (input sockets)
OUT of the mixer (output sockets)
IN to the amplifier (input sockets)
OUT of the amplifier (output sockets)
IN to each of the loudspeakers (input sockets).

To record music the sound needs to travel:

OUT of the keyboard (output sockets) and/or the microphone
IN to the mixer (input sockets)
OUT of the mixer (output sockets)
IN to the tape recorder (input sockets).

Note that, if we then wished to replay the recorded sound tape, we would have to link the *output* sockets of the tape deck to the *inputs* of the mixing desk, which would then be connected to an amplifier and loudspeaker, as in the PA example.

Systems and Symbols

Sound system components can be represented in diagrams by using schematic symbols.

Never unplug a speaker whilst it is being driven by an amplifier as this will cause damage to the equipment. Always turn off the amplifier before connecting or reconnecting loudspeakers.

Figure 5.3   *Sound system schematic symbols*

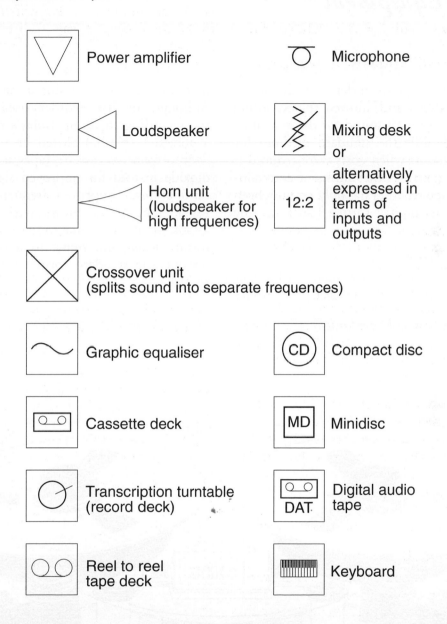

	Power amplifier		Microphone
	Loudspeaker		Mixing desk or
	Horn unit (loudspeaker for high frequences)	12:2	alternatively expressed in terms of inputs and outputs
	Crossover unit (splits sound into separate frequences)		
	Graphic equaliser	CD	Compact disc
	Cassette deck	MD	Minidisc
	Transcription turntable (record deck)	DAT	Digital audio tape
	Reel to reel tape deck		Keyboard

TASK

Study a range of audio equipment and establish where the input and output connections are to be found. Look at the following pictures to establish what type of connectors will be required in each case. Work out if the signal will be mono or stereo.

Sound Equipment

THE TAPE RECORDER

The magnetic tape recorder was developed during the 1930s and allowed the recording and precise editing of sound for the first time. It quickly became the standard medium for broadcasting, and when costs were reduced it began to be used in other forms of entertainment. The tape recorder has only recently been superseded by digital formats such as the MiniDisc.

Magnetic Tape

Analogue sound can be recorded onto a continuous medium which is coated in a surface that is capable of retaining a magnetic signal. Although the first recorders used iron wire as the recording medium, today's machines use a polyester (plastic) coated in an iron oxide. More expensive cassette tapes use chromium dioxide instead for improved signal to noise ratio and an improved frequency response. Metal tapes were introduced in the late 1980s for even greater improvements in distortion levels and signal to noise ratios and became the standard format for digital tape recordings.

Figure 5.4   *A reel-to-reel multi-track recorder*

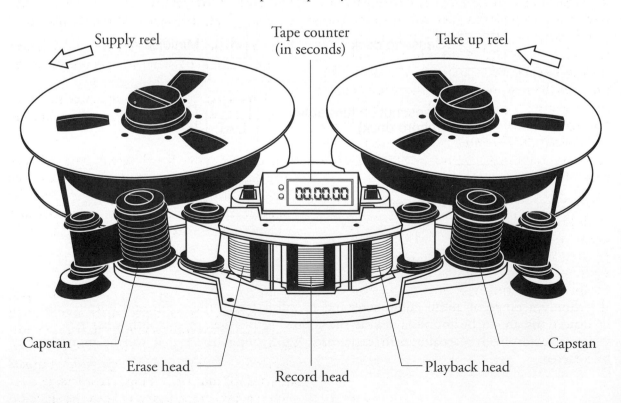

Tape transport system

A Guide to Tape Speeds for ¼ inch Reel-to-Reel Recorders.

Tape speed	Use
¹⁵⁄₁₆ i.p.s. 2.375 cm/s	Poor quality recording. Often used by radio stations to record the output, which they must do for legal reasons.
1⅞ i.p.s. 5.75 cm/s	Loss of high frequencies. Only really suitable for dictation purposes for future transcription. Although this speed is not suited to open reel recordings, it is the same speed which is used to transport domestic compact cassettes and digital audio tape which, with additional circuitry, are able to produce hi-fi and digital quality sound.
3¾ i.p.s. 9.5 cm/s	Useful for long background effects. Loss of high frequencies means this speed is inappropriate for music. Editing effects can be tricky.
7½ i.p.s. 19 cm/s	Hi-Fi recording possible. This is the standard tape speed for theatre playback. Gives a good frequency response and wide dynamic range. The amount of tape required for such a recording is not excessive, so it makes a good cost-effective compromise.
15 i.p.s. 38 cm/s	Excellent quality of recording, but seldom used for theatre replay due to the excessive amounts of tape required to run a show. Use is restricted to recording and mastering in professional recording studios, however, has been largely replaced by digital recording technology.
30 i.p.s. 76 cm/s	Used only in professional recording and mastering situations. Now largely replaced by digital recording technology.

i.p.s = inches per second

Bias, Recording and Playback

The recording head of a tape recorder is like an electromagnet which creates varying intensities of magnetism on the tape as it passes. In order to achieve high quality recordings, a high frequency **bias signal** is added to the tape. This provides the minimum force that is required to make the magnetic tape behave evenly. The bias signal is inaudible, since it has a frequency of between 30 kHz and 80 kHz and it is filtered out of the replay signal by dedicated **bias trap filters**.

The process of playback is the reverse of the recording method. The magnetised tape is drawn past the playback head at exactly the same speed as it was recorded. When the magnetic flux on the tape flows through the gap in the playback head, it induces a current and, therefore, an electrical signal. The pattern of voltages is then amplified by a playback amplifier and fed to the loudspeaker or headphone socket.

Tape Speed

The tape speed governs the frequency range and, therefore, the quality of the recording:

- The slower the recording speed, the longer the running time of the tape, but the worse the recording quality.
- The higher the speed, the better the quality of recording but the recording time becomes shorter.

The playing time for different types of tape varies according to the manufacturer and the thickness of the tape, as well as the size of the reel. Precise recording times for speeds and sizes of tape reels are usually given on the packaging of the tape box.

Tape Formats

Magnetic tape was first used on spools or open reels, commonly using 1 inch and 2 inch widths. As electronic circuitry has improved, the size of the tape required to record sound signals has reduced. Although wider formats are used for multi-track tape recorders, quarter inch magnetic tape has long been the standard format in the broadcast and entertainment industry to record stereo sources.

Professional machines now tend to use digital audio tape, but semi-professional analogue recorders are still available that allow 8 tracks to be recorded onto quarter inch tape and 16 tracks onto half inch tape. This type of machine is valuable to the theatre Sound Designer since it allows complex effects to be recorded and mixed down (see page 208).

Tape Track Configurations

1 **Full track recording** – the magnetic flux pattern produced by the record head covers virtually all of the surface of the tape.
2 **Half track** (mono) – the head covers less than half of the surface area and is off-set to allow for a second mono track to be recorded. The tape must be recorded in the opposite direction and the reels interchanged to allow this to happen.
3 **Half track stereo** – two recording heads are aligned so that each covers just less than half of the width of the tape. This allows for the left channel and the right channel of the stereo image to be recorded simultaneously. The tape is recorded in one direction only

and most recorders allow the two tracks to be recorded either simultaneously or separately. This is the format for most reel-to-reel recorders used in theatre sound.

4 **Quarter track stereo** – two record heads are aligned to record two tracks on the tape in one direction and another two tracks when the tape is reversed and recorded in the opposite direction. Stereo recordings can be made by using tracks 1 and 3 simultaneously in one direction and 2 and 4 in the other. Alternatively, four separate mono recordings can be made.
5 **Four track** – four record heads are positioned to allow four separate signals to be recorded across the full width of the tape in a single direction. This is the basis for professional multi-track recording and heads can be isolated to allow a single track, or two, three or all tracks to be recorded together at the same time.
6 **Eight track** – works in the same way as the four track, but eight heads are aligned across the width of the tape allowing eight signals to be recorded separately or in any combination.

The reel-to-reel tape recorder

Reel-to-Reel Tape

For many years, the reel-to-reel tape recorder was the standard replay machine in the theatre. It uses quarter inch tape and allows two-track high quality recording. Precise editing can be achieved through physically cutting and splicing the tape and the addition of coloured leader tape allows cues to be identified and played back precisely.

The standard tape speed for general theatre use is 7½ inches per second.

It would not be uncommon to find two (or more) reel-to-reel machines in a theatre control room. Although they may look like antiques,

Revox tape players are expensive, high quality audio equipment costing over £1000 each. In a theatre production capacity, they would usually be supported by two or more cassette machines or tape cartridge players (**carts**) to allow for a complex playback of several sound sources at the same time. Increasingly, reel-to-reel tape recorders are being replaced by recordable compact disc and relatively cheap MiniDisc equipment. These provide digital recordings at a fraction of the price of the analogue reel-to-reel tape recorder.

In spite of these developments, it is still useful to know how to record and edit on tape, and the ability to compile a show tape gives a valuable insight into making sound. Simple tricks with tape speed, splicing, loops and playing effects backwards can create sounds which would be difficult to make on more sophisticated electronic equipment.

Lacing a Tape

It is important to understand the tape head configuration of a tape recorder and how to lace a tape.

Compact Cassette Tape

The compact cassette is a ubiquitous sound reproduction format. However, for most performance use, where accurate cueing is required, cassettes are not acceptable. This is partly why reel-to-reel tape machines are still commonplace.

Introduced in the early 1960s, the compact cassette format has used a narrower (3 mm) track tape running at a slow speed (1.875 inches per second) and encased within a plastic housing that protects the tape and spools. The cassette allows for a stereo recording on each side of the tape, but the cassette must usually be taken out of the player and reversed. The miniature size is convenient and means that the size of the cassette recorder/player is also relatively small.

Always remove the plastic tab once you have completed recording. This prevents accidental over-recording of the tape. Future recordings can still be made by sticking sellotape back over the relevant hole.

Quality portable cassette recorders allow the Sound Designer to gather sound on location with comparative ease. This can be re-recorded (dubbed) onto an appropriate format for editing, processing and replay in performance.

Cassette tapes are regularly used in live performance situations, but because of cueing difficulties, are primarily reserved for the replay of pre-show and interval music. Because it is difficult to ensure that a particular sound will be reproduced right on cue, the cassette is reserved for cues which can be faded up gradually and for longer duration background sound effects such as birdsong.

Portastudios

Portastudios are multi-track cassette machines that were introduced in the late 1970s. To allow for good quality recording on four separate tracks they need to run at high speed (3.75 inches per second), work in a single direction only and use the full width of the cassette tape.

Tape Formats

Common cassette formats:

C5	2.5 minutes per side
C10	5 minutes per side
C30	15 minutes per side
C60	30 minutes per side
C90	45 minutes per side.

C120 allows 60 mins per side, but uses very thin tape to fit it within the plastic cassette housing. The tape is extremely flimsy and does not last well, often being caught within the transport mechanism of the player and consequently stretching or being chewed up. It is, therefore, not advisable to use this length of tape.

When using cassettes for recording or the replay of sound in performance, buy the best quality of tape that you can afford e.g. a chrome or metal tape from a well-known manufacturer.

TAPE CARTRIDGE OR NAB CART MACHINES

Originally developed for the domestic market to allow continuous playback of music, the cartridge system was adapted by the broadcast-

ing industry which used small cartridges containing a continuous loop of tape. The format was popular because of its small-size, noise-free instant start, and the possibility of accessing sound effects and music at random.

Many professional theatres adopted this system for the replay of sound effects, particularly where a show was destined for a long run or an extensive national tour. This system involves recording separate cues onto individual carts, which automatically cue themselves up after playback. It is also possible to record several cues onto the same cartridge with appropriate stop signals placed in between effects. The tape speed is usually 7.5 inches per second and a variety of tape lengths are available. Common sizes are 10, 20, and 40 seconds but longer versions up to 10 minutes are available.

This format was commonly used on radio for playback of adverts, jingles and radio news items because the machines are virtually silent when working and the tapes reset themselves automatically. The absence of audible clunks and other mechanical noises allowed theatre sound operators to work from the auditorium without annoying the audience. Also, the cart machine has the facility to create a truly endless loop, so that an effect of seawash, wind or birdsong can be recorded without a gap and played continually throughout a performance if desired!

Although still found in some radio news rooms, the cart has largely been superseded by digital equivalents, Sonifex systems which use floppy discs, and the development of specialist hard disk recording, editing and playback systems.

Head Cleaning and Demagnetising

To maintain a high quality of tape recording, it is important to clean and demagnetise the recorder tape heads and transport system on a regular basis. Cleaning should be undertaken prior to any important recording and at least once for every eight hours of use. Dirty tape heads cause loss of the magnetic signal and a reduction in the high frequency response.

Cleaning is carried out with a professional cleaning fluid such as isopropyl alcohol and cotton wool buds or equivalent. All parts which come into contact with the tape should be cleaned until any oxides are removed and discolouration is no longer seen.

Heads, capstan spindle and guide posts should also be demagnetised (or degaussed) once for approximately every 50 hours of use. This procedure requires a professional demagnetiser unit and instructions should be followed carefully. All pre-recorded tapes should be removed from the area before the device is used.

DIGITAL AUDIO TAPE RECORDER, DAT OR R-DAT

Open reel digital multi-track recorders are limited to professional recording and broadcast fields. Smaller, portable machines are available. These offer a cassette-based digital tape format which has been widely adopted for recording purposes. Replay can be unsatisfactory as there is a delay between pressing the play button and sound. In addition, many domestic machines do not allow the digital copying of CDs. Digital inputs may have been modified so that analogue inputs must be used for recording CDs, or a serial copy management system (SCMS) is built in.

However, professional DAT machines and controllers which link two or more DAT machines together do not have these problems. This allows for seamless digital audio edits, negating the need for the razor blade and splicing block. The desired sounds are edited and re-recorded digitally onto a master tape with no degradation of sound. Unlike editing with analogue tape, the proposed edits can be previewed, amended and rehearsed before the actual edit is performed.

Record player, turntable or transcription deck

Despite being apparently outdated technology, the record deck can produce good quality sound and is still an essential piece of equipment for the Sound Designer. However, as more vinyl recordings are transferred to CD, and vinyl discs deteriorate through use, the turntable will soon become obsolete.

There are three main parts of a record player:

1 The **turntable** (or platter) which is driven either directly by a motor or by a motor and a belt allowing the standard speeds of 33⅓ and 45 rpm. More sophisticated turntables will offer 78 rpm as well as the facility to vary the speed as necessary. Professional turntables allow for back-cueing which means that the platter can be rotated backwards by hand to line up the next track on the record. Instant starting and stopping also aids replay.
2 The **pickup arm** which is weighted so that it will track across the surface of the record, exerting an even pressure in the groove.
3 The **cartridge** which is located at the end of the arm and holds the **stylus**. As the stylus reads the information in the groove of the record, the small movements induce a current in magnets or coils in the cartridge. This signal is amplified, either internally or externally. Hi-fi record decks tend to have a pre-amplifier built-in, as well as a main amplifier to send the signal to the loudspeakers. Professional decks may require a separate pre-amplifier unit to boost the signal before it reaches the mixing desk.

If you are planning to use sound effects or music that is supplied on vinyl, it is essential that the recording is as clean as possible, and that the cartridge and pick-up arm are balanced correctly to give the correct tracking weight.

Compact disc

The digital compact disc or CD has become the standard modern format for pre-recorded music and the main storage medium for computer program data (CD-ROM). The CD has replaced the vinyl gramophone record, providing clear digital sound without the noise associated with analogue replay methods (clicks, hiss, scratches, etc.). Because of the quality of sound, CDs are excellent for playback of sound and music. However, direct playback in a live situation can prove difficult if the player does not allow you to access appropriate tracks easily or quickly. Professional models allow automatic cueing and incorporate features such as loops, section repeat, vari-speed and a manual search wheel. These are very useful facilities for the Sound Designer and Engineer.

The CD incorporates digital information in the form of a minute spiral of pits and bumps in an aluminium layer on one side of the disc only, beneath a transparent protective surface. A laser within the CD player is focused to read this information and, unlike the vinyl record, it ignores minor blemishes on the outer surface to maintain the original quality of the recording. Also, unlike the gramophone record, the data spiral begins at the centre of the disc and runs to the outer rim, allowing for up to 80 minutes of sound to be accommodated. The disc rotates at different speeds between 200 and 500 rpm according to which part of the disc is being read. The slower speed is used at the outermost part of the disc.

The digital information within the disc also incorporates a subcode to ensure that the player maintains the correct speed, error correction data and other information such as track times, locations, index points, total running time and a table of contents which is read immediately by the player as soon as the CD is inserted.

Recordable CDs

CD-R or recordable CDs are becoming cheaper and many productions now use this technology and format instead of tape. The mastering process can be aided by a computer with appropriate hardware and software applications, but can also be achieved with a CD-R recorder linked to any sound output.

Although the CD-R may be a good choice for the *replay* of sound in performance, once a CD has been recorded, it cannot be changed. So, effects cues cannot be added, removed or re-sequenced without recording an entirely new CD. The playback of a CD in performance requires an industrial CD player which can access tracks and index points instantly. Domestic and hi-fi CD players may be fine for rehearsals, but usually prove unsuitable for

cueing sound in performance. Delays in selecting individual tracks may be mitigated by the use of the pause button, but generally this is unsatisfactory.

Other variants of the CD format are:

CD-E	a recordable and erasable format
CD-I	used for interactive multimedia and games
CD-ROM	standard format for the storage of computer data and distribution of software. Up to 600 MB of information can be stored on a single disc, nearly 300 times the amount that can be squeezed onto a high density 3.5 inch floppy disc.
DVD	Digital Versatile Disks can hold 8 GB (Giga bytes) of data equivalent to over 1,000 minutes of audio.

MINIDISC

The newest technology from Sony is fast gaining popularity. It provides quality and flexibility of use at a relatively low cost. MiniDisc is like a miniature, recordable CD, but with greater versatility, since it is possible to edit and record tracks easily. This seems to be the immediate future for sound recording and re-

production. One drawback is the small size of the portable (walkman-type) units which can be a little awkward to operate. Professional playback decks are available however, and MiniDisc is quickly establishing itself as a preferred format for replay in performance.

HARD DISK (DIGITAL) RECORDING

Increasingly computer-based systems are being used to sample, record and mix sounds. This relies on the capability of the hardware (the computer, its memory capability and storage mechanism) and the software (the computer programme that allow the recording and manipulation of sounds). Some computers such as the Apple Macintosh are manufactured to work easily with sound and multi-media programmes. PCs need additional sound cards to be fitted. Examples of common sound software

packages used for composition and recording include;

- Steinberg's Cubase VST which combines MIDI (see page 210) and audio recording techniques in a virtual studio with multiple tracks of CD quality digital audio. It also allows sophisticated alterations to sound, mixing and effects. Cubase Score will even write the music score for you to print it out if desired.

- MOTU Digital Performer is a powerful MIDI sequencer package designed for the music professional, allowing recording, playback and editing, with numerous audio effects.

- Logic Audio Pro-Tools is a sophisticated multi-track digital audio production system.

MICROPHONES

As we have seen, a microphone is a device for converting acoustic power, in the form of sound waves, into electrical power, which has similar wave characteristics. A microphone enables 'live' sound to be converted into electrical energy which can then be handled by the sound system. It works in a similar way to the human ear, with a diaphragm that responds to vibrating air in the same way as the eardrum does. The movement of the diaphragm is converted into electrical pulses which mirror the changes in air pressure caused by the original sound.

The **transducer** is the device that carries out this physical to electrical signal conversion. The way it works depends on the type of microphone.

Unlike most of the other sound sources described above, which supply signals at the line level, most microphones are fed through a pre-amplifier to boost the signal strength to a level that the mixing desk can use. Therefore, they have separate input sockets on the mixer which divert the signal through a pre-amplifier before it reaches the main input channel controls.

Figure 5.5 *A condenser microphone and its pick-up pattern*

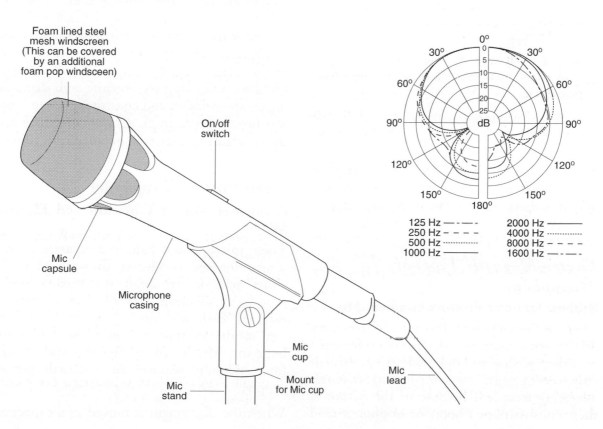

A microphone consists of a **capsule**, which holds the **diaphragm**, and various electrical coils and magnets, depending upon the precise workings of the unit. These are protected by a metal **grille** or **screen**. This may be filled with foam to reduce (attenuate) wind noise and popping or 'p-blasting' from the performer's mouth. Additional pop screens may also be introduced over the metal screen to give added protection from unwanted noise.

Microphones vary in size and the body may be used to conceal batteries, a mount switch or additional electronic circuitry, such as transistors and pre-amplifiers.

Microphones can be classified in three ways:

1 **generically**, in terms of the way in which they are used. For example, radio mic, gun mic, boom mic, float mic, etc.
2 the way in which they are **constructed** and, therefore, how they work mechanically. For example, dynamie condenser, ribbon, moving coil, etc.
3 by their **directivity** or pick-up characteristics. For example, cardioid, omni-directional, etc.

Not all microphones pick up sound in the same way. Some collect sound from all directions equally, whilst others will favour one or more directions. These characteristics depend on how each microphone is manufactured and how it is designed to work. It is important to select the correct microphone for use in a given situation.

Electro-Magnetic Types of Microphone
Ribbon Mmic or Pressure Gradient Mic

These are usually very delicate and expensive instruments, used extensively in professional recording studios and in broadcasting, particularly where acoustic instruments and orchestras are being recorded. Because of the nature of their construction, ribbon microphones tend to be larger than other types of microphones. They are constructed with a thin metal ribbon which is fixed between the poles of a magnet. Pressure waves move the ribbon within the magnetic field, generating a small electrical signal.

Due to the way in which the ribbon mic is manufactured and operates, it is **'bi-directional** and has a characteristic **'figure of eight'** pick-up pattern, making it very sensitive at the front and back, but relatively 'dead' at the sides. It does not require a power supply.

Dynamic Mic or Moving Coil Mic

The dynamic mic is widely used in the audio industry, since it is robust and does not transmit noise when hand-held. It is particularly good for vocals and is often used to pick up bass drums. Like the ribbon mic, it does not require a power supply to generate a signal, but the signal that is produced is small and needs amplification at the mixing desk. The diaphragm is attached to a moving coil which is housed within a magnet. The movement of the diaphragm causes the coil to move in relation to the magnet, which creates a small current. Dynamic mics are very versatile and, depending on their design and construction, can have any form of directivity. Commonly, they are either **omni-directional** or **cardioid** (directional).

Electrostatic Microphones
Condenser Mic or Capacitor and Electret Mic

These microphones require a separate power source for the condenser to work. This is either provided through the mixing desks (known as 'phantom power') or by a separate external, dedicated power supply. The electret condenser type has an internal battery, built into the handle of the mic and, therefore, doesn't require an external power supply.

When the diaphragm is moved in a capacitor

microphone, varying, voltages are created between the diaphragm and a counter electrode. These are proportional to the acoustic signal. Electronic circuitry alters and balances the signal and, in many types, also amplifies the signal, so that it is supplied to a mixer at line level and is less prone to interference. The condenser or capacitor is a common form of microphone which can be manufactured to have virtually any pick-up pattern. They have a high sensitivity, a wide frequency response and excellent noise performance. The best condenser mics offer the highest quality of recording, but are expensive and require gentle handling. Cheaper electret mics are built into small portable cassette recorders and more sophisticated versions are used for miniature tie-clip type radio mics.

Other Types of Microphone

Carbon (Contact Resistance) Mic

These are cheap and very robust, but poor quality. They are not directional and have a limited frequency range. Therefore, they are not suited to professional work. This type of microphone works by the diaphragm literally squeezing carbon granules to create an electrical resistance. An internal battery or low voltage mains supply is required.

Crystal or Piezo-electric Mic

These are very similar in construction and characteristics to the carbon mic, except piezo-electric crystals are used instead of carbon. They can be manufactured cheaply and in small sizes, so they are appropriate for use as inbuilt mics on domestic audio equipment, telephone handsets, etc. They are not directional and have a limited frequency range. This type requires an internal battery or low voltage mains supply. They are rarely used for professional audio work.

Pick-up Patterns

The variety of available directional patterns means that particular types of microphone can be selected for specific applications. Manufacturers supply **polar diagrams** which indicate the directivity of each model of mic, usually at a variety of frequencies.

The polar diagram is a two dimensional map with the microphone's diaphragm positioned at the centre. Contour lines show the directivity of the microphone at different angles with 0 degrees to the front and the 180 degrees, the rear (see Figure 5.5 on p. 183).

Microphone type	Advantages	Disadvantages
Cardioid	High gain before feedback and, therefore, good in live PA work where speakers are involved. Good compromise for general purpose work.	Doesn't pick up well from a distance (proximity effect). Output is lower than other types of mic.
Omni-directional	More natural sound, immunity to handling noise and proximity effect. Useful for conferences and whole stage pick-up.	Not selective and, therefore, limited number of uses.
Bi-directional/Figure-of-Eight ∞	Good quality and very sensitive. Useful where two people need to share a microphone. Excellent for miking most classical acoustic instruments.	Subject to the proximity effect, not very robust, prone to wind noise and, therefore, useless outdoors. Expensive.
Hyper-Cardioid	Very directional, picks up sound at a distance.	Large size, limited pick-up from sides.

TASK

Which type of microphone pick-up characteristics would usually be best in the following situations?

1 To help prevent feedback in a live PA application, e.g. for a lead vocalist.
2 To record the general atmosphere in a school playground.
3 To mic separate elements of a drum kit, keeping each adjacent sound separate.
4 To pick up the singing of a small group of performers on a stage that is full of chorus members.
5 As a show relay microphone.
6 As a microphone for a stand-up comedian.
7 To record a solo violin in a studio environment.
8 To record a herd of elephants.
9 To record all of the conversation at a large meeting.
10 As a trail microphone for a compere of a cabaret performance.
11 To pick up the tap dancing of the lead performer at the front of a stage.
12 As a miniature lapel or tie-clip microphone.
13 To record two voices in a radio play.
14 In news gathering applications, where a speaker needs to be isolated from the surrounding atmosphere.

Answers on p. 224

SPECIALIST MICS

Stereo Mics

Stereo mics use two microphones within a single unit, which can be set to offer a combination of pick-up patterns, e.g. cardioid and figure of eight. This produces a stereo signal.

Two conventional microphones can be mounted (crossed) at 90 degrees to each other to produce a stereo signal. This is called a stereopair.

Ultra-directional Mic, Gun Mic or Rifle Mic

The 'shot-gun' mic is used if the microphone has to be positioned at a distance from the sound source, e.g. over the stage. This type has a very narrow response, since the mic capsule is mounted at the end of a long tube, which has holes along it and built-in acoustic delays. It is very useful for isolating individual areas of the stage and, for this reason, can also be found rigged downstage, along the front of the stage.

A single overhead rifle mic might be used in conjunction with a reverberation unit to create an echo effect as performers move to an area of the stage which must suddenly become a cave.

Parabolic Mic

This is an ultra-directional mic which uses a dish similar to a satellite receiving dish to focus sound waves from a distant point. This type of mic is commonly used in the broadcasting of sports events such as cricket where the microphones cannot be positioned close to the source of the sound. They are also useful in pinpointing birdsong and other animal noises in the wild, since they can be 'focused' to pick up sound only from a specific point in the distance.

Boundary Effect or Pressure Zone Mic (PZM)

Often used in conferences and on the downstage floor of a stage where they are not visible to an audience. They will only work when placed against a flat area (boundary) such as a floor, wall or table that is at least a metre square. They can be described as an omni-directional mic, with half of the sphere cut off at the boundary.

Contact Mics

Contact mics attach to musical instruments and are specifically manufactured to suit the characteristics of the instrument they are designed to be used with. Usually of the moving coil or piezo-electric type, they convert the physical vibrations of the instrument or its strings into an electrical signal that can be handled by a mixing desk. This microphone technique does not reflect the true sound of the instrument without considerable equalisation of the frequency response. Common contact mics include the guitar 'pick-up' and those known as C-Tape. These attach with flexible adhesive plastic tape to most musical instruments, from a drum to a flute.

Radio Mics

These are increasingly used in performance work as their quality improves and costs reduce. They solve the need for the conventional trailing microphone cable, which can appear unsightly, and which creates restrictions for performers on stage. They can be lavalier type (suspended around the neck), attached to clothing or the head, or hand-held in the conventional manner. Radio mics provide enormous freedom for performers and have become an essential requirement of most large scale musical productions, allowing the performer to be heard easily above the band. The miniature capsule type of radio mic requires the performer to wear a belt-pack which contains the transmitter, aerial and batteries to power it. The hand-held version uses a conventional microphone with a transmitter and aerial built into the handle. Each radio mic transmits on a specific frequency. An aerial and a receiver are positioned elsewhere in the auditorium to receive each frequency and to supply the resulting signals to the mixing desk. Batteries on radio mics have to be replaced frequently and this can be expensive.

PROXIMITY EFFECT

Cardioid and ribbon microphones, which are pressure gradient types, produce a characteristic known as the **proximity** effect when the sound source is located very close to the microphone. This results in a boosting of the low (bass) frequencies and occurs due to the construction of these microphones. The path lengths of the sound waves reaching each side of the diaphragm are slightly different and this effect is exaggerated at close distances (e.g. under 5 cms). The proximity effect is used to advantage by many vocalists to give a richer sound.

MICROPHONE RECORDING TECHNIQUE

Tips to Avoid Feedback

1 Keep the number of microphones used to the minimum number required. Fewer mics at a higher gain may be less susceptible to feedback than more microphones at a lower gain level.
2 Place the microphones carefully in relation to the loudspeakers. Keep sources on-axis.
3 Position microphones as close to the source as possible. This requires less gain at the mixer.
4 Turn down microphones when they are not in use.

Selecting the Right Microphone

To select the right microphone it is important to consider the type of sound source, the type of recording required and the directionality of the proposed microphone.

Using the Right Microphone Correctly

Vocals – for studio recording, position the mic in front of the nose, pointed downwards into the mouth. Use of a pop screen between the mouth and the microphone will reduce 'popping' sounds from the performer's mouth. Thin tights (e.g. 15 denier) stretched on a wire frame make a cheap and effective pop screen!

Stage use will require a stand which places the microphone slightly in front and below the mouth. If the microphone is to be handled, a dynamic mic will reduce unwanted noise. Omni-directional microphones can be used by a singer since they can be placed further away from the mouth and do not pick up breathing noise.

Piano – use a PZM inside the middle of the lid or at least two separate microphones; one to cover the high notes and another for the bottom end.

Acoustic guitar – point a microphone directly at the hole in the sound box or use a pick-up mic.

Synthesiser – these are not miked. They are connected direct or use a direct injection box (see p. 192).

Electric guitar – Direct injection box (see p. 192).

Drums – specialist mics should be used for the kick drum. A mic placed above the snares and high hat cymbals may be sufficient to pick up both instruments. Ideally, each element of the drum kit should be miked separately. Often this will not be possible. If only a single mic is available, place it away from the kick drum and closer to the higher drums and cymbals. In addition two microphones are positioned above the kit to pick up an overall balanced sound.

THE MIXING DESK

The mixer is the heart of any sound system and facilitates precise control of individual sound sources. Even relatively simple mixing desks can handle a number of different sound inputs and mix the signals together as a single blended output.

The mixing desk is used in two main ways for performance:

1 To prepare recordings for later use by routing signals from a variety of sources so that they can be modified and then recorded on appropriate equipment.
2 To mix and replay sound in performance, so that the correct levels are reproduced and the sound is distributed correctly around the auditorium.

A mixing desk has two main sections; the input channels and the output section.

Input Channels

Mixers are specified according to the number of inputs and outputs that they have. A simple mixing desk might have twelve input channels and two outputs and this is described as a 12 into 2 mixer and is indicated as 12 × 2, 12/2 or 12:2. The input channels accept a single mono signal and allow a variety of source equipment to be connected to the desk.

Microphones plug in to a single input channel via a three pin socket at the back of the mixer. Stereo sources, such as a cassette deck or a CD player require two adjacent input channels and connect to the line input socket at the back of

Figure 5.6 *A simple mixing desk with mono and stereo input channels and two output channels*

the mixer, using either phono or jack connectors as appropriate. Two channels are required for all pieces of equipment that supply a stereo signal; one input channel for the left signal and one channel for the right signal of the stereo image. Therefore a 12:2 mixing desk will allow up to six stereo source units to be connected at any one time. If microphones are also to be used, this will reduce the number of input channels available.

Output Section

The output section controls the volume of the sound leaving the mixing desk and where the sound is to be routed to. In playback, this determines the volume of the final mixed signal which is to be sent to the amplifiers and to the loudspeakers in the auditorium.

Sub-master or Group Outputs

Larger and more complex mixing desks are common, both for recording purposes and for playback in theatre venues. Most professional mixers also have a separate output section known as the sub-masters. A typical configuration might be 24:8:2. This mixer has 24 input channels, 8 sub-masters and two master outputs. Incoming signals may be routed to the sub-masters and/or the master faders. In a recording environment, the eight sub-masters might be linked directly to the inputs of an 8 track tape recorder, allowing the 24 incoming signals to be divided down or grouped to one or more of the eight tracks. In a performance context, the sub-masters may well be used to distribute the sound to different banks of loudspeakers. This allows particular cues to be routed to individual speakers if required, and also for levels to be balanced between different speaker clusters in the auditorium.

The Input Channel Controls

Inputs

There is usually a button to select either the line or the microphone input socket.

Gain

This control allows the operator to alter the strength of the incoming signal to the mixer. For microphones this control may need to be turned up, whilst line level sources will require a lower gain. A careful note of the level of the gain setting is essential when plotting sound levels as this will affect the final volume of the sound. Often there is a 'PAD' switch associated with the input gain. This reduces the level of the incoming signal by a set amount.

Phantom Power Switch

Some microphones require an external power source before they will work. This switch enables the mixing desk to supply power to selected microphones down the connecting cable.

EQ

This section of the input channel allows the incoming signal to be modified in tone. Basic mixers may have a 3 band EQ section allowing high (HF), mid (MF), and low frequencies (LF) to be altered separately. A 4 band EQ usually splits the mid frequencies into high-mid frequency (HMF) and low-mid frequency (LMF) bands. More sophisticated equalisation sections may be 5 or 6 band. Parametric equalisation allows individual frequencies to be selected and either boosted or cut.

Greater sophistication of equalisation is possible using an external graphic equaliser or dedicated computer software. Sound sources can be routed to these external units via Auxiliary send and return controls on the mixer (see below).

TASK

Experiment with the equalisation section on the mixer. How can you alter the incoming sound? Establish exactly how the EQ works. Are there simply HF, MF, LF controls, or is it more complex? Can you isolate individual frequencies and cut or boost them? Compare your equalised signal with the original 'flat' input signal.

Panning

The 'pan pot' control (or panoramic potentiometer) is a dial that positions the signal in the stereo spectrum. If the dial is turned entirely to the left it will route the signal only to the left master output and, therefore, only to the left loudspeaker(s). Conversely, panning the signal to the right will ensure that the sound is only heard on the right loudspeaker(s). A centre position ensures an equal mix of the signal to both outputs and is in effect a mono sound. Microphones are often panned to the centre, whilst stereo inputs, e.g. from a CD player, require one input channel to be routed to the left and the second channel to be routed to the right, if the stereo signal is to be preserved. There may be situations where it is impractical to provide stereo playback in the performance situation and input channels may be deliberately panned to mono to achieve a uniform output.

This control is also important in the recording

environment and the sound engineer may wish to position a particular sound so that it appears to come from a particular direction. A recording of an orchestra, for example, might attempt to position the instruments according to their perceived location on a stage, i.e. violins to the left, woodwind in the middle, brass slightly to the right, etc.

The pan pot control is also useful for making a sound appear to move across the stage. This can be achieved at the recording stage, or may be created live with the operator physically moving the relevant pan pots before or during the cue. Depending upon how the loudspeakers have been arranged, it is possible to route the signal to a single speaker to give the impression that a dog is barking off stage left for example. Moving the pan pots during the cue allows effects such as trains, aircraft, etc. to be heard to move across the stage or auditorium.

Fader

The input channel line fader sets the level or volume of sound that is to be sent to the sub-masters and master sections of the mixer. The fader is usually calibrated in decibels and may need to be marked more precisely for performance work. On more complex mixing desks, the line fader works alongside the pan control and routing buttons to determine exactly where the signal is passed to next. The signal can be sent independently to any sub-master or master outputs or to combinations of outputs as appropriate.

PFL

Pre-fade Listen (PFL) is usually in the form of a button which, when depressed, allows the operator to listen to the channel on head-phones or on monitor speakers without the need for the fader to be up. This is useful in performance situations, since microphones can be checked without the signal passing to the loudspeakers and the audience hearing the sound. Similarly, tapes and CDs can be checked and cued prior to replay.

Solo

This works in a similar way to PFL, but on some mixers may not work with the fader down. Instead it allows a single channel to be isolated and monitored on headphones or on control room monitor speakers. Again this is useful in the performance situation to detect problems with a single microphone in a large musical for example.

Foldback

This is a way of sending a specially mixed signal back to the performers on stage. A sophisticated blended mix can be fed or 'folded back' to performers with these controls to allow them to hear the sound on headphones, ear-pieces or monitor speakers via a dedicated amplifier. In musical theatre, foldback is often used to send voices of the performers to musicians in the pit, whilst also ensuring that music from the band is separately folded back to the performers on the stage.

During a soundcheck, individual singers or musicians on stage may complain that they are unable to hear themselves. Using foldback subtly will solve this problem and give the performers more confidence.

However, when using foldback via monitor speakers, the sound operator must be careful to avoid feedback, and loudspeakers should be placed with care to avoid pick-up from the microphones. Foldback is often achieved by using an auxiliary control on the mixer, which might be labelled as 'Foldback' or simply intended for use as a Foldback control.

Auxiliaries

These controls allow for greater flexibility in the use of the mixing desk. Auxiliaries can be set up in a number of different ways to send signals to external equipment, such as reverberation units. Some auxiliaries may be designed to route the signal before the EQ section or before the line fader affects the level of the sound. This is known as a pre-fade Aux.

Other auxiliaries may be designed to work only post-fade. On more sophisticated mixing desks, each auxiliary may be independently switched to work either pre-fade (for foldback) or post-fade (for effects).

Auxiliaries are identified as Aux Send, if they are routing the signal to other units, and Aux Returns, which control the level of the signal returning to the mixing desk.

TASK

Try to insert effects using the Auxiliary controls. What is the difference between a pre and post send and return?

TASK

Draw the input channel to a mixer that you are familiar with. Alternatively obtain a technical drawing from a manual. Make sure that you include all of the input sockets, buttons and controls. Label each control and establish what it is used for.

The Mixer Output and Submaster Controls

The output section of the mixer allows the mixed sound to be distributed to a number of different places at the same time. The master faders control the main output of the desk, which is sent to the main PA in the perform-ance situation or to the recorder in a studio set-up. Most mixers allow the main output to be routed to two or more locations at the same time, so that a show can be recorded as well as being replayed to an audience, for example.

Submasters or 'groups' can be used in per-formance to route sound to different sets of amplifiers and loudspeakers, allowing subtle effects to be created off-stage and volume levels to be balanced around the auditorium.

In the studio environment, submasters are used to assign input channels to specific tracks on a multi-track recorder. Submasters are also used to mix down multi-track recordings to create a master recording.

The Direct Injection (D.I.) Box

This unit is used frequently in stage work since it allows electronic keyboards, electric guitars and other musical instruments to be connected to the mixing desk. It accepts signals that may be at a pre-amplified level or of a high impedance and then provides a balanced output at line level (150 ohms) for a mixer or recording equipment. Many units also incorporate a 'ground lift' switch which disconnects the ground signal be-tween the unbalanced input and the bal-anced output to help prevent 'earth buzz'.

Signal Processors

There are a wide variety of units which enable the Sound Designer to modify audio signals in specific and often sophisticated ways. These dedicated units are introduced into the sound chain either before the signal enters the mixer, or, more often, at the control stage when the signal is routed from the mixer via an auxiliary send. It is useful to be able to switch between the original 'dry' signal and the processed 'wet' one, to compare them.

Common types of outboard processor units

used in recording and live PA applications are described below.

- Mic pre-amp – enhances the quality of signal from professional microphones in a studio environment Some units may incorporate a de-esser to provide increased clarity from vocal mics.
- Compressor – ensures that all sounds are between the noise and distortion limits of equipment or sound medium. A compressor levels out extreme peaks and troughs in the dynamic of a sound, working above a set threshold to gradually reduce the upper volume range of the audio signal in proportion. If used carefully, a compressor can squeeze the overall dynamics of a sound to prevent distortion without the effect of being noticed. In performance, a compressor might be used to reduce the overall dynamic range of a sound effect like seawash. Waves breaking on the shore may be audible but the backwash involves a considerable drop in level which can be inaudible due to the level of ambient noise in the auditorium. To avoid constant alteration of levels, a compressor can be set to automatically reduce the higher levels of the effect. Compression is particularly helpful when replaying gunshots, explosions and sounds replayed from digital sources.
- Expander – operates like a compressor in reverse, to give more precise control of the dynamics of a sound.
- Compressor/Limiter – reduces the overall volume range, but also limits the signal to prevent overloading equipment by holding unexpected high peaks at a set level. It will also boost low level signals to a usable working range of the sound system, but will also increase associated background noise.
- De-esser – reduces sibilance. Useful in the studio environment when recording vocals.
- Equaliser or EQ unit – allows tonal adjustment of sound by boosting or cutting specific audio frequencies. Careful use of equalisation can achieve realistic effects such as radios, a telephone conversation, intercoms, etc.

Digital Delay and Reverberation Units

These units are an essential tool of the Sound Designer, since they allow virtually any acoustic environment to be created. The shorter the reverberation time, for example, the smaller the perceived space. Most units are supplied with a multitude of pre-programmed settings which are accessed by a menu, e.g. cave, church, cathedral, concert hall, etc. Subtle reverberation is frequently added to many vocalists to give them added presence in performance. Slap or repeat echo can be added to live sound such as stage fights and battle scenes to enhance the confusion and chaos on stage. Digital reverb units offer effects such as multiple repeats with slightly delayed timing and pitch changes (flange effect and phasing). This has the effect of 'thickening' the sound.

Noise Reduction Units

These units use a variety of techniques to minimise distortion and reduce the background sound on a recording by filtering it. The resulting effect is an improvement in high frequency signal-to-noise ratio.

AMPLIFIERS

An amplifier is an electrical circuit which transforms small voltages and currents (line level), into much larger ones that are sufficient to power a loudspeaker.

Amplifiers are classified in terms of watts, either in terms of peak power or RMS (power expressed as Root Mean Square). However, manufacturers' figures can be misleading, since the output volume is determined by the *resistance* of the loudspeakers (measured in ohms) and the *power rating* of the amplifier. The lower the resistance of a speaker, the greater the power of the amplifier and the higher the quality of sound reproduction.

Most power amplifiers are capable of supplying speakers at 4-ohm, 8-ohm or 16-ohm loads and most produce an output of two channels, a left and a right. In a simple stage set-up, this may equate to a stereo replay with one signal being sent to a speaker on the left of the stage and one to the right. However, there are several different ways in which an amplifier can be connected to loudspeakers. The number of speakers connected to a single amplifier will depend upon the ohm rating of the system (see below). Ideally, each loudspeaker should have its own amplifier. However, the additional costs of this type of system may be prohibitive, and for most non-music performance events, is unnecessary.

The rear panel on the amplifier provides both input sockets to receive the output signal from the mixing desk and usually a variety of outputs. Outputs may be provided on posts, requiring bare wire termination, similar to a hi-fi system, but larger power amplifiers tend to use locking connectors.

Power amplifiers get hot when they are working and require good ventilation. Many amps have a fan built into the unit. Care should be taken when switching these units on and off.

To turn on an amplifier:

1 Ensure that all source equipment is switched on.
2 Turn mixing desk on, ensuring that all faders are down.
3 Check amplifier volume controls are set to zero.
4 Turn on power to the amplifier rack and check that the fans are working.
5 Turn on individual amplifier power switch and set volume controls.
6 Bring up faders on the mixing desk.

To turn off an amplifier:

1 Bring down all faders on the mixing desk.
2 Turn the amplifier volume control to zero.
3 Switch individual amplifiers off.
4 Turn off all power to amplifier racks and fans.
5 Wait until amplifier lights go out before switching off mixer and other audio equipment.

LOUDSPEAKERS

A loudspeaker works in the opposite way to a microphone. Whereas a microphone converts sound waves to electrical signals, a speaker converts the electrical energy back into audible sound waves.

In a sound system, these electrical signals have been processed by the mixing desk and magnified by the power amplifiers to a level which is sufficient to drive the loudspeaker cones.

There are three main parts inside a typical loudspeaker:

1 magnet
2 cone or driver
3 cabinet or baffle.

The quality of the loudspeaker housing is also important. Baffles are required to assist in directing the sound and to prevent low frequencies from re-entering the loudspeaker at the rear of the cabinet. The housing or cabinets are made from heavily absorbent materials and include air vents which serve to equalise the air pressure and prevent vibrations which would give unwanted resonance to the sound.

Loudspeakers, like microphones, are designed to respond in specific ways. A speaker with a single cone (similar to a typical car stereo speaker), cannot be expected to respond accurately to a wide range of sounds. Many loudspeakers incorporate two or more cones of differing diameters within a single cabinet. Typical hi-fi speakers work in this way with small 'tweeters' and larger 'woofers', placed together in the same cabinet. These are designed to respond to high frequency sound and low frequency sound respectively.

TASK

Examine a hi-fi loudspeaker. Study how the audio signal is connected to the cabinet. Remove the front screen and identify the size and type of speaker cones.

Some professional loudspeaker units, like hi-fi speakers are manufactured to provide a good response to all frequencies. These, therefore, incorporate a variety of cones within the speaker cabinet. Other loudspeaker units are designed to respond to specific frequencies. Horn units are used for high frequency sound reproduction, whilst larger bass bins are dedicated low frequency units.

The Bose 802 loudspeaker is a popular 'general purpose' loudspeaker designed specifically for the theatre and entertainment market. Whilst loudspeakers such as the Bose 802 are sufficient to provide the main sound for smaller theatre spaces, larger venues require more powerful systems with dedicated loudspeakers for separate frequencies.

More sophisticated sound re-inforcement involves splitting the audio signal into separate frequency bands and feeding these signals to separate loudspeaker units designed to respond to high frequency, mid frequency and low frequency sounds. In permanent sound installations these speaker units are often built into the building, around a proscenium arch for example. This is known as a **line source column**.

In rock concerts and other events where a temporary sound rig is required, a range of loudspeaker units are built on top of each other in a 'stack'.

Crossover Units

The crossover unit is required to split the audio signal so that the appropriate frequencies are sent to the relevant speaker cones. Some crossovers are built into the loudspeaker cabinet, but in professional sound PA installations, the crossovers are separate external units.

Crossovers can either be passive (set at a fixed frequency) or active (able to be set to respond at a variety of alternative frequencies).

Biamplification

This is a process whereby the crossover splits up the frequencies before the signal is amplified. This process gives a better quality sound with less distortion. However, it is more expensive since it requires a separate amplifier for each individual loudspeaker unit.

MATCHING AMPLIFIERS TO LOUDSPEAKERS

Difficulties may occur when trying to connect loudspeakers to amplifiers, since speakers may have an impedance of between 2 and 30 ohms, whilst, as we have already established, amplifiers supply signals at 4, 8, or 16 ohms.

Manufacturers' data will help to establish the optimum performance levels for combinations of amplifiers and speakers.

An 8 ohm amplifier could supply two 4 ohm loudspeakers, if they were wired in series. Although there would be a slight loss of quality, the speakers would match the amplifier's output.

A better way of connecting more than one speaker to a single amplifier is to wire the speakers in parallel. In this scenario, two 16 ohm speakers would need to be used to match the 8 ohm output of the amplifier.

Incompatible equipment causes problems.

Amplifiers can usually accept a loading from half to double the one specified, but the output performance will be affected. Always consult the manufacturer's guidelines and recommendations.

HIGH VOLTAGE SYSTEMS

Paging and show relay systems use a 100 volt line system to solve the problem of feeding large numbers of speakers from a single amplifier over relatively long distances. The high voltage system negates the difficulties associated with long cable runs and also allows different types and sizes of speakers to be used in an installation.

Special amplifiers 'step up' the voltage from 10 volts to 100 volts before sending the signal to the loudspeakers. Transformers built into each speaker in the system then 'step down' the voltage from 100 volts to 10 volts. The high

Fault Tracing

To determine whether a loudspeaker or the amplifier is faulty follow these steps:

1 Turn down the amplifier volume controls before connecting and re-connecting the speakers.
2 Unplug a speaker and test the cable by plugging it to an amplifier that you know to be working. If it works, the problem must be with the original amplifier, the cable or connectors.
3 If the speaker is damaged, it may be because the amplifier has 'gone DC', producing a direct current.
4 Check the amplifier fuses and replace them if they are blown. It is important *not* to re-connect the speaker. Instead, use a volt meter to test the output. A reading of over 0.5V DC means that the amp needs urgent repair and will destroy any speakers connected to it.

voltage system works because stepping up the voltage ten times actually increases the impedance by 100 times, and so makes the cable resistance far less important.

Show relay systems in venues use the 100 volt line system to allow a variety of speaker types to be connected to the same source. A transformer is required for each speaker, but this allows small (e.g. 10 W) speakers to be used in toilets and dressing rooms whilst larger 20 W speakers can be used with appropriate transformers in a noisier room.

Cables and Connectors

A variety of connector types are used to join sound equipment together. Some connectors simply push in to connect, others can lock

in place for added security and durability. These are released by pressing on a small lever.

Examples of connectors

- Most source units use phono connectors.
- Most microphones use 3 pin XLR connectors.
- Quarter inch jacks are used extensively to connect items of sound equipment. Headphones and electric guitars use stereo jacks of this nature.
- Miniature variations of the jack (e.g. 3.5 mm plug) are found on small professional and domestic equipment such as portable MiniDisc and personal stereos.

- Loudspeakers use a variety of types of connectors. some connect simply with bare ends of wire to binding posts. Others require small banana plugs or quarter-inch two-pole jack plugs, but locking connectors such as the XLR type or Speakon locking connectors are preferred, since they are more secure.

Jackfields and patchpanels

In sound installations, such as a recording studio or theatre control room, where the equipment is installed on a permanent basis, each unit of the sound chain is permanently linked to a patch panel (patchbay or jackfield). This is a set of sockets that allows a sound operator to connect and disconnect equipment quickly and easily, without the need to struggle with the connectors at the rear of each unit. The outputs and inputs of each piece of equipment in the sound chain are, therefore, permanently wired to the back of the patch panel and individual patch cords or jack leads are used to link the equipment as desired on the front of the panel. Every input and output of the mixing desk and of external equipment will appear on the patch panel, making it a comprehensive and versatile method of interconnecting equipment. A thorough understanding of the sound chain and signal path is, therefore, essential. However, this method of connecting equipment together is a neater alternative to having to find the correct lengths and types of cable each time the equipment has to be set up.

The layout of a jackfield should appear logical to the user. It should try and follow the signal path down the panel with outputs at the top and inputs at the bottom. It should also be clearly marked.

Normalling or normalisation

Normalling is a method of permanently connecting those sockets on a jackfield which are likely to be used together frequently. Eight sub-master outputs of a mixer, for example may well be normalised at the patch panel to eight corresponding inputs of a multi-track tape recorder. The sockets will be permanently linked behind the patch panel, saving the need to use patch cords.

On a standard patchbay, eight separate patch leads would be required to physically link the output from sub-masters 1–8 to multi-track inputs 1 to 8. A normalised jackfield will therefore require less patch cords, and, if designed carefully, may not need any inter-connecting patch leads at all in some circumstances. Signal paths can still be routed elsewhere on a normalised patch panel simply by inserting a patch lead in the appropriate socket. This will break the normalling connections and send the signal to the new location instead. This is known as semi-normalisation.

Mic and tie lines

In a theatre space or recording studio, mic and tie-line outputs also appear on the patchbay, allowing signals generated in the performance space to appear automatically at the patch panel for easy connection to the mixer. Speakers can be connected to the amplifiers in a similar way, although the signal is travelling in reverse from the control room to the performance space. Speakers require a different type of audio cable which needs to be clearly marked. Tie-lines are connection sockets found in various locations around a theatre which enable equipment to be connected to the control room, without the need to run long cables, or multicores. Due to the diverse requirements for the positioning of mics, speakers and other audio equipment for performance, it is difficult to ever have enough of these types of outlets for flexibility in the performance space.

Signal levels and cable

Very small signal voltages (typically from 1 mV – 1/1000th of a volt – to 3 V) are used to transmit sound between units in the sound system. Even when these signals are amplified, they rarely reach 30 volts. Because the signal voltage is so small, the sound signal can be prone to interference (noise) from electrical devices, radio waves and magnetic fields. This may be heard as audible humming, buzzing, clicks and hissing. Screened cable should always be used for long cable runs, since this encases the signal wires in a metallic shield and helps to prevent interference (see troubleshooting below).

Try and keep sound equipment and cables away from sources of electricity, including electrical cables. Audio cables are particularly susceptible to electrical interference, which can ruin the replay of sound in performance. Where sound cables need to run near electrical cables, keep them as far apart as possible and where they need to cross (e.g. on a lighting rig), make sure that they cross at right angles to minimise interference. Never run audio signal cables directly alongside electrical cables.

Line Level

Small signal levels are used in sound to avoid the need for large and heavy amplifiers at the end of the sound chain. The standard sound signal level is around 1 volt (actually 0.775 volt) and is known as line level or 0 dB. There is a direct correlation between input/output levels, which are expressed in volts, and the decibel scale.

Decibels	Volts	
+20	7.75	
+2.2	1	
0	0.775	line level
−17.8	100 m	
−20	77.5 m	
−37.8	10 m	
−40	7.75m	
−57.8	1	mic level
−60	0.775	

Cable

Audio cable is far more vulnerable to damage than its lighting counterpart. Multicore cables are often used in sound installations, since they group together a number of individual cables within a single larger cable. Multicores are particularly useful on stage, where a number of microphones may be required. A single multicore cable, therefore, allows a large number of mics, instruments, DI boxes, etc. to be connected to the sound system on stage with a single cable run to the mixing desk.

Cables, particularly sound cables, should always be handled with care. Never place heavy objects on top of a cable and always coil cables by hand avoiding the 'elbow wrapping' method which causes wires within the cable to break. Try and establish the natural loops of the cable when coiling it and secure it with a small piece of PVC tape.

TROUBLESHOOTING UNWANTED NOISE

If you have followed the above advice and are still experiencing unwanted noise or 'hum' on the sound installation, you will need to troubleshoot the situation in a logical manner. Try and develop a systematic approach to analyse where the unwanted noise may be coming from. A set of headphones will be useful in attempting to isolate where the signal is being corrupted.

1 Listen to the output of the mixing desk to establish whether the signal is clean. If it does not have interference at this point, then the problem lies after the desk and means that you will need to concentrate on:
   - the cabling between the mixer and the amplifier
   - the amplifier(s)
   - the cabling from the amplifier to the loudspeakers
   - the loudspeakers.
2 If the interference is audible at the mixer, check the original signal from the source machine. The problem may be:
   - the source machine itself or the original recording
   - the cable and connectors between the source machine and the mixing desk
   - the mixing desk itself.

In the majority of cases it is the cables that are at fault, since electrical current produces 'hum' which can be added to the signal path. Check all of the connectors to ensure that they are in good condition. Wiggling the connectors may stop the hum or create a change of tone. If this is the case, it is also the problem! Change the cable, repair or replace the faulty audio connectors. A professional cable tester is an invaluable piece of equipment that can isolate continuity problems in connectors and cable.

If individual items of equipment are at fault, they will have to be replaced or repaired by a qualified technician. It might be fairly easy to swap a faulty cassette replay machine, but a noisy mixing desk will require servicing. If the problem seems to lie within the mixing desk, it may be corrected by bypassing the EQ section if this is not required. Alternatively, connect the source machine to alternative input channels to see whether this makes a difference. This often solves the problem and points to faulty components or input sockets on individual input channels.

If the precise cause of the interference proves difficult to find, it may be possible to minimise the noise by routing the signal through a graphic equalisation unit or a noise gate. Whilst this may reduce the unwanted noise, it may also affect the quality of the rest of the sound adversely.

To Avoid Creating Unwanted Noise

Use professional quality equipment and cables.

Ensure that audio equipment is cleaned and serviced regularly.

Ensure cables and connectors are in good working condition.

Reject any cables and connectors that don't pass a visual inspection.

Look after audio cables by coiling and storing them carefully.

Keep power cables as short as possible.

Don't coil power cables near sound equipment or cabling.

Keep audio signal cables away from mains electrical cables.

Where audio cables need to cross electrical cables ensure that they do this at 90 degrees.

Keep audio cables away from other electrical equipment, e.g. lanterns, dimmers, working lights, etc.

Keep the main amplifiers away from other audio equipment.

Feedback

Feedback or 'howlround' is the painful high pitched scream that is caused when an output signal is fed back into an input. This most common cause of feedback occurs in the live PA situation when a microphone level is increased to such a level that it picks up sound from a loudspeaker. Careful choice of the type of microphone, and the location of the loudspeakers will minimise the risk of feedback.

Some microphones are manufactured to give a high gain *before* feedback and are, therefore, particularly suited to live PA work. Always try and ensure that microphones are not pointing directly towards loudspeakers. Changing the angle or altering the position of the main loudspeakers may be all that is necessary to reduce the chance of feedback in performance.

When feedback occurs it is necessary to fade the volume down immediately. The sound operator should always ensure that a sound check is carried out before a performance, as this will demonstrate how much 'headroom' is available before feedback occurs. Gain input controls and fader levels should be marked carefully and microphones should be faded up gradually one at a time. A good sound operator will listen for the characteristic 'ringing' quality of the sound and be able to reduce microphone levels just before feedback occurs.

To Avoid Feedback

Use as few microphones as possible since increasing the number of mics increases the potential for feedback.

Keep microphones as close as possible to the intended sound source. Close miking requires less gain at the mixer.

Turn off mics that are not being used. Bring down the fader until the microphone is needed again.

Position the main loudspeakers downstage of the microphones.

Choose an appropriate mic that is suited to the task.

BALANCED AND UNBALANCED SYSTEMS

It is important to recognise whether equipment needs balanced or unbalanced connectors and cable.

Unbalanced systems use two pin connections; one pin carries the signal (conductor) and the other provides the screen, a braided wire mesh which encloses the signal cable.

Balanced systems use three pins and consist of two conductors and one screen. (This is often known as **twin screened cable**)

Balanced systems are the preferred method of connecting professional sound equipment and are essential for any long cable runs. Unbalanced systems are only acceptable for linking together pieces of equipment in close proximity to one another, e.g. mixing desk and source machines.

As mentioned, all cables pick up hum and other forms of electrical interference, but the balanced system is better at cancelling out unwanted noise.

Earth Loops

Major problems occur when connecting unbalanced equipment together. The screens within the cables link the cases of the equipment, say the mixing desk and the amplifier, which for safety reasons are also connected to earth. This causes an earth loop running from the mains plug of the mixing desk via the case of the mixing desk, the screen cable, the amplifier chassis, its mains plug and back to earth. The continuous flow of an earth current combines with the sound signal and, when amplified, causes a constant background hum. The solution in this scenario would be to remove the earth connection on the relevant **audio** cables, never on the mains cables.

In a balanced system, the earth loop is less likely to occur because there are two signal wires completely independent of the earth connection (screen). However, a noticeable earth hum can still be a problem if the screens of interconnecting items of sound equipment form earth loops by coming into contact with mains earths. For this reason, always arrange the equipment so that cables are separated. If this doesn't work, the solution would be to sever the earth loop by disconnecting the screen at one end of a cable only, e.g. at the mixing desk.

Power Phases

Always ensure that all items of equipment in the sound chain are powered from the same electrical phase (see page 137). Using more than one phase of electricity will increase the mains noise and may tempt people to remove earths from equipment. This is extremely dangerous.

The Recording Process

MAGNETIC RECORDING PRACTICE AND SIGNAL-TO-NOISE RATIO

Pages 176 and 180 cover tape and tape recorders in more detail.

It is essential that the signal which is supplied to the recording head of a tape recorder is of a good quality, since it cannot be improved after the recording has been made. In the magnetic recording process the audio signal is added to a tape which already has inherent tape noise (a hiss in the background). On playback of the recorded sound, the tape noise is amplified. Therefore, if the original recorded signal is too low, it will need to be amplified on playback to such an extent that the background noise will intrude.

A taped recording with lots of 'hiss' is caused by a poor signal-to-noise (S/N) ratio. When making a recording it is essential to achieve the optimum level that will give the best signal-to-noise ratio, without the signal distorting. Overloading can occur if the signal is too high (loud).

Some recording equipment includes electronic circuitry which automatically limits the amount of overload, to prevent damage to the machine. However, the recorded sound is affected adversely as a result of this process and levels should be re-adjusted accordingly.

Monitoring Sound

Most professional sound equipment is provided with meters to enable the sound levels to be balanced.

A VU (volume unit) meter or a LED bargraph is used to monitor sound levels. These scales are marked in decibels (dB) or Volume units. An ideal signal should peak just into the red area of the scale at 0 dB to +1 dB.

Volume Unit Meter

The VU meter has a needle which responds to the incoming sound levels by moving from left to right. Although it doesn't indicate all of the peaks of an audio signal, it measures the *overall loudness* of the input signal. A PPM, or **Peak Programme Meter**, is a more accurate way to measure individual variations in the signal, since it responds far quicker. It is a more expensive device, usually reserved for broadcasting and professional recording studios. A red area on the scale, sometimes accompanied by a peak warning light, warns the engineer if the signal is likely to distort.

LED Bargraph Meter

The LED bargraph meter, sometimes referred to as a 'ladder' consists of a line of light emitting diodes (hence LED), often coloured green, yellow and red to indicate the parts of the dB scale. The efficiency of electronic bargraphs depends upon how many LEDs are used in the 'ladder'. The display tends to provide a more accurate measurement of sound than the VU meter, since it is able to respond to changes instantly. Some bargraph meters also retain peak levels every few seconds, which can be useful to a recording engineer.

How to Achieve a Good Signal-to-Noise Ratio

1 Connect equipment so that the audio signal is fed to the input sockets of the recorder.
2 Adjust the input controls so that the sound can be monitored visually on the meters. It may be necessary to depress Record, Play and Pause buttons to register the incoming sound on the meters.
3 Connect the headphones, so that the sound can be monitored aurally as well.
4 If using a mixing desk that generates a calibrating line-up tone or 'slate', generate an oscillator signal (usually 1 kHz) to line up the outputs of the mixer, to the input of the recorder.
5 Monitor the sound to be recorded by watching the meters and listening for distortion. Pay particular attention to the loudest parts of the sound that you need to record.
6 Adjust the input controls accordingly, so that a strong signal is recorded and the signal peaks just into the red at the loudest point. Check that the signal is strong, but not excessively overloading or distorting.
7 Monitor the signal visually on the meters and also on headphones. By switching a monitor switch on some recorders you can compare the quality of the incoming signal (monitoring at the record head) with the recorded signal, a moment after (monitoring at the playback head.) By continual switching between the two settings, it is possible to check that the signal-to-noise ratio is satisfactory and that there is not a noticeable drop in quality or volume in the recorded sound.

Following this process should result in a good signal-to-noise ratio, although with some sound sources (e.g. classical music) it is notoriously difficult to get the levels right. Sometimes a slightly higher recording level may need to be selected if there is a large dynamic range in the sound. To compensate for the quieter moments, where the signal may only just be visible on a meter, it may be necessary to tolerate occasional higher peaks. Listen to the recording and if you are not satisfied, re-record the sound with different recording levels. Remember, do not rely solely on readings from the meters – it is important to listen to the sound to monitor a recording properly.

Recording Tips

Unless you wish to *record* a fade, you should not adjust levels whilst recording. Fades may be required on some effects, but unless the timing is certain, it is best to perform these changes *live*. This allows for greater flexibility and a better chance of the sound matching the on-stage action. A pre-recorded fade can not be altered once it is recorded.

How to achieve quiet sounds! Never attempt to make a quiet recording. This will result in a poor S/N ratio and exaggerated noise on playback. Record the sound at an optimum level and adjust the level on playback.

RECORDING AND EDITING ON REEL-TO-REEL TAPE MACHINES

The reel-to-reel tape machine has been the standard item of recording and playback equipment in the performing arts field for a number of years. It allows the precise recording, editing and cueing of effects, since the tape is accessible at the recording and playback heads.

The path of the tape passes three heads: erase, record and playback.

The tape will always pass the heads in this order during recording or playback. (Some cheaper machines, including some cassette decks, may combine the erase and record head functions into a single head.)

Reel-to-Reel Tape Machine Features

Erase head – removes any pre-recorded signal from the tape by randomising the magnetic particles on the tape. Only works when the record button is depressed.

Record head – works in tandem with the erase head in record mode to imprint a new signal on the magnetic tape.

Playback head – works in isolation from the other heads to read the information on the audio tape to allow it to be converted back into an electrical signal.

Tape tension arms – maintain tape tension so that tape is transported smoothly through the head assembly.

Guides – ensure that the tape is aligned correctly when entering and leaving the head assembly.

Tape pins – keep the tape away from the heads in fast forward, stop and rewind modes. The pins retract to allow the tape to sit against record, erase or playback heads when required.

Pinch roller – a rubber coated wheel that presses the tape against the capstan spindle to move the tape in the direction required.

Capstan spindle – the capstan is a sophisticated mechanism within the tape deck, which precisely controls the speed of the tape transport mechanism. A spindle or shaft protrudes to interact with the tape medium and moves the tape smoothly once the pinch roller has pushed the tape into contact.

Infrared light gate – works in conjunction with a photo-electric cell on the opposite side of the tape path to detect auto-stops (see page 205) or the absence of a tape. Once the photo electric cell senses the light it shuts down the transport mechanism of the machine and the reels stop turning.

Cue button – retracts the tape lift pins to allow the tape to rest against the playback head. The signal on the tape can be monitored by moving the reels backwards and forwards by hand. This is essential when finding the correct point to cut the tape during editing. The cue button is also used in performance conditions to prepare a cue for playback.

Editing Quarter Inch Tape

Once individual sounds have been recorded onto tape and meet all the technical and artistic requirements, the show tape is compiled. This involves sorting out the individual sound cues so that they appear in the correct order in the final tape and editing the sounds so that extraneous noises, clicks, interference, unwanted recordings, etc. are all removed. There should be no sounds left on the show reel that are not required in the performance.

The Editing Kit

To begin editing quarter inch audio tape an editing kit is required. This should comprise of:

- a sharp single-sided razor blade
- a quarter inch professional splicing block with a 45 degree angle
- a chinagraph pencil
- splicing tape
- appropriate colours of leader tape
- a set of headphones
- a number of spare open reels.

1 Locate the beginning and ending of the sound cue and mark it with a chinagraph pencil against the centre of the playback head. It is essential that the beginning of the sound is located precisely. This is achieved by using the cueing button to bring the tape into contact with the playback head without the play button being depressed. Move the take-up reel and supply spool by hand to hear the beginning of the sound as it slowly passes the playback head. Shuttle the tape backwards and forwards until the start of the sound has been identified. Turn the tape back slightly (a quarter of a turn of a reel is sufficient) and mark the tape with a clear vertical line with the chinagraph pencil. Before physically cutting the tape, check the edit point by lining up the chinagraph line so that it is about to pass across the playback head. Then press play and listen for the beginning of the sound. If it plays almost immediately, the edit is perfect. If the sound is clipped, the mark needs to be adjusted to the right. If there is more than a fraction of a moment of silence, the edit point is not close enough to the beginning of the sound and needs to be remarked to the left.

2 Once the edit point has been located accurately, lift the tape away from the machine and carefully place it into the splicing block, so that the chinagraph line is resting on the 45 degree groove.

3 Using a corner of the single-sided razor blade, cut the tape. Draw the blade *smoothly* through the splicing block groove. Discard the portion of tape that is unwanted (the part to the right of the splice in this instance). Slide the other part of the tape to the left, away from the splicing groove.

4 Put the desired colour of leader tape in the splicing block groove. (See below for colour coding.) Using a corner of the single-sided razor blade, cut the leader tape by drawing the blade smoothly through the 45 degree groove. Discard the left portion of the leader tape.

5 Slide the right portion of the leader tape to meet the spliced audio tape. Both 45 degree cuts should match and provide a smooth splice.

6 Using the single-sided razor blade, cut 2 cm of splicing tape and carefully align it across the splice so that it sticks the audio tape to the leader tape. The leader tape should be placed so that the matt side of the plastic passes against the heads of the tape recorder. This reduces the build up of static. It is important that the splicing tape *does not* overlap the top or bottom of the tape in the splicing block. Press down with a finger to ensure that any air bubbles are expelled and that the splicing tape has adhered properly. Although this part of the editing process is the most tricky, it does become easier with practice. Try not to let fingers come into contact with the sticky side of the splicing tape as this affects the adhesion. It is worth making sure that the splice is secure because a poorly spliced tape can come apart in performance, with disastrous consequences!

7 Gently peel the edited tape out of the splicing block. Do this *slowly*. Doing this too quickly can damage the edges of the tape which affects the recording.

8 The leader tape can be wound onto an empty take-up spool and the end of the sound cue can then be found, marked and spliced to another length of leader tape.

9 When marking the end of a sound effect, do not worry about identifying the end of the sound precisely. If the splice is made near the recording it may sound clipped as the reverberation of the sound is not allowed to die away. It is far better to allow a couple of seconds of silence, before the splice is made. However, clicks and other sounds may need to be edited out.

An experienced editor will be confident enough to mark the beginning and ending of a cue before undertaking any cuts. This saves time, particularly if the marks are made clearly. Horizontal chinagraph marks help to identify the unwanted portion of the tape and are useful for finding the edit point again.

Instead of following the procedure exactly as outlined, time can be saved in steps 2, 3 and 4 by first laying down the leader tape in the splicing block and then placing the audio tape on top, with the edit point aligned against the 45 degree groove. A single cut with the blade will therefore cut through both tape media and create an identical splice.

Playing a Spliced Tape

When preparing a cue for playback, line up the splice so that the magnetic tape is about to pass the playback head. Then press the cueing button so that the tape lies against the head. This will create an instantaneous and a smoother start to the cue. Never press the cue button in the opposite direction. To release the tape, press the play button or move the pinch roller towards the capstan spindle.

Leader Tape

Leaders (also known as spacers or trailers) are colour coded to assist in the replay of sound in performance. The **beginning** of a show reel should have around 2 m of either **white**

or green leader tape joined to the beginning of the first sound cue. The spliced join should be within 1 cm of the beginning of the sound.

At the **end** of the reel there should be a tail of 2 m of **red** leader tape, which should be spliced to the magnetic tape well after the last reverberation of sound ends. The position of this join is not critical, but should not clip the recorded sound. It is always useful to allow a few seconds of blank tape before joining it to the red leader.

Coloured leader tape should also be spliced between individual cues on the reel. **White** or **yellow** leader is used for this and a minimum of 4 seconds of leader tape is required. At 7½ inches per second this equates to a minimum of 30 inches, or around 80 cm of leader between cues.

Adding Auto Stops

Adding auto stops or clear tape 'windows' to the leader tape is very useful when working with a reel-to-reel machine that has a light gate (see page 203). Care should be taken to ensure that the clear window is positioned correctly. Inserting it too near the beginning of the leader tape will cause the machine to stop before the last of the previous sound cue has passed the playback head. The addition of 3 cm of clear leader towards the end of each coloured leader tape will automatically stop the tape just before the next cue to allow the operator to turn the reels by hand to line up the next cue against the replay head.

Auto stops can also be created by removing the coloured surface of the leader tape by scratching with a single-sided razor blade, or by rubbing the coloured tape with a cotton wool bud soaked in acetone. These methods both remove the colour and leave a patch of clear tape as a window.

Finally, once the sound tape has been plotted at a technical rehearsal, each cue should be numbered on the leader tape with indelible ink.

Advanced Editing

In addition to splicing in leader tape to identify separate cues, individual recorded sounds may also have to be edited for a variety of reasons. Unwanted noises can often be removed by careful editing. Precise sound can be identified and edited out by exactly the same method as described for splicing cues.

Editing does require practice, however, and confidence will only accrue over time. Try not to be hesitant. Although removing a 2 cm length of audio tape may seem drastic, at 7½ inches per second it will only shorten the recording by a tenth of a second!

TASK

Record a friend reading a report from a newspaper, or ask them to respond to some questions that you have prepared for an interview. Listen to the recording that you have made and think about how you might be able to edit the recording to change the sense of what the speaker has been saying! Experiment with editing the recording to remove entire words with a view to changing the meaning of what has been said. If the editing is undertaken carefully, the edits will not be noticed.

You will have to concentrate on the rhythm of speech to ensure that you leave the correct space between the words. Too much silence, or not enough, will betray the edit point. This technique was used extensively in radio journalism until recently. Digital techniques have now overtaken tape-based editing methods. Replay the edited recording and see whether the edit points are noticeable. Can any of your edits be improved?

RECORDING TECHNIQUES

Close Up Recording

Recording sounds at different distances can often reveal radically different qualities. In particular, some sounds recorded close up sound completely different. This technique can be used to create 'cheats'. A typical example of a cheat is recording the manual manipulation of cellophane close to a microphone to create the sound of fire. Lateral thinking is often required to create the right type of sound and experimentation is often the key. Once sounds have been captured they can be modified by a variety of signal processors (see page 192).

Altering the Speed

Recording an effect at a different speed to that at which it will be replayed causes a relative pitch shift. This alters the sound considerably.

For example, recording a mantelpiece clock ticking at 15 inches per second and replaying the effect at 7½ inches per second can transform the mantelpiece clock into a grandfather clock, with a slower and lower sounding mechanism! Recording the same clock at 3¾ inches per second and replaying it at 7½ inches per second produces a quicker, almost manic watch-like ticking.

Modern digital audio equipment allows for the speed of recordings to be changed without the pitch variation, or for the pitch to be altered without affecting the speed and, therefore, the duration of the sound. These modifications are impossible with analogue equipment.

Loops

Looping enables effects of long duration to be achieved from a short recording. The technique involves joining the end of a sound (or segment of sound) to its beginning to create a continuous loop. This is used frequently to create long, continuous atmospheric tracks such as weather effects. Care must be taken to ensure that the edit point is not distinguishable; the sound at the beginning and end must be matched in terms of level, pitch and rhythm.

Looping is now very easy to achieve using digital equipment, but analogue methods are a little more awkward and time consuming. Reel-to-reel tape machines require the tape to be spliced and rejoined to create a physical loop. Most effects do need a considerable length of recording to prevent the audience realising that the sound is being regularly repeated.

Long tape loops can be achieved by passing the tape around an empty spool positioned at a distance from the reel-to-reel machine. A pencil can be used through the middle of an empty spool and secured to the edge of a table or back of a chair with some gaffa or PVC tape. The chair can be easily moved towards the tape machine or away from it to establish the correct tape tension.

TASK

Create a loop of some of the following sounds. Try and use both tape and digital methods. Take particular care that the edit point is not detectable.

- waves breaking on a beach – here it is important to get the rhythm correct.
- birdsong – a longer loop is required so that the pattern of the repeated birdcall is not audible.
- insects – should be easy since the sound is naturally repetitious.
- wind – pitch alteration and rhythm are important.
- tolling bells – be careful to allow the sound of the bell to decay before the next bell rings.
- an urban atmosphere – again relatively straightforward unless there is a noticeable noise such as a car passing, an individual voice, or horn which will highlight the loop.
- a piece of music – music is extremely difficult to loop successfully, but a solo instrument such as a trumpet fanfare shouldn't be too difficult.

Play the final sound and see if others can detect the loop point.

TASK

Think about the use of the tolling bell in performance. Can you foresee any difficulties? What about ending the cue?

Consider the use of the insect loop or other continuous background track. What would be required to make the sound appear more realistic in performance?

Using Signal Processors

The characteristics of a sound can be radically altered by the addition of effects to a recording. The Designer needs to be careful when they add the effect. If the effect is added at the recording stage, it cannot be removed without re-recording the original. One way of safeguarding this situation is to record the original untreated effect onto one channel of a stereo recorder and the modified or 'wet' signal onto the other channel. This allows the operator to balance the amount of processed signal by adjusting the relative levels of the two tracks.

Composite Effects

This involves linking two or more sounds together to create a new effect. If an absurd play requires the sound of a hippopotamus falling off a bicycle, the Sound Designer would have to explore possible sounds and link them together to create a believable effect. Using two or more tracks will allow the various components of the final effect to be overlapped.

TASK

Try to create this effect yourself. Replay the final sounds to others and ask for their response. Can they identify what the effect is? How humorous did they find it? How funny did you intend the effect to sound? Did your audience react to your sound in the way that you intended?

MULTI-TRACK RECORDING

Multi-track tape recorders allow several sounds to be recorded on to separate tracks. This facilitates the layering of sound and the ability to create unique effects, even when working only from commercial library effects material. Most open reel tape multi-track recorders are 4 track and 8 track machines, although professional music studio recorders rarely use less than 16 tracks and often use 32 or 64 digital tracks. One or more tracks can be recorded simultaneously. Digital multi-track recorders have now superseded the analogue tape-based technology.

Individual sounds can be laid down on separate tracks, so that a complex layer of sounds can be built up. Mistakes on individual tracks can be rectified without re-recording the whole piece. A simple music track might consist of these elements:

Track 1	drums
Track 2	percussion
Track 3	lead vocals
Track 4	backing vocals
Track 5	lead guitar
Track 6	acoustic guitar
Track 7	bass guitar
Track 8	saxophone.

As discussed, each of these elements could be recorded separately, allowing the precise balance between tracks to be set later when the track is 'mixed down'. The mixing or re-mixing involves adjusting the relative volumes of each track and refining the EQ, setting the location of the sound, adding filters and effects as necessary. Once the processing and blending of the tracks has been achieved, the resulting mix is recorded on a master tape or in digital form.

The Sound Designer can use the facilities of multi-track machines to create innovative effects for performance work. The opening scene of Shakespeare's *The Tempest*, for example, requires a storm at sea that causes a shipwreck. It is unlikely that an appropriate effect exists on a library effects disk, but a range of sounds that fit the scene could be mixed together to achieve the desired effect.

In this example, the Sound Designer found 7 pre-recorded tracks from library effects and created an original, 'cheat' which was recorded onto track 8:

Track 1	heavy seawash
Track 2	storm at sea
Track 3	thunder
Track 4	distant thunder
Track 5	howling wind
Track 6	wind and rain
Track 7	creaking timber
Track 8	flapping/tearing sails

If the final sound effect must last for a considerable time, these tracks would have to be recorded several times over. The ending of each effect would be disguised by the seven other tracks playing at the same time. The final storm sequence can be mixed down with differing proportions of each track over time to suggest a gradually worsening storm. The new mix would be recorded onto whatever format would be used for the playback in the show itself.

Improvising Multi-track Recording

If multi-track recorders are not available, it is still possible for the Sound Designer to create original effects by making use of several source machines, the mixing desk and a recorder. By setting off the source machines together and altering the line faders, an instant mix is created. Practice will be required before the effect is perfect! Alternatively, any stereo recorder with separate recording facilities on the left and right channels will create new sounds by mixing two sources. (The two-track reel-to-reel tape recorder, as well as digital equipment could be used for this.) For example, a less sophisticated tempest could be achieved by recording 'storm at sea' on the left channel and 'creaking timber' on the right. Similar unique effects can be achieved by combining two different pre-recorded sources, e.g. for a rubbish tip, tracks of seagulls and heavy lorries moving or reversing could be combined. By recording each sound on to a separate channel, the desired effect would be achieved.

When replaying an effect in performance that has been created by mixing two mono sources, care should be taken to balance the levels as it is unlikely that they will be required at the same volume. Also the pan controls on the mixer should be set to the centre to create a mix of the two tracks. Otherwise you will hear one track from one loudspeaker and the second track from the other!

Multi-track recording is also possible, and usually very easy, with software packages on computers.

TASK

Create your own unique effects by using pre-recorded library effects and a recorder with two (or more) tracks. Try and provide an imaginative response to some of these sound-scapes:

a jungle atmosphere
a blustery day
an eerie wasteland
a commentary of a sporting event or public occasion
someone falling off a cliff
the magic kingdom
summer in the countryside
the laboratory
a journey
a moonlit night.

The Digital Recording Process

The major differences between analogue and digital audio are discussed on page 170.

Sampling

Sampling is the name for the technique of recording and storing a digital sound source into a memory. A sampler is a computer that stores data in the form of digital sound. This data can be recalled and manipulated. It can be permanently stored on hard disk, floppy disk, or on removable drives, such as Zip or Jaz drives. External mass storage media are usually linked to the sampler by **SCSI** (Small Computer System Interface, or 'Scuzzi') which is an industry standard data transfer system.

The sampler has been called the audio equivalent of a film camera. A movie camera takes 24 pictures or frames per second, and a projector plays these back to give the illusion of motion. Working at 44.1 kHz, a sampler takes 44,100 digital snapshots of an audio signal every second and stores them separately. These can be played back in order to recreate the original sound, but they can also be edited, reversed and manipulated to create entirely new sounds.

A sampler can be used on its own as a record and playback device in a recording studio, or linked to a keyboard to provide samples that can be activated by individual keys. Alternatively, if linked to a computer with appropriate software, the sampler can be controlled on screen via a mouse. In fact, this is the way many Sound Designers prefer to work. Setting up and using such systems requires a good working knowledge of the sampler, the software and of **MIDI** (musical instrument digital interface) protocols.

The sampler is able to playback effects live in performance and can be triggered by a keyboard, computer or a MIDI controller. MIDI control programs enable sounds to be assigned to keygroups on a keyboard, so variations of a sound can be triggered by a single note. Four variations of sea effects such as lapping waves, gentle seawash, breaking rollers and storm force crashing waves could be accessed simply according to how hard the note is played. Other modifications may be achieved by assigning variations on the same sounds to other notes on the keyboard. The pitch, volume and the way in which a sound begins, is sustained and ends (known as the sound 'envelope') can easily be assigned to keys and accessed in this way.

Editing Sound on a Sampler

Editing sound which has been sampled involves digital modifications. The techniques have the same terms as the analogue tape techniques but do not involve any physical cutting or splicing:

- **Truncating** – setting the start and end of each sample.
- **Splicing** – linking separate samples together.
- **Mixing** – blending two samples together to form a third sound.
- **Expanding and compressing** – changing the duration time of a sample.
- **Looping** – joining the end of a sample to its beginning to create a continuous sound. With some effects only a short section of the sound is required to create a longer effect, e.g. rainfall.

Many samplers have a multiple loop or auto loop function which allows the repetition of a sound to be achieved relatively easily. Just as in tape-based editing, it is important to select the loop point carefully to ensure that the join cannot be heard. With music in particular, a 'glitch' is easy to detect if the volume, pitch, and timbre of the sounds either side of the edit point are not matched.

Storing Digital Audio

Good quality, digital audio takes up considerable computer memory space. At a sample rate of 44.1 kHz, approximately 1 MB of memory is taken up for every 12 seconds of recorded sound. This means that around 5 MB of memory is required for a minute of audio and double that amount is required if the sound is to be recorded in stereo!

Because of the difficulties in storing large amounts of digital audio, a hard disk with a large capacity is required for recording and editing digital audio. Finished effects are usually downloaded and stored on other media (e.g. digital audio tape, CD or MiniDisc) for playback in performance.

Editing Digital Sound

In most cases, digital sound can be edited relatively easily. Editing of digital audio takes place in three main ways:

- **Re-recording** – With compact disc and digital tape formats, digital sound is usually not edited but re-recorded. Unlike the equivalent analogue process, there is no loss of quality after duplication.
- **Reorganisation** – MiniDisc and other re-recordable media allow recorded sounds to be edited and reorganised on the disc. **Digital splicing** is relatively straightforward and sound effects can be renumbered to be replayed in a different order.
- **Remixing** – hard disks with appropriate computer software programs allow complex editing and remixing of audio, without affecting the original track. Many software packages allow audio tracks to be laid down independently and altered substantially in terms of volume, speed, EQ, etc. Many also provide digital effects to process the sound such as expanders, compressors, pan controls, etc. The editing is all done on screen using mouse controls on a graphic representation of a mixing desk and of the audio tracks themselves. Editing is achieved by moving the mixer controls and highlighting, dragging, dropping, cutting and pasting segments of audio. The combination of audio tracks can be played together just like a multi-track tape recorder. However, the advantages of computer-based systems are that once the general controls are understood, they are quick and easy to use and experimentation in modifying the sound is much simpler.

The Role of the Sound Designer

The Sound Designer is more than simply a technician or engineer, although these terms are often used instead. The Sound Designer must have technical skills, however, to understand and operate types of audio equipment and systems in order to respond creatively.

The Sound Designer must be able to design a sound installation in a venue, since the location of speakers and the selection of equipment determines how well the final sound design will be realised in performance. However, the Sound Designer is not only concerned with the technicalities of how the equipment works. They must respond artistically to the brief and work collaboratively with the Director and other members of the design team. This demands that the Designer understands the concepts behind the production, the stylistic implications of design decisions and how to research, select and create sound.

The Sound Designer needs to have a wide knowledge of musical styles and to understand how the audience is likely to respond to particular sounds on both a conscious and a sub-conscious level. Many Sound Designers are also musicians and composers who take a more holistic approach to sound design for performance. Other Designers may work collabora-tively with a composer or Musical Director.

SOUND IN PERFORMANCE

We can identify six areas in which sound contributes to on stage action:

1 sound reinforcement
2 establishing settings
3 atmospheric effects
4 underscoring
5 transitional sound
6 spot effects.

Sound Reinforcement

This is the simplest, practical contribution of sound to performance, but can easily ruin a show if it is not realised correctly. Voices of performers and 'live' sound from musical instruments have to be balanced, amplified and replayed to an audience. A typical set-up might involve a microphone for the vocals and a separate microphone rigged to pick up an acoustic guitar. For dramatic presentations, microphones may be rigged at the front of the stage or overhead to pick-up specific parts of the action. Mics are also used extensively in musicals, to balance the orchestra or band and to reinforce the vocals so that the audience can hear the performers above the music.

Establishing Settings

The sound of children shouting and a ringing hand bell can communicate a school playground. Background traffic noise and pedestrians indicate an urban environment, and the addition of carol singers to this track provides a clue about the time of year and possibly the country. Birdsong can signify a range of information:

- An owl hooting may be all that is required to signify night.
- A cuckoo indicates late spring or summer, depending on it's call.
- A specific mix of birdsong indicates time of year, region and time of day, e.g. a southern England, woodland, spring dawn chorus.
- Seagulls may communicate a coastal location.

Atmospheric Effects

Weather effects are, perhaps, the most common way of establishing a particular atmosphere. Howling wind may suggest an empty wasteland, but could also create an eerie environment. Individual sounds, such as a single creaking door, may be a more economical or appropriate way of creating an ominous atmosphere. A short regal fanfare may enhance the overall atmosphere of a court scene, as well as helping to establish the setting and create anticipation for the arrival of an important character. Distant rumbling thunder can communicate an oppressive atmosphere. The Designer may choose to use continually chirping cicadas (crickets) to communicate evening and heat. Depending on the precise texture and volume of this sound, the cicada noise could create an unbearably tense atmosphere. This technique is known as underscoring and moves away from merely creating atmosphere (see below). Complex environmental soundscapes create dramatic ambience and are often used in film.

Don't forget that silence can be more effective than a sound. In a production of Shakespeare's *Cymbeline*, chirping cicadas were used in the boudoir scene, for the reasons mentioned above. Suddenly cutting the chirping heightened the dramatic tension, as well as highlighting a particular action. In the same production, one of the characters loses his head in a fight. In this instance, the fight scene was underscored with drumming, which reached a crescendo and was suddenly cut in time with a blackout. The audience was left in no doubt as to what had occurred, and moments later the evidence was visible. The sound prevented a difficult moment from appearing comical.

Underscoring

This technique, aimed at provoking an emotional response is borrowed from the cinema and involves using sound to support the action. Music is the most common form of underscoring and easily stimulates an emotional response in the audience, but more abstract sounds can also work well. Extreme care is needed to select pieces that are suitable and which work perfectly with the action on stage. Sound Designers have to build up a knowledge of a broad range of musical styles. It is important to be aware of the connotations associated with a particular piece of music before selecting it for use in performance.

TASK

Assess the impact of sound by studying a horror movie on videotape. Select a scene and view it with the volume turned down. Repeat the exercise with the sound track audible. How complex is the mix of sound and music? What separate elements can you identify? How do they work together? Does the scene work without the sound? What is lost?

Transitional Sound

This helps to link scenes and to mask scene changes. Music or other atmospheric effects may be used as a practical way of hiding on stage activity, but should also contribute to the development of the performance by maintaining the momentum of the production. Transitional sound is an easy way of signifying place and/or time. A piece of music played on a sitar might signal the sudden change of location to India, for example. A relentless heavy drum beat might communicate increased tension and an impending military battle, as well as bridging scenes and masking the noise and business of a scene change.

Pre-show sound also falls into this category. The audience, entering a theatre to the sound of gentle seawash, will automatically begin to make associations, before the performance has begun. A Beatles track may help to set the scene by placing the action in the 1960s. This use of sound is also known as a **framing effect** and, when used between Acts or as a coda at the end of the performance, can contribute to an audience's response to the performance. *She Loves You* might be played to end an Act on a positive, energetic, upbeat mood, but alternatively, could be used as an ironic comment on a relationship that has broken up. The convention of framing effects is that they are *not* part of the world of the play and, therefore, are not heard by the characters. The Sound Designer must consider whether it is appropriate to locate the sound outside the stage area so that it communicates directly to the audience.

Spot Effects

These effects occur at specific moments of the performance. They reproduce physical events that are part of the script or are inserted as part of the dramatic interpretation, e.g. a door bell, a clock chiming, an explosion, etc. Spot effects are very common but are difficult to get right. They can easily sound comic, which destroys the atmosphere on stage. In addition, they must be cued accurately.

APPROACHES TO SOUND DESIGN

The Designer must experiment to find out which sounds work for a particular piece and which don't. Collaboration in the rehearsal environment is an ideal way to establish whether sound works alongside the action.

Involvement in rehearsals can help to avoid hours of wasted effort in the recording studio, creating effects that are cut because they do not work alongside the action in performance.

TASK

Think about a piece of music that, when you hear it, always reminds you of a person, place or an experience in the past. Can others have any way of understanding this personal response?

The use of sound effects should always be selective and appropriate. A poorly chosen sound effect will destroy the world created on stage by reminding the audience of the artificiality of the event. An inappropriate sound can provoke laughter!

In a national touring production of *Pride and Prejudice*, the sound operator hit the play button on the tape deck by mistake. The next effect, which was meant to establish a countryside setting, was played. A cow's 'moo' was heard over the top of Leslie Phillips' opening speech. The audience laughed so much that the effect was kept in for future performances!

FINDING A STYLE AND ESTABLISHING CONVENTIONS

The Sound Designer has to establish the overall style of the sound contribution to a performance and to decide which conven-

tions are to be followed. If a production is to have an underscore, are the characters aware of the sound? If so do they respond to it? Is it replayed over the main loudspeakers, only from onstage positions or solely in the auditorium? Does all music emanate from the world onstage and, therefore, have to come from practical speakers built into the gramophone or radio on the set? Close work with the Director and other members of the design team will ensure that the style of sound integrates with the other production elements.

Realistic Sound

A realistic or naturalistic production is probably the least interesting in terms of the contribution that sound can make artistically. However, this style does provide a challenge to the Designer, since the sound must mimic true life as far as possible. Research is vital and a great attention to detail is required. There will always be a trainspotter in the audience who complains that a particular class of steam locomotive wasn't even built until 1948 and that the sound has totally ruined his enjoyment of the performance! Whilst this may be a little extreme, the Sound Designer should always seek to avoid such anachronistic errors. (However, the Designer may ultimately decide that the quality of the sound outweighs the historical accuracy!) As has already been noted, the selection of birdsong should be undertaken with careful consideration of location, time of year and time of day. There are even more ornithologists than steam train enthusiasts who notice such mistakes.

The role of music in realistic productions needs particular consideration and a convention needs to be established and followed through the performance.

Representational Sound

This approach tends to take a more selective view of realistic sound effects which are pared down to communicate specific ideas. A single crow may be sufficient to convey the mood of a bleak, rural, winter landscape, for example. Similarly, the selection of the sound of rattling iron chains or the slamming of a heavy cell door may be sufficient to represent the idea of imprisonment. The Designer must search for individual aural elements that are able to communicate a wider context to an audience. When this approach works well the effect is of a neat, apparently simple contribution which allows the audience imaginative scope.

Stylised or Abstract Use of Sound

This stylised theatrical form uses elements of reality in an exaggerated or distorted way and is particularly appropriate to non-narrative performances and plays with a symbolic, surrealist, expressionist or absurd nature. These performance styles can provide enormous creative scope for the sound designer.

Individual aspects of the drama can be used as inspiration to create a heightened dramatic effect. In Kafka's *The Trial* a human heartbeat can be replayed in response to the events on stage to heighten the dramatic tension. The individual style of such effects will often be exaggerated through treatment involving signal processors such as reverberation units. In this way, the sound effect evolves by abstracting qualities from an original source to communicate atmosphere in an expressionistic way. Although this type of approach will not be suitable for all performance work, it can provide a strong creative contribution to the drama.

TASK

Study Tennessee William's *A Streetcar Named Desire*. Consider the role that sound could play in a production. What do you think this play is about? Note down your ideas and responses to the main themes. Do these inspire possibilities or suggestions for sound? Note down the sounds *required* by the script, but also think about how sound might *contribute* to the world of the play. How realistic does the sound need to be? Clearly, the sound needs to portray the atmosphere of New Orleans. How could the sound assist in reflecting the emotional response of the characters? How can the sounds of the railroad and the 'streetcars' (trams) be used to underscore the action? When should they be heard? What about the role of live sound and music? Where could you go to research the musical effects for this play? How can sound emphasise shifts in the action? A Director might wish to emphasise the sense of a gathering climax to the action – how could sound assist dramatically?

Make a provisional sound cue synopsis for your design. Discuss your response to sound in a small group. How do others' designs differ from your own?

SOUND DESIGN TECHNIQUES

Using Sound to Create Focus
Cueing, Volume and Mix

The pacing and timing of sound cues is crucial to their success. Spot effects, such as door knocks, ringing telephones and crashes are nearly always best performed live backstage. Effects that are referred to by characters should always be handled subtly and introduced carefully before the appropriate line in the text. If weather effects are cued on or immediately after a line such as 'I see it's started raining again' the audience may laugh. In an absurd play, however, this effect may well be absolutely appropriate. Alternatively, a sound such as squeaking mice might be substituted for the rain, to provide a designed response to the absurd world of the events on stage.

As a general guide, weather effects should be introduced to a scene around 30 seconds before they are referred to in the script.

Volume levels are also very important and care should be taken when deciding on the correct levels. Very loud sound can be used for deliberate dramatic effect if exaggeration is re-

quired, but usually the sound contribution to a performance should be quieter rather than louder. For dance and physical theatre presentations, loud volumes of sound may be appropriate, but volume levels which are too high will intrude on the drama, annoy the audience and make the performers inaudible. Increasing the volume of sound can help punctuate a performance by injecting pace into scene transitions. Reducing volume levels can focus attention on a particular moment and make an individual action or soliloquy more prominent. Cutting an atmospheric sound track, which has been running underneath a scene, can be dramatic in itself and may serve to heighten the tension on stage.

Sound can work well on the subliminal level; underscoring a scene so that the audience are barely aware of the sound at all. A recent production of *The Seagull* at West Yorkshire Playhouse used a complex mix of natural sounds, such as crickets, dogs and birds, which were replayed at very low levels to create a subtle countryside evening atmosphere for Act 1. The audience were, therefore, able to believe in the location beside a lake which they could not see. Individual sounds which provide subconscious emotional trigger points can, therefore, be buried in an overall sound mix.

Establishing an Effect

A common technique for replaying a sound effect is known as 'establish and fade'. Often sound effects need to be established at a relatively loud level for the audience to experience the sound fully, before fading to a lower level so that the actor's voices can be heard.

Although fading down the effect once it has been established seems very artificial, it will be accepted by an audience if the fade is handled subtly and cued carefully. In fact, sound played like this works in the same way as we perceive noise in real life. We are suddenly aware of a particular sound, but after it has been registered we tend to push the sound into the background. If coordinated carefully, the sound level can also be faded back up at appropriate moments, to reinforce the effect.

A Sound Design Chronology

The sound design process has been discussed throughout this book. It is given in summary here with cross references to relevant sections.

The discussion below is based on the design process for a dramatic play text and it is important to note that the sound design process for other performance types such as music, dance and devised pieces may differ significantly, especially due to the way in which they are developed through work in rehearsals.

During the design process, the Designer should frequent rehearsals as often as time allows and maintain a close relationship with the Director and co-designers throughout. In this way, the sound contribution can evolve with the rest of the production and the Designer can respond quickly and imaginatively to changing ideas and new requirements.

TASK

Study *Macbeth*. List the range of noises which are included in the text of the play. Draw up an initial sound cue synopsis. Include all sound that you consider appropriate. State which sounds are to be performed live by actors or musicians, and which will be prerecorded. What is your justification for your decisions? Have you added any sounds which are inspired by the text but which are not actually referred to? What do you expect each effect to communicate?

PRE-PRODUCTION PLANNING

1 From a combination of research and early design ideas, the Sound Designer draws up an Initial Sound Scene Synopsis in preparation for early planning meetings.

2 At this stage in the production process, the Sound Designer may record early samples of material to play to the Director and/or to the rest of the design team. Make sure that everyone is aware that the sound effects are still 'rough'.

3 As the Designer works they may consider these aspects of the play:
- What is the style of the production?
- How do the other design elements work? What do they communicate? What is the precise role of sound in this production?
- How does the stage area change throughout the play? What implications do these shifts have for the sound?
- Are live microphones required? If so, where can they be located?
- Where are the loudspeakers likely to be located? Use a plan to check the available rigging positions. Are there sufficient speakers to cover all areas of the auditorium sufficiently?
- Where will the control position be?

DEVELOPING THE DESIGN SCHEME

1 Following the initial planning and design stage, the Sound Designer draws up a detailed preliminary cue list which outlines the intended sound design contribution to the production.

2 During the rehearsal period, they will begin recording effects according to the proposed cue list. Cues may, however, be deleted and added throughout the period leading up to the first performance.

3 During the rehearsal period the Sound

SOURCING SOUND

1 The Sound Designer undertakes extensive research in order to locate specific sounds that are appropriate to the production. Extensive field recordings are often required, whilst others are achieved through exploration in the studio. Some effects may be sourced from professional recordings or libraries.

2 Where sourced effects are unsuitable or in-

- How will the sound be cued?

4 The type of venue that the performance is to be staged in will have major implications for the replay of sound, since the audience will be seated differently in each case.

Practical and Technical Considerations

1 The Sound Designer has to consider whether there are any practical restrictions that are likely to limit what they will be able to achieve. For example, they may or may not be working with assistance.

2 The availability of equipment may limit what is technically possible.

3 If the production is on tour, different considerations will apply to each venue.

Designer should receive regular communications from the Stage Management team in the form of rehearsal notes. These will keep everyone informed of progress in rehearsals on a daily basis. Rehearsal notes will detail any new sound requirements or changes.

Production Meetings

Throughout the rehearsal period the Sound Designer should attend regular production meetings. These are attended by all of the production team. Progress is monitored, problems are raised and solved.

appropriate, even when modified, the Sound Designer may:

- make their own original live recordings
- generate sound electronically, e.g. using a synthesiser
- create 'cheats'
- experiment!

Figure 5.7   *A preliminary cue list outlines the proposed sound design. This is an example from Woyzeck by Georg Büchner*

Scene No & location	Page	Effect	Description/Purpose/Duration	Notes
Prologue	N/A	Odd Music	Uncomfortable, expressionistic music – emphasise fairground theme? spinning type effect – out of control	Compose or research appropriate material?
1 The Captain's House	107	Gusting wind	Atmospheric (wind = madness) Enough required to underscore entire scene	Modify BBC CD Fx or generate with keyboard sampler?
2 Open Countryside	108	Crows/Rooks	Introduced over scene change. Lose before Andre sings	Existing effect – use the rocks from King Lear
2\3 Scene Change	109	Drum Beat	Ominous, regular – deep but in distance. Volume increases over scene change	Live recording needed
	110	Change EQ + Pan	As soldiers march past window	Live pan and fade
4 Fairground	111	Crowd Noise + Music	Crowd heightened + slightly distorted. Music – needs to feel uncomfortable – slightly grotesque	Modify existing effect. Music – live and/or recorded? barrel organ? accordion?
5 Fairground Booth	112	Hideous circus-type music	Underscores entire scene	Compose or research
	113	Clock Ticking	Builds into scene change and runs throughout Scene 6 – represents pressures inside Woyzeck's mind	Not naturalistic.
6 Marie's Bedroom	114	Foetal Heartbeat	Runs throughout scene. Consider how to realise this in performance. Transitions need to be subtle.	Record at local maternity unit?
7 Doctor's	115			
8 Marie's Bedroom	116	Human 'panting' and Ticking	Grunts – human or more animalistic runs into Scene 9	Live recording required

RECORDING

1 At this point the Designer begins to think about playback methods and cue organisation. How many replay machines are required and of what type and format? What is available or suitable? What tape speed, if any, is appropriate?

2 They will also be considering the likely volume level and direction of each sound. Whether it will be in stereo or mono. The number of loudspeakers and amplifiers that are available. What about the mixing desk? Are there a sufficient number of outputs? Where can loudspeakers be located? Should specific cues be routed to individual speakers? Do any effects need to be panned? Is this an issue at the recording stage or can you pan the effects live (see page 190)?

3 It is important to record a sufficient length of sound for each cue. Some sounds may need to play for substantially more time than you think will be required. Plans change and it is easier to cut sound at a later stage than to record a lot more!

4 Recording of sound cues is covered on pages 201–211.

5 At this point, it is necessary to think about the sequencing of cues. If two or more effects are to be replayed together or soon after each other from separate sources, it is essential to consider carefully which replay machine each sound needs to be located on. The sound effects need to be recorded onto the correct tape, reel or MiniDisc to facilitate easy playback. Whilst digital sound can be relocated quite easily, tape-based show reels require substantial reorganisation and re-editing to adjust the order or positioning of cues.

EDITING

1 Having decided which effect is to be replayed by which source machine, the editing process can begin.

2 Effects should be edited and compiled in the correct order. MiniDisc technology allows straightforward and relatively speedy digital editing and ordering of sounds.

Conventional reel-to-reel recording requires time-consuming marking and splicing of tape to leader tape and then arranged in cue order (see page 203).

3 As the recording and editing process continues, the sound cue sheet is continually revised.

SOUND MEETING WITH THE DIRECTOR

1 The Director and Sound Designer listen through the recorded sounds and discuss the effects. It is important to convey how the specific effects will be used.

2 The Director may be unhappy with individual sound cues. If the Sound Designer really wants to retain a sound, they may agree with the Director to review it at the sound plotting session and the technical rehearsal.

PLANNING THE SOUND INSTALLATION

We have already discussed the importance of organising the replay equipment and deciding how effects will be replayed (see above). A **system plan** should be drawn up in diagrammatic form, and a plan showing the actual location of the loudspeakers should also be realised.

Locating Loudspeakers

Loudspeakers need to be directional to distribute sound to an audience in a venue.

There are three main issues associated with selecting loudspeakers:

They have to be matched with an amplifier.
They need to be appropriate for the task.
They have to be positioned with careful consideration.

Each loudspeaker has to be 'focused', a bit like a theatre lantern. Speakers produce a beam of sound which is a known **pattern of sound radiation**. This beam varies according to the frequency of the sound emitted. Low frequencies are omnidirectional (go in all directions) and high frequencies are more directional.

Manufacturers provide radiation data for specific frequencies, so that the optimum position for loudspeakers can be determined and overall sound coverage assessed.

The decision about where loudspeakers should be located will depend on both practical and aesthetic considerations.

Practical Considerations

- *The nature of the space and the location of the audience*: is the audience in a single block and all at the same height? Are there galleries, dress circle, balconies or steeply raked seating?
- *Space at the side of the performance area*: can speakers be flown? If there are scenic elements what form do they take? Box set? Scenic drops? Open stage? Trucks?
- *Safety*: are the prospective loudspeaker positions safe? Can they be rigged or flown securely, with adequate secondary suspension systems? Can they be cabled without affecting performer's entrances and exits? Are they out of the way of other technical workings and backstage equipment?

Artistic and Aesthetic Considerations

- *Direction*: where should each sound appear to come from? Does sound travel during a cue? Does sound have to appear to come from inside a TV set or radio? Can you cable this up to your control position and disguise the cable run? If a small speaker cannot be concealed on stage, can the effect be cheated?
- *Appearance*: ideally, loudspeakers should appear invisible to an audience. Make sure that sound units do not affect the visual impact of the stage design.

THE GET-IN

1 The loudspeakers have to be rigged according to the plan and cabled correctly to the amplifiers.
2 The operating position has to be established with appropriate source machines connected to the mixing desk.
3 Cabling between the source decks, mixer and amplifiers is also established.
4 Other audio equipment, such as mics and cables, aerials and receivers may be rigged overhead.
5 Safety procedures are of paramount importance when working at height (see page 127). All audio equipment rigged overhead should be fixed securely and have a secondary suspension mechanism such as a safety chain or steel cable.
6 Once the equipment has been rigged a

sound check should establish whether all of the equipment is working correctly. There is no need to test the audio equipment by replaying sound at a high volume level at this stage.

7 If there are problems with the routing of the sound, investigate this in a logical manner. Trace the route of the signal through the system.

8 Ensure that the correct number of communication sets and cue light boxes are provided for the operator and other members of the sound crew.

9 Blank sound cue sheets are prepared prior to the plotting session.

10 It is essential to identify the line faders and output faders on the scribble pad provided on most mixing desks or by using masking tape along the bottom of the faders. This makes it easy to see at a glance which faders operate the CD player, etc. Where there are two or more source machines of the same type, these should also be clearly labelled, e.g. MiniDisc 1, MiniDisc 2, etc.

11 If several microphones are to be used in performance, it is useful to identify them by using different colours of PVC tape around the stem. Miniature radio mics will need the belt packs marked in this way instead. Corresponding coloured tape should identify the mics at the mixing desk underneath the relevant line fader.

SOUND PLOTTING SESSION

1 This involves the Sound Designer, a sound operator, the Deputy Stage Manager and the Director. The Musical Director will also be present if the production has one. Individual sound cues will be established in a quiet environment. No other work should occur in the space during this session.

2 Prior to beginning the sound plotting session, the amplifier volume controls should be set at a specific level and recorded on cue sheets. The mixer gain controls should be set to zero and the EQ should be flat. This information should be included as part of an extensive pre-show checking routine. Any adjustments to these levels during the plotting session have to be recorded clearly on the cue sheets and will be replicated during every performance.

3 It is important to establish whether the sound operator will always be cued by the Deputy Stage Manager or whether they will follow their own cue sheets. In musical presentations the sound operator will not be listening to the Deputy Stage Manager, but to the sound on stage. In this case cue lights can be used instead of communication headsets.

4 The Sound Designer begins with the pre-show music and works through each sound effect to establish:
- level, pan and EQ settings
- the timing of any fades
- the number of the cue
- the positioning of the cue in the prompt copy.

5 It is best to set sound cue levels on the line faders on the mixing desk whilst keeping the sub-master and master faders at 0 dB or equivalent. Use the masters to fade sounds in and out and not the line faders. The master faders often travel further, which enables smoother fades to be performed. In this way, the operator can pre-set line faders precisely in advance and always fade in with the masters to a pre-set mark.

6 The volume of sound cues should be set with the knowledge that the acoustics of the space will alter when filled with an audience. Because human bodies absorb sound, volume levels should be set to a slightly higher level when the auditorium is full. They must also be monitored in performance.

7 Cue sheets are, of course, vital documents to ensure that all of the relevant sound information is written down logically and in a form that is easy to read.

8 If microphones are to be used, then relevant cast members and/or musicians will be required during the plotting session. A separate music sound check will usually be held for live bands.

9 Following the plotting session, each cue is allocated a number (see page 81). Separate cues are numbered sequentially with any alterations to the cue level being given an additional letter.

TECHNICAL REHEARSAL

1 All sound effects should be replayed in their entirety. Strictly, if the sound runs throughout an Act, the entire Act should be played through to ensure that the sound works for the whole duration.

2 The technical rehearsal should not be stopped until the sound operator has prepared the next cue. This is particularly a problem if the production is using tape-based technology, as the operator has to spool through unwanted tape to find the next cue. If two or more replay machines are available, the next cue can be prepared and played back from the second replay machine.

3 Difficult sequences, involving playback from multiple sources have to be practised and cannot be rushed. Operators need to gain confidence in the cueing and realisation of these sequences.

4 During the technical rehearsal there is likely to be substantial revision of cues which were plotted. Most of the changes will involve levels, positioning and timing. Some cues may also need to be cut at this late stage, whilst additions are also a real possibility!

5 The Sound Designer should check the levels and quality of sound from different areas of the auditorium.

THE DRESS REHEARSAL

1 Pre-show checks should be undertaken carefully as detailed on cue sheets. All loudspeakers and source equipment should be tested and levels established. Check amplifier and mixer gain settings if there seems to be a problem. All microphones should be tested and batteries replaced in radio transmitters.

2 Microphones should not be left rigged on stage, but should be replaced in protective boxes or pouches when not in use. They, therefore, have to be rigged as part of the pre-show set-up and de-rigged after every performance.

3 The dress rehearsal is the first true reflection of how the sound works under performance conditions. The Designer may alter the levels, fade times, cue position or location of cues at this point. Amendments have to be made in the prompt copy and on the sound operators cue sheets.

PERFORMANCES

1 The sound operator runs the show according to the cue sheets.

2 The Sound Designer monitors the volume levels and sound quality.

STRIKE

1 De-rig all overhead equipment.
2 Return all mics, control and source equipment.

3 Ensure control room or operating position is clear, clean and tidy.
4 Return hire equipment.

POST-PRODUCTION

- All sound source media are labelled correctly.
- Multiple reels of tape can often be spliced together to fit onto a single 10 inch reel which should be logged and stored.
- All recorded material is archived and catalogued.
- Cue sheets should be stored with the prompt copy.

- Completion of PRS Returns to ensure copyright.
- Evaluation: What worked particularly well? Which aspects were disappointing? How could the sound design be improved?
- How could the operation have been improved?

Answer Task on page 104

The fuses in this example are the same fuses that would protect any piece of equipment connected to this socket.

- fuse or trip switches in dimmer pack
- fuse in 13 amp plug
- fuse or trip switches in a distribution box located somewhere nearby and which controls the ring main.

Answers to Task on page 186

1 cardioid
2 omm-directional
3 cardioid
4 hyper-cardioid
5 omm-directional
6 cardioid
7 bi-directional
8 hyper-cardioid
9 omm-directional
10 cardioid
11 hyper-cardioid
12 cardioid
13 bi-directional
14 hyper-cardioid

USEFUL ADDRESSES AND CONTACT NUMBERS

Arts & Entertainment Technical Training
Initiative (AETTI)
Lower Ground
14 Blenheim Terrace
London NW8 0EB
0171 328 6174

Association of British Theatre Technicians
(ABTT)
47 Bermondesey Street
London SE1 3XT
0171 403 3778

Association of Lighting Designers (ALD)
PO Box 95
Worcester Park
Surrey KT4 8WA
0181 330 6577

Broadcasting Entertainment Cinematograph
and Theatre Union (BECTU)
111 Wardour Street
London W1V 4AY
0171 427 8506

Equity
Guild House
Upper St. Martin's Lane
London WC2H 9EG
0171 379 6000

Independent Theatre Council
12 The Leather Market
Weston Street

London SE1 3ER
0171 403 1727

Institute of Entertainment & Arts
Management
Rustles
9 Bushetts Grove
Herstham
Surrey RH1 3DX
01737 644432

Metier Training Services
Glyde Gate
Bradford
01274 738800

Professional Lighting and Sound Association
(PLASA)
38 St Leonards Road
Eastbourne
East Sussex BN21 3UT
01323 642639

Society of British Theatre Designers (SBTD)
47 Bermondsey Street
London SE1 3XT
0171 403 3778

Stage Management Association
Southbank House
Black Prince Road
London SE1 7SJ
0171 587 1514

FURTHER READING

General

Designing for the Theatre (2nd
 edition)
Francis Reid
A&C Black 1996

Stagecraft
Published in USA as
**Practical Theater: How to stage your own
 production**
Trevor R. Griffiths
Quarto Publishing (Chartwell) 1982

The Staging Handbook
Francis Reid
A&C Black 1978

The ABC of Stage Technology
Francis Reid
A&C Black 1995

Theatre from A to Z
Norman Boulanger & Warren Lounsbury

Univ of Washington Press 1992

Effects for the Theatre
Edited by Graham Walne
A&C Black 1995

**The Focal Guide to Safety in Live
 Performance**
George Thompson
Focal Press 1993

Control systems for live entertainment
John Huntington
Focal Press 1994

Stages for Tomorrow
Francis Reid
Focal Press 1998

Stage Management

Stage Management – A Gentle Art
 Daniel Bond
 A & C Black 1991

**Stage Management & Theatre
 Administration**

Pauline Menear and Terry Hawkins
Phaidon 1988

Create Your Own Stage Props
Jacquie Govier
Bell & Hyman Ltd. 1985

Lighting

The ABC of Stage Lighting
Francis Reid
A&C Black 1992

**Stage Lighting Design, The Art, The craft,
 The life**
Richard Pilbrow
Nick Hern Books 1997

The Lighting Art: The Aesthetics of Stage Lighting Design (2nd ed)
Richard H. Palmer
Prentice Hall 1994

Discovering Stage Lighting
Francis Reid
Focal Press (Butterworth-Heinemann) 1993

Stage Lighting Handbook (5th edition)
Francis Reid
A&C Black 1996

Lighting the Stage
Francis Reid
Focal Press (Butterworth-Heinemann) 1995

Stage Lighting for Theatre Designers
Nigel Morgan
Herbert Press 1995

Create Your Own Stage Lighting
Tim Streader and John A. Williams
Bell & Hyman Ltd. 1985

Stage Lighting Design
Richard Pilbrow
Studio Vista, Cassell Ltd. 1986

Lighting and Sound
Neil Fraser
Phaidon 1988 (revised 1993)

Concert Lighting; Techniques, Art and Business (2nd ed)
James L. Moody
Focal Press 1997

Theatre Lighting in the age of Gas
Terence Rees
The Society for Theatre Research 1978

Theatre Lighting before Electricity
Frederick Penzel
Wesleyan University Press 1978

Light on the subject Stage lighting for directors and actors and the rest of us
David Hays
Limelight editions, 3rd ed. 1992

The Art of Stage Lighting
Frederick Bentham
Pitman 2nd ed 1970

Stage Lighting
Richard Pilbrow
Studio Vista, Cassell 2nd ed 1979

Lighting in the Theatre
Gosta M. Bergman
Almqvist & Wiksell/Rowman & Littlefield 1977

Stage Lighting Practice and Design
W. Oren Parker & R. Craig Wolf
Holt Rinehart & Winston 1987

Stage Lighting Revealed: A Design and Execution Handbook
Glen Cunningham
Betterway/F&W Publications 1993

Designing With Light An Introduction to Stage Lighting
J. Michael Gillette
Mayfield Publishing Co. 2nd ed 1989

Lighting Design Handbook
Lee H. Watson
McGraw-Hill Inc 1990

Theatrical Design and Production
J. Michael Gillette
Mayfield 2nd ed 1992

Lighting
D.C. Pritchard
Longman 5th ed 1995

Practical Stage Lighting
Rex Bunn
Currency Press 1993

Lighting By Design: A Technical Guide
Brian Fitt, Joe Thornley
Focal Press 1992

Lighting Technology: A Guide for the Entertainment Industry
Brian Fitt, Joe Thornley
Focal Press 1997

Projection for the Performing Arts
Graham Walne
Focal Press 1995

Stage Lighting Controls
Ulf Sandstrom
Focal Press 1997

Stage Lighting Step-by-Step
Graham Walters
A&C Black 1997

Sound

Sound for the Theatre
Graham Walne
A&C Black 1990

Stage Sound
David Collison
Studio Vista, Cassell Ltd. 1976

The Sound Studio (6th edition)
Alec Nisbett
Focal Press 1995

Sound and Recording – An Introduction
  (3rd edition)
F. Rumsey & T. McCormick
Focal 1997

The Art of Sound Reproduction
John Watkinson
Focal Press 1998

The Use of Microphones (4th edition)
Alec Nisbett
Focal 1994

Sound and Music for the Theatre
D. Kaye & J. Lebrecht
Backstage Books 1992

Sound for the stage – A Technical
  Handbook
Patrick M. Finelli
1989 Drama Book Publishers, NY

Concert Sound and Lighting Systems (2nd
  ed)
John Vasey
Focal Press 1994

An Introduction to Digital Audio
John Watkinson
Focal 1994

The Art of Digital Audio (2nd ed)
John Watkinson
Focal Press 1993

MIDI Systems and Control (2nd ed)
Francis Rumsey
Focal Press 1994

Sound Recording and Reproduction (3rd
  ed)
Glyn Alkin
Focal 1996

Handbook for Sound Engineers – the New
  Audio Cyclopedia
G. Ballou
Howard W. Sams & Co. 1991

Sound Recording Practice
John Borwick (ed)
Oxford University Press 1987

Loudspeaker and Headphone Handbook
  (2nd ed)
John Borwick (ed)
Focal Press 1994

Sound Synthesis and Sampling
Martin Russ
Focal Press 1997

WEBSITES

ABTT

http://www.abtt.org.uk
Association of British Theatre Technicians website. Lots of useful technical theatre information and industry links

PROFESSIONAL LIGHTING AND SOUND ASSOCIATION

http://www.plasa.org.uk/

A comprehensive site with links to all major UK and International manufacturers of theatre equipment. Training information, Technical bookshop, product information, etc

PRODUCTION SERVICES ASSOCIATION

http://www.psa.org.uk/
Production, design, touring, technical and support services for the live entertainment industry. Health and safety guidelines

SBTD SOCIETY OF BRITISH THEATRE DESIGNERS

http://www.theatredesign.org.uk
Society of British Theatre Designers website

USITT

http://www.ffa.ucalgary.ca/usitt/
US Institute for Theatre Technology. An association of design, production and technology professionals

BECTU

http://www.bectu.org.uk
The entertainment union's website with information on health & safety, regulations, etc

OISTAT

http://www.oistat.nl/

International Organisation of Scenographers. Concentrating on design for performance

ASSOCIATION OF LIGHTING DESIGNERS

http://www.ald.org.uk/
Organisation for professional lighting designers and students. Lots of links to related lighting sites, suppliers, manufacturers, etc

SOCIETY OF PROFESSIONAL AUDIO RECORDING SERVICES

http://custwww.xensei.com/spars/
US based site focuses on innovations in audio technology & techniques

INTERNATIONAL LASER DISPLAY ASSOCIATION

http://www.ilda.wa.org/
Association dedicated to advancing the professional use of laser displays. Safety and technology info

THEATRE SOUND DESIGN DIRECTORY

http://theatre-sound.com/
Richmond Sound Design's audio reference site

AUDIO ENGINEERING SOCIETY

http://www.cudenver.edu/aes/
University of Colorado audio technology website

ICMA

http://coos.dartmouth.edu/~rsn/icma/icma.html
International Computer Music association for composers, designers, musicians involved in computer music

ESTA

http://www.esta.org/
US based Entertainment Services & Technology Association site includes suppliers of stencils & CAD symbol libraries

ENTERTAINMENT TECHNOLOGY ONLINE

http://www/etecynt.net
US based Entertainment Services Association publishers of Entertainment Design Magazine (TCI Magazine), and Lighting Dimensions Magazine

INSTITUTE OF ELECTRICAL AND ELECTRONICS ENGINEERS

http://www.ieee.org/
Membership, products and services

APRS ASSOCIATION OF PROFESSIONAL RECORDING SERVICES

http://www.aprs.co.uk/index.html
Recording industry, audio resource, technology, training courses, etc

Web-based resources for theatre and live performance

TECHNICAL THEATRE GLOSSARY

http://www.ex.ac.uk/drama/tech/glossary/html
The largest theatre glossary on the web! Search for technical theatre terms alphabetically or by subject; Stage management, lighting, sound

UK THEATRE WEB

http://www.uktw.co.uk/
British theatre website with lots of related links

THE STAGE NEWSPAPER

http://www.thestage.co.uk/
British theatre industry's weekly newspaper. Site with lots of useful information and links

BACKSTAGE WORLD

http://www.stagelight.se/backstage/
Swedish based technical theatre resource

MCCOY'S GUIDE TO THEATRE & PERFORMING STUDIES

http://www.stetson.edu/departments/csata/thr_guid.html
US academic site with lots of related links including stagecraft and technical theatre

CANADIAN INSTITUTE OF THEATRE TECHNOLOGY

http://www.ffa.ucalgary.ca/citt/clbd/wais/html
Site includes a stagecraft digest which allows a contextual search of archives

THEATRE CENTRAL

http://wwwl.playbill.com/cgi-bin/plb/central?cmd=start
US based theatre news site. Reputed to be the largest compendium of theatre links on the internet

WWW VIRTUAL LIBRARY, THEATRE & DRAMA

http://vl-theatre.com
Drama/theatre section of the world wide web virtual library, broad range of theatrical resources across the world

THE INTERNET THEATRE BOOKSHOP

http://www.stageplays.com
On line catalogue of stage plays and texts

ARTS INFO DATABASE

http://www.arts-info.co.uk/

UK performing arts database with details of venues, companies, festivals, practitioners, jobs, services & technical glossary

MICROPHONE HOMEPAGE

http://members.aol.com/mihartkopf/
Database of major manufacturers and technical information on professional microphones. Links to manufacturer's sites

MP3

http://www.mp3com/
All you need to know about the new digital format for the electronic transmission and storage of sound. What it is, how to use it, where to get it

STUDIOGURU: THE PRO AUDIO RESOURCE

http://www.studioguru.com/
Resource site linking to hundreds of other audio related sites

HARMONY CENTRAL

http://www.harmony-central.com/
Useful internet resource archive for musicians

SOUNDSITE

http://www.soundsite.com/
Audio technology, manufacturers, products, technical information and links

THEATRE SOUND DESIGN

http://theatre-sound.com/tsindex.html
Theatre Sound design directory of sound designers and resources

ONLINE SOUND EFFECTS

http://www.soundogs.com/index.htm
The first online sound effects library. Search, listen and order over 35,000 sounds

LIGHTING LINKS

http://waapa.cowan.edu.au/lx
Western Australia Academy's guide to lighting links on the web.

The most comprehensive worldwide listings of manufacturers, organisations, effects, forums, health & safety, publications, etc

STRAND ARCHIVE

http://www.ex.ac.uk/drama/strand/welcom.html
Listings and technical details of all Strand Electric equipment. Handy reference index of lantern pattern numbers

LIGHTING ARCHIVE

http://www.psu.edu/dept/theatrearts/archives/index.html
Listing of Penn States School of Theatre archives of lighting materials

BRETTON HALL UNIVERSITY COLLEGE OF LEEDS, SCHOOL OF DANCE & THEATRE

http://www.bretton.ac.uk/dt
Resources for stage design and production management, Lighting and sound cue sheets, and related material

THE STAGE TECHNICIAN'S PAGE

http://www.geocites.com/Broadway/3738/
Dedicated to all of those interested or involved in stage technician work

THE LIGHT NETWORK

http://www.lightnetwork.com/
Site devoted to discussion of lighting for professionals and students

LIGHT NETWORK

http://www.lightnetwork.com
Meeting place for lighting professionals and students. Latest information in the lighting field and discussion forums

BACKSTAGE WORLD

http://www.stagelight.se/backstage/

Swedish based technical theatre and live entertainment resource. Equipment specifications, touring details, etc

INDEX